Principles
of Church Growth

ENGLISH VERSION OF INTERTEXT #1

of the

LATIN AMERICAN COMMITTEE FOR THEOLOGICAL TEXTS (CLATT)

Published with the official approval of the following organizations:

Assemblies of God (PECS)
Advisory Committee for Self-study Texts (CATA)
Church of the Nazarene
Instituto Evangelistico de Mexico
Conservative Baptist Seminary of Argentina
Christian and Missionary Alliance United Biblical Seminary
    of Ecuador
United Biblical Seminary of Colombia (Mennonite, Latin
    America Mission, Evangelical Covenant, SEPAL, etc.
George Allen Theological Seminary (Evangelical Christian
    Union, Andes Evangelical Mission, Evangelical Union of
    South America)

PRINCIPLES

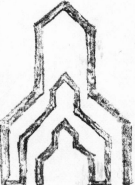

OF CHURCH

GROWTH
(preliminary edition)

Wayne Weld
&
Donald A. McGavran

William Carey Library
South Pasadena, California

Library of Congress Catalog Card Number: 71-96752
International Standard Book Number: 0-87808-108-9

Published by the William Carey Library
533 Hermosa Street
South Pasadena, Calif. 91030
Telephone: 213-682-2047

PRINTED IN THE UNITED STATES OF AMERICA

CONTENTS

The authors of this book are Dr. Donald McGavran, Dean of the School of World Mission and Institute of Church Growth of Fuller Theological Seminary, and Wayne Weld, professor in the Seminario Bíblico Unido (United Bible Seminary) of Colombia. The basic ideas of the book and much of its structure originated in the writings and conferences given by Dr. McGavran. Nevertheless, the adaptation for Latin America and the programming have been the responsibility of Mr. Weld. Any criticism or suggestion for improving the content or presentation of the book should be directed to him.

This text was prepared in Spanish for those who had completed primary school. In the English edition no effort has been made to keep vocabulary at that level. The book is offered as an aid to those who do not read Spanish, but who will be able to translate from English into the language in which they work. This manual is also presented as an example of cultural adaptation. Some sections of this book may be compared with corresponding sections of Understanding Church Growth by Dr. McGavran.

Many people have contributed to the Spanish and English editions of Principles of Church Growth. May all those to whom it is due accept this grateful recognition. Special thanks go to Mary Anne Weld who has typed the major part of both manuscripts and contributed in many others ways to the production of the present volume.

FOREWORD

The publication of the present work represents a triumph
for many brethren in Latin America who for various years have
been working in the theological education by extension movement.
The principal impulse for the movement was given in a consulta-
tion carried out in Armenia, Colombia, in September 1967. On
that occasion two functional committees were formed: The Latin
American Committee for Theological Texts (CLATT) and the Advisory Committee for Autodidactic Texts (CATA).

The most important work of CLATT/CATA after the consulta-
tion was the assignment of more than twenty-five subjects (generally part of the curricula in seminaries and Bible institutes in
Latin America) to the respective authors; the assistance in the
technicalities of programming; the approval on the most general
scale possible of the content of the intertexts; and the publication by means of the publishing houses most widely accepted in
Latin America. Several authors are working conscientiously to
write other intertexts, but the first to appear has been Principles of Church Growth, for which in the name of CLATT the most
cordial congratulations are extended to Professor Wayne Weld of
the United Bible Seminary of Colombia.

All the intertexts are directed toward the person who has
finished six years of primary school. Investigations in this
matter have revealed that the majority of Latin American pastors
are at this level. The reader should take into consideration that
the average student who uses the intertext is not a child in the
sixth grade, nor even a youth, but rather an adult already recognized as a leader in his local church. Of course his maturity
will help him to understand certain subjects that younger persons
with the same academic preparation possibly would not fully
understand.

More and more seminaries and Bible institutes are adopting
extension programs to supplement present residence programs for
ministerial training. It is calculated that more than 2000 persons are studying theological courses by extension this year and
almost monthly the number rises. All are found in Latin America,
but also in other parts of the world an increasing interest in
theological education by extension is noted and projects else-

where are underway.   Precisely to fill this enormous demand for
self-teaching materials the Clatt/CATA intertext project was
initiated.

        The format of this book is not that of a traditional book.
The reader must work while he reads, and thus he becomes personally involved in the book's message and learns more.   This form
of instruction conforms to the best standards of modern educational psychology.   For greatest benefit from the book the reader
should enroll in one of the many institutions in Latin America
which have extension programs and thus enjoy the assistance of a
properly qualified instructor.   Nevertheless, if this is not
possible, the reader should study alone, but being diligent to
do all the exercises which the book demands.   You will be sur-
prised at how much you learn!

                                C. Peter Wagner
                                Ad-hoc Secretary
                                CLATT

Cochabamba, Bolivia
December, 1970

INSTRUCTIONS
FOR THE STUDENTS

This manual is different from others that the student may have used. Part of the content is in the form of programmed instruction, one of the most modern educational techniques. This system is based on three principles: 1) The student must respond actively to the information given. 2) He must respond correctly so that an incorrect answer is not remembered. 3) His answer should be confirmed immediately. Some variation will be found in the types of instruction used in this manual, but only the programmed part needs special explanation.

In order to make full usage of this program the student must read the information and the question carefully. Afterwards he should write his answer. There are clues of various kinds in the questions so that the student can choose or compose the correct answer. One type of clue is that of sequence or context. If the student can not think of the answer he should read the question again. If he still needs help he should review a few of the preceeding questions. It may be necessary to reread the paragraph before the series of questions. Some questions require the student to use information given in another section or previous lesson. These questions will show whether the student should review that material before proceeding.

Since the correct answers are found on the same page there is always the temptation to look at them before answering the question. In order to prevent the student from reading the answer to the next question when he confirms another the order of answers is mixed. Because the order of the answers is not the same as that of the questions it is necessary to use the key indicated.

The student is advised not to look up the answer before making his own. Learning is better and more permanent when one thinks about the answer before looking for it. This will be evident on the weekly and final examinations.

In order to help you in these examinations there are certain questions which review the material in sections. Some of these questions are indicated by the box which encloses them. Examinations are not limited to these questions, but the student who can fill in the boxes from memory will have dominated the majority of the material which the authors consider of primary importance.

During the weekly class a short quiz will be given over the lesson studied the previous week. The rest of the time will be dedicated to the discussion of questions which require the opinion or experience of the students. You will note that the space after these questions is divided by a vertical line. While he studies the lesson the student will answer in the space at the left of the line. In class he will add on the space to the right supplementary ideas of the teacher and other students.

If the student does not understand or does not agree with the answer given to the objective questions he should discuss it in class. It is not expected that everyone will be in agreement in all the diverse aspects of this study. It is more important that the student think for himself and that he not be bound by tradition or prejudice.

Really, success in this study does not depend on the grade earned by means of examinations or other requirements. The most significant criterion will be the growth that results in the church in which the student serves his Lord. Therefore the final goal is not passing the course, but fulfilling the will of God for His glory.

1
THE EVANGELICAL CHURCH IN LATIN AMERICA

Church growth is a topic which includes various aspects of the Church's activities and purpose in the world. We must see it in historical perspective, primarily because a knowledge of what has happened in the past will help us to know what to do now and in the future. The lessons of the past are applied to the present. In particular, they are applied to the student's situation.

Another aspect is evangelistic. The strategies and methods which have been used to extend the kingdom of God must be analyzed. The study of church growth requires a rather wide concept of evangelism. It is not limited to winning souls. The promoters of church growth have to recognize that man is more than a soul. He is a complete and complex being and the Church needs to minister to man in his entirety.

The study of church growth implies also a knowledge of sociology because man is a social being. He does not live in isolation but in community. The social, political and economic factors which operate in the life of the individual must be studied if we are to formulate a faith which can be an integral and integrating part of the person and the community.

Many evangelicals oppose the inclusion of Seventh Day Adventists in a discussion of the Evangelical Church. They are included in this study because they represent an important work in many Latin American countries. We should learn from what the Adventists can teach us with regard to methods and the importance of social factors to produce religious changes.

In considering church growth there is a certain emphasis on numbers. If the Church grows, this means that individuals are added and that these individuals can be counted. Man can not be reduced to a cipher. But he can be counted among those that God has redeemed and added to the Church.

The quality of Christians is equally as important as the quantity. Size is not the only criterion of the Church. It needs true disciples of the Lord who know how to live and work for Him. In the midst of all the problems that Latin Americans must face, the Church must proclaim with prophetic voice the implications of the gospel for all of life. This implies not only the redemption of the individual, but also changing the structure of society.

In spite of all that church growth can include, this book does not pretend to give the answer to all the problems inside or outside the Church. If in some areas it seems to be superficial, it is because it can only introduce some topics. By no means is it expected that all those who study this book will be in agreement with everything that is said. Of greater importance is that it stimulate critical thought concerning the Church, its message and its mission. Our hope is that men will not only think of these things, but that they will act, directed by the Holy Spirit and instructed in human wisdom for the glory of God.

The table of contents indicates what this book is about. If a reader is impatient to find out what it says about a certain topic he can look ahead. However there is a logical order of presentation of subjects, chapter by chapter and section by section. It is hoped that the emphasis of each aspect will not cloud the vision of the whole. The first chapter or lesson treats the worldwide growth of the Church and particularly its extension in Latin America. The emphasis is on numbers and how faithfulness to God is reflected in numerical and qualitative growth of the Church.

The Reality of Worldwide Growth

The Church is growing tremendously today. The number of Christians is higher than ever. This growth is a phenomenon that is seen throughout all the world. It is certain that in some places Christianity has suffered defeat. Some countries have closed their doors to Christian missionaries. But outside of these few exceptions the Christian faith is extending throughout the world. In the midst of non-Christian populations new congregations are born. Many of the congregations are small and do not have a full-time pastor. Nevertheless, they are local expressions of the universal Church. (In this study "Church" with a capital C refers to the universal Church or a denomination, while "church" with a small c indicates a local congregation.) Each year the number of congregations and their members increases greatly.

1.   A notable fact in our days is the advance of the religion which is called

_____ .   see /

2.   According to the experience of the student the Church is growing in the land in which he lives, that is
                    see ///   _____ .

3.   Christians organize themselves into new _____ . see $$

4.   The increase in the number of congregations is the result of the conversion of many persons to

_____ . see &&&

5.   These congregations are local expressions of the universal

_____ .   see //

        In the three sentences that follow write <u>Church</u> or <u>church</u> according to its use in this book.

6.   The evangelical community in Paraguay is indicated by _____ .
                                            see $

7.   For a Baptist congregation in Cali, Colombia we may use the term

_____ .   see &&

8.   The Christian and Missionary Alliance in Colombia is an example of

_____ .   see &

        The universal Church grows by means of the affiliation of individuals with local churches. This numerical growth occurs for various reasons. In some sectors the excess of births over deaths in the Christian community contributes to church growth, but only if these children come to mature faith in Christ. To these that grow up in the Church we must add the many who are converted from the world.

9.   The Church grows only through the conversion of _____ .
                        see $$$

/   Christianity
/   Church
///   the name of
    your own
    country
    Eg. Peru
&   Church
&&   church
&&&   Christianity
$ Church
$$ churches,
    congregations
$$$ individuals,
    persons

10.   Some believers grow up in the Christian community because their

_____ were Christians.   see /

11.   If all the evangelicals had large families, probably in the next generation the Church would have

see &&   _____members.

12.   This biological or natural growth is very slow. What is needed is the conversion of people outside the Christian community, that is, from the

_____ .   see ///

There are social factors that operate in many of these cases. For example, a young man marries a Christian girl and later accepts her religion. There are many reasons why men in contact with the evangelical community decide to enter into the communion and faith of the Church. There are also dramatic conversions of large numbers of people that were before not identified in any way with evangelical Christianity. All these ways of entering the Church have been seen in Latin America and other parts of the world.

13.   Some accept the Christian faith not only for spiritual reasons, but also because of friendship with Christians or other factors which are

_____ in nature. see &&&

14.   Of these ways of accepting a biblical faith, in Latin America it is possible to find

_____.   see //

15.   In every case conversion can not take place without a knowledge of the

_____ .   see &

It has been said that in 1850 the number of Christians, whether genuine or nominal, in the world was 500,000,000 and the number of non-Christians was 1,000,000,000. In 1950 the numbers had increased to 1,000,000,000 Christians and 2,000,000,000 non-Christians. In view of this situation answer the following questions.

16.   For every Christian in 1850 there were _____ non-Christians.   see $

/   parents
// all or SIMILAR WORDS
/// world
&   gospel or SIMILAR WORDS
&& more
&&& social
$ two

17. For every Christian in 1950 there were _____ non-Christians.
                                                    see &&

Note: In questions 18-20 and others of this type later, the student must put an "X" in the space before the most correct answer. With a few exceptions, which are indicated, you should mark only one answer. There may be an element of truth in two or three of the answers. Therefore you must select the best word or phrase.

18. With regard to the numerical growth of Christians and non-Christians until 1950

_____a) The number of Christians had decreased.

_____b) The number of non-Christians was twice as large.

_____c) The number of non-Christians had not changed. see //

19. With regard to the proportion of Christians to non-Christians

_____a) The proportion of Christians increased.

_____b) The proportion of Christians decreased.

_____c) The proportion of Christians remained the same. see &

20. This evidence indicates that the Church of Christ

_____a) Will win the world.

_____b) Will die out.

_____c) Keeps up with the demographic explosion. see ///

21. If the same proportion between Christians and non-Christians should continue, when there are 2,000,000,000 Christians there will be
                    _____ times as many non-Christians. see /

two
b o o
two
/ // /// & &&

22. In addition to social and natural factors - war, famine,
epidemics, false theology, migration and oppression - there are
personal and spiritual reasons for lack of church growth. Based
on your experience and reading of the Bible and other books,
state some causes of lack of growth or of success in the Lord's
work.

The Facts of Growth in Latin America

Although we are interested in the progress of Christianity
throughout the world, it is natural for anyone to be more concerned with his own sector of the world. Therefore, we will pay
more attention to the Latin American Church. In the second lesson
we will examine some examples of growth. But before this we
must consider the overall state of the Church from the Rio Grande
to Tierra del Fuego. The following data of the total population
and the number of baptized evangelicals for various years are
presented for all of Latin America.

	1911	1938	1960	1967
Total population	72,000,000	125,000,000	195,000,000	250,000,000
Evangelicals (baptized)	103,000	452,000	2,744,000	6,019,000

One of the purposes of this study is to teach the student the value of graphs. Therefore a graph is given below based on the data on the preceeding page.

| 1911 | 1939 | 1960 | 1968 |

Note: The black column indicates the evangelical population and the white column the total population. Note that the white columns are ten times as wide as the black ones.

23. The numbers and the graph indicate that the evangelicals still represent a

_____ percentage of the total population. see /

/ small

24. Nevertheless, if there was one evangelical for every 720 persons in 1911 and later one for every 40 in 1967, the proportion of evangelicals has

_____ .   see $

25. Between 1938 and 1967 the total population increased _____ times. (Compare 125,000,000 with 250,000,000) see &&&

26. During the same period the number of evangelicals increased some thirteen times. This tells us that the number of evangelicals was increasing

_____ rapidly than that of the total population.   see %

27. Between 1960 and 1967 the number of evangelicals more than doubled. If the number of members doubles every seven years there will be twice as many as in 1967 by
(1967 plus 7)   see //   _____ .

28. These figures represent the area of the world in which we have the greatest interest, that is
see $$ _____ .

29. In the preceeding section of this lesson we noted that the number of Christians worldwide doubled between 1850 and 1950 or a period of

_____ years.   see &&

30. But in Latin America the same proportion of growth was reached between 1960 and 1967 or

_____ years.   see ///

31. If the world growth of the Church has continued at the same pace we can see that the rate of evangelical growth in Latin America is

_____ .   see &

32. Between 1911 and 1938 there was a period of _____ years.
see $$$

33. During this period the Latin American Church grew a little more than
see / _____ times, that is it doubled every 13 years.

/ 4
// 1974
/// 7
& greater, higher
&& 100
&&& 2
$ increased
$$ Latin America
$$$ 27
% more

34. In recent years the Church has required _____ time to double its membership.   see &

35. This indicates that the Church is growing _____ rapidly than at the beginning of the century.   see ///

36. We must consider many factors in regard to these figures. However, we may deduce in general terms that, by the end of this century, the proportion of evangelicals will be much
                                        see &&   _____ .

37. We can think of the future of the Evangelical Church in the Latin American countries with
                                    _____ hope.   see /

        The figures in the preceeding section were taken largely from various editions of the World Christian Handbook. There is another reference book which is indispensable for the serious student of the Evangelical Church in Latin America. <u>Church Growth in Latin America</u> by Read, Monterroso and Johnson not only presents many data concerning the Churches, it interprets them. We will cite this book frequently in this study. Although it is not obligatory that the student buy the book for this course, it is strongly recommended. In spite of the fact that the book appeared in Portuguese in 1969 and in Spanish in 1970, the latest figures are from 1967. Therefore the reader should not expect that they reflect the present situation. The student is encouraged to make his own supplement to the book and determine if the tendencies indicated have continued.

38. The observations in the preceeding sections are based on

_____ taken from various books.   see //

39. The most important book for the student of church growth is

_____ in Latin America.   see &&&

40. One aspect of the book which is of great value for us is its
_____ of the data.   see $

/   much
// data, figures
/// more
&   less
&& higher or
    SIMILAR
    WORDS
&&& Church Growth
$ interpretation

41. Although the book appeared in Spanish in 1970, the latest figures are from three years before or

_____ . see ///

42. For this reason the data do not indicate exactly the size of the Church

_____ . see //

43. The task of suplementing these data will be the responsibility of the

_____ . see /

Church Growth in Latin America contains many data and graphs which reveal much about the Church in the Latin American countries. They indicate not only the size but also the rate of growth. Below there is a list of the seventeen countries included in the study with the membership of the Evangelical Churches and the annual growth rate of the Church in each of these countries. The membership total is not the same as that given on page 1-6. The sources of information are distinct and the total below includes fewer countries.

COUNTRY	EVANGELICALS (MEMBERS)	ANNUAL GROWTH RATE BETWEEN 1960 and 1967
Argentina	249,500	5.0%
Bolivia	45,400	11.5
Brazil	3,313,200	11.0
Chile	441,700	8.5
Colombia	73,900	12.0
Costa Rica	14,200	7.0
Ecuador	12,600	15.0
El Salvador	35,800	5.5
Guatemala	77,200	9.0
Honduras	18,800	8.5
Mexico	429,900	11.0
Nicaragua	19,800	3.0
Panama	37,500	5.5
Paraguay	15,200	11.0
Peru	61,900	6.5
Uruguay	21,800	7.0
Venezuela	46,900	14.0
TOTAL	4,915,400	10.0%

/ student
// now, today
/// 1967

44. One of the most notable facts is that two thirds of the evangelicals in Latin America live in the country of
                          see /   _____ .

45. Since that country has less than two thirds of the total population, the percentage of evangelicals in Brazil is

_____ than the average for the Spanish speaking nations. see &&

46. The Latin American country with the fewest evangelicals is

_____ . see //

47. But that republic has the _____ rate of growth. see &

48. The two countries that follow Ecuador in rate of growth of the Protestant Church are
        see &&&   _____ and _____ .

49. It would seem that in the countries where the proportion of evangelicals is still very low the Church is growing

_____ rapidly.   see ///

50. If there are 4,915,400 evangelicals in Latin America and the rate of growth is 10%, we may calculate that the Church should add 491,540 members per year. It is calculated as follows:

         4,915,400   We must multiply the present number of
              .10   members by the percentage of growth. In
        491,540.00   this case we multiply by ten and divide
                       by 100 (per cent). This division is
                       done by moving the decimal point two
                       places toward the left.

/   Brazil
/// Ecuador
&   more
&&   highest
&&   higher
&&& Colombia, Venezuela

Calculate the number of evangelicals which should be added to the Church in your country in a year according to the percentage of growth indicated on the list on the preceeding page.

51. How many believers are there in your local church? _____
If it grows at the national rate, how many new members should be added to your church in a year?

Although the Latin American countries have a similar cultural heritage, there is much diversity. The differences result in part from economic and political influences. Nevertheless, the most important factor has been the racial and social composition of the people. In the Andean republics and some of the Central American countries a considerable percentage of the population is of Indian blood. In some areas these Indian groups have preserved almost completely their culture. At the other extreme are the River Plate republics. Argentina and Uruguay have experienced a continual immigration of Europeans for more than a century. Many of the immigrants came from the north of Europe where the Protestant faith dominated. Particularly where the recent arrivals established communities which retained their language and other aspects of their old culture, the inherited religion was preserved also. These communities which do not mix with the rest of the population are called ethnic communities. An ethnic church is one that attracts and ministers principally to members of its own culture. Some Latin American countries have stimulated the immigration of such peoples because of their contribution to the economy. In order to attract Protestant Europeans the governments had to decree religious liberty for them and later for all.

52. Racial, economic and political differences have produced

_____ diversity in Latin America.   see /

cultural

/

53. The nations that formed part of the Inca, Maya and Aztec empires have a

_____ percentage of Indians.   see /

54. Some Indian groups have retained the customs and beliefs that are part of their

_____ .   see &&

55. Protestantism entered some nations by means of immigrants who came from the north of

_____ .   see ///

56. Many of the immigrants were craftsmen or businessmen and the governments welcomed their contribution to the

_____

of the countries to which they immigrated.   see &

57. Some colonists preserved their language, customs and the

_____ faith which they had brought from their native lands.   see &&&

58. As a result the Roman Catholic governments had to permit the practice of

_____ .   see $

59. The River Plate republics were among the first to decree

_____ liberty.   see //

60. In this case the entrance of the gospel to certain countries was aided by

_____ interests on the part of the governments.   see $$

     Argentina is an example of a country dominated by Europeans.
Several of the largest denominations were formed by Germans,
Italians, English and other ethnic groups. Of the 250,000 members
of the evangelical churches, some 90,000 belong to the ethnic de-
nominations (Read, 1969:82). Their growth has been limited by the
desire to maintain their own culture. Therefore their churches
have not attracted other elements of the society. The Italian
or German speaking churches can not communicate the gospel to
those who speak only Spanish. Now that the immigration has
slowed and the second and third generations demand the use of
Spanish in the churches, there is hope for greater outreach in

/ higher
/// religious
    Europe
&   economy
&& culture
&&& Protes-
    tant,
    religious
    evangeli-
    cal
    Protes-
    tantism
    or
    SIMILAR
    WORDS
$ economic
$$

evangelism. The largest Church in Argentina, that of the Plymouth Brethren, suffers now because many people associate it with the English who founded it. The two denominations which are growing most rapidly at present are the Seventh Day Adventists and the Assemblies of God.

61. Argentina received immigrants from various European countries. Almost all the Italians professed the

_____ form of

Christianity. see &

82. From Germany, the home of Luther, many brought the _____ faith. see //

63. A great number of the denominations represent peoples which have preserved the culture of their home land. These are called

_____ Churches. see &&

64. The Italian churches did not attract Argentines who spoke only

_____. see /

65. Now that these groups are mixing more with the rest of the population there is

_____ opportunity for growth. see &&&

66. Today the ethnic churches grow _____ than the more indigenous groups such as the Adventists and the Assemblies of God.   see ///

Bolivia gives an entirely different picture from that of Argentina. Most of the people live on the high plateaus. Only in the last few years has the economy been developed in some sectors of the country. Bolivia has attracted few Europeans and at least 50 per cent of the population is of pure Indian blood. There we find ethnic churches of another type. Instead of being made up of Italians or Germans they are composed of Quechuas or Aymaras.

With the exception of the Adventist Church that still counts for a third of the evangelicals in the country, growth of the Church was very slow before 1950. Between 1915 and 1934 many of the Aymaras became Adventists. Since 1960 other groups have also found them to be responsive. In comparison with other countries the pentecostals have had relatively little success in Bolivia.

/   Spanish
// Lutheran
    Protestant
/// less OR SIMILAR WORDS
&   Catholic
&& ethnic
&&& more, greater

On the other hand the Methodists, giving emphasis to the planting of new congregations, grew 150 per cent between 1960 and 1967 (Read, 1969:111).

67. In contrast with Argentina, Bolivia received few immigrants from

_____. see ///

68. The majority of the population consists of descendents of the original inhabitants of the country, the

see $ _____.

69. In addition to the Spanish speaking churches, congregations have been formed of those who speak

see & _____ and _____.

70. Before 1950 the greatest growth occurred among the _____ people. see //

71. The non-Catholic group which has retained its advantage gained in the early years of this century is the

Church. see $$ _____

72. Today the Aymaras are _____ to the gospel. see &&&

73. Bolivia's example shows that the _____ groups do not always grow fastest. see /

74. It also indicates that evangelistic emphasis among responsive peoples can result in

_____ see &&

The development of the petroleum industry in Venezuela has brought prosperity to the country. It has also produced a largely urban population. More than in other Latin American countries the evangelical work in Venezuela has been dominated by missionaries and directed from the stations and institutions which they founded. The largest Church is that of the Plymouth Brethren which has emphasized lay testimony. Some missions with fifty years or more of work in the country have persisted in following policies and methods which have impeded growth. Therefore some congregations have broken off from the missions to form independent churches. In recent years the more traditional churches have tried to make up for lost opportunities.

/ pentecostals
// Aymaras
/// Europe
& Quechua, Aymara
&& growth
&&& responsive
$ Indians
$$ Adventist

75. In an earlier section we learned that Venezuela has one of the

_____ rates of growth. see &&

76. One of the reasons that the proportion of evangelicals changes so rapidly is that the evangelical community is relatively

_____. see //

77. In part, the development of the oil industry has been the reason that so many Venezuelans have left rural areas to work in the cities. This movement has produced a population that is mainly

_____. see &

78. The evangelical work in Venezuela has been less indigenous than that in other parts of the continent. It has been directed in large measure by

_____. see ///

79. The Church that has grown most is that which has emphasized the responsibility to evangelize of the

_____. see /

80. In spite of the opportunities presented, growth has been slight due in part to the fact that missions have employed certain

_____ and _____. see &&&&

        In Central America one of the important elements of the population is that of the Negroes who came from the West Indies and speak English. Nicaragua offers an example of the division of the churches between English and Spanish speaking congregations. The Moravians began missionary work among the Negroes at the turn of the century and have the largest Church in the country. But this Church is isolated from the Spanish speaking peoples and is ineffective in disseminating the gospel in the rest of the country. Other Churches have experienced good growth but their progress has been limited by conflicts between leaders, and other factors such as the occupation of the country by the U.S. Marines. Even those pentecostals which have done so well in neighboring countries have had less success in Nicaragua.

/ laymen
// small OR SIMILAR WORDS
/// missionaries
& urban
&& highest OR SIMILAR WORDS
&&& policies, practices, methods

81. In the list of figures on page 1-9 we noted that Nicaragua has the

_____ rate of growth. see &

82. One of the important elements of the population is that of the

_____ whose forefathers came from the West Indies.
                                                            see //

83. The Negro Churches don't attract the Latins because of

_____ differences.   see &&

84. For this reason the large Negro Moravian Church has _____ influence in the rest of the country. see ///

85. Sometimes the work is obstructed by disagreements between leaders. Church extension in Nicaragua has been limited by con- flicts between its

_____ see /

86. The pentecostals have grown less in Nicaragua than in the other

_____ countries. see &&&

87. Now that we have finished our consideration of various Latin American Churches write your observations concerning the reasons why the Church grows more in one area than in another or within one denomination than another.

/   leaders
// Negroes
&   little
    lowest
&& language,
    cultural,
    racial
&&& Central
    American

Church Growth as a Reflection of Faithfulness to God

We have seen enough evidence to convince us that the Church is growing. However there are some basic questions that should be answered. Is all this emphasis on numerical growth pleasing to God? Is it in agreement with the divine will? Does it reflect God's purpose in the world? The conviction of the authors is that the extension of the Body of Christ on earth is an essential part of God's purpose for today. It is not all His plan, but it is an essential part. In another chapter we will examine the biblical evidence for this position. Anticipating these arguments we declare that church growth reflects faithfulness to God. This faithfulness takes various forms which are:

Faithfulness in proclaiming the gospel
Faithfulness in finding the lost
Faithfulness in gathering and feeding the believers
Faithfulness in multiplying churches
Faithfulness in relating to the world

88. We must be sure that church growth conforms to the divine will. We must know if it is pleasing to

_____. see /

89. The authors of the text are convinced that the extension of the Church is the

_____ of God. see &&

90. The figures indicate that the Church is growing in _____.
see ///

91. If God wants church growth, those that promote this cause demonstrate their

_____ to God. see &

92. Later we will see how the concern for numerical growth is not just the idea of certain men, but that it rests on

_____

evidence. see //

In the first place, the believer has to proclaim faithfully the good news of salvation in Christ. There are at least two motives for the believer. One is the command of the Lord in Matthew 28 and other passages, that is called the Great Commission. It is an external impulse that requires obedience. We

/ God
// biblical
/// numbers OR
& faithfulness OR SIMILAR WORDS
&& purpose, plan

also have an internal impulse which is the Holy Spirit. The promise of Acts 1:8 is that the disciples of Christ would receive power and that they would be witnesses. Constrained by the Holy Spirit "we cannot but speak of what we have seen and heard" (Acts 4:20).

Where there is no faithfulness in proclamation, there is no growth. The Church is not extended unless the multitudes hear, obey and follow Christ. And they cannot hear where Christians don't show their loyalty to Christ and the power of the Holy Spirit in proclaiming the good news of salvation.

93. The first kind of faithfulness is the proclamation of the

_____. see &&&

94. One reason for preaching is the command of Jesus in Matthew 28 that is called the

_____. see /

95. Another reason for evangelizing is the presence of God in the believer through the person of the

_____. see $

96. In addition to the external command there is an _____ impulse. see ///

97. Two motives for evangelism are:

see &&

98. The multitudes can not hear and follow the gospel where the gospel is not

_____. see //

99. The first aspect of our faithfulness to God is _____

_____.see &

The second aspect of our faithfulness to God is the act of searching for and finding the lost. It is possible to preach to deaf ears. A common experience is to proclaim the gospel in

/ Great Commission

// preached, proclaimed

/// internal

& to preach the gospel OR SIMILAR WORDS

&& The Great Commission,

&&& The presence of the Holy Spirit OR SIMILAR WORDS

&&& gospel, good news

$ Holy Spirit

almost empty churches. A mere homiletic exercise doesn't accomplish God's purposes. If I drop my keys while opening a door, just looking for them is not sufficient. Merely looking doesn't interest me; I want to find them. There is a biblical illustration that treats the same point. It is not sufficient to look for the lost sheep. God wants it to be found. His purpose is finding, not seeking. Some "sheep" don't want to be found. If they continue in their rebellion against God without repenting, God's servant is not responsible for their condemnation. But the is obligated to seek the lost with intelligence and zeal, doing all that he can to find them.

100. The first aspect of faithfulness to God is to _____.
see &&&&

101. But it is possible to preach under hostile conditions in which the proclamation is

_____ .   see /

102. Although the message is very good, if the people do not respond, the preaching has not accomplished the purpose of
see $
_____.

103. God desires that the sheep not only be sought, but also

_____ .   see ///

104. No man can come to God without _____ of his sin.
see &&

105. Nevertheless, if someone doesn't respond to the message, it may be the fault of the

_____.   see //

106. Doing everything possible to find the lost demonstrates

_____ .   see &

107. Two aspects of our faithfulness to God are:

_____

_____

see $$

/ vain or SIMILAR WORDS
// preacher or SIMILAR WORDS
/// found
& faithfulness to God
&& repenting
&&& preach the gospel
$ God
$$ preaching the gospel, finding the lost or SIMILAR WORDS

Following the illustration of the sheep, we note that it is not sufficient to find them. Church growth occurs when the lost are not only found, but also restored to the fold. Faithfulness in gathering and feeding the lost is essential for permanent growth of the Church. When Church leaders let those who have made decisions, often with great sacrifice, slip back into the world, churches do not grow. Besides faithfulness in preaching and finding there must be faithfulness in gathering and feeding.

108. God's purpose is not to leave the sheep in the field without restoring it to the

_____ .   see /

109. In human terms, this means that a person should enter into the fellowship of a

_____ .   see &&

110. Without the support of other Christians many converts revert to the

_____ .   see ///

111. A part of the responsibility for those that fall away from the gospel belongs to the

_____ .   see &

112. Helping the new believers in becoming part of the congregation is faithfulness in

_____ .   see //

113. Giving biblical instruction is carrying out faithfully the responsibility of

_____ the believers.   see &&&

114. The three aspects of faithfulness to God that we have seen so far are:

•—————————————————————————————————•

•—————————————————————————————————•

•—————————————————————————————————•

see $

/ fold
// gathering
/// world
& leaders
&& Church
&&& feeding
$ preaching, finding, gathering and feeding or SIMILAR WORDS

God seeks not only the greatest number of Christians, but
also of Christian groups organized into congregations. Faithfulness in multiplying churches nourished on the Bible and full of
the Holy Spirit is essential to carry out the purposes of God.
The New Testament indicates that the normal Christian life is
found within the Christian community. It is developed through
companionship, instruction and mutual exhortation. Although it
is not possible to identify the Kingdom of God with the Church
and although there may be legitimate differences between the
visible and the invisible Church, God wants His sons to identify
with the visible Church. There is nothing spiritual about re-
maining outside an organized church.

115. God wants believers to organize into _____ . see &&&

116. The number of these churches should _____ . see $

117. Life in fellowship with others of like faith is normal for

_____ . see /

118. The totality of those that have accepted Christ as their Savior and Lord is the
　　　　　see &　　　_____ (visible/invisible) Church.

119. The local congregation is part of the _____ Church.
　　　　　see $$　　　(visible/invisible)

120. In a nominally Christian community the Church _____
(visible/invisible) would be larger. see ///

121. One of the purposes of the Church is to instruct the believers
in the things of God. Therefore every church should offer spi-
ritual nourishment based on the

_____ . see &&

122. The true Church is characterized also by the presence and
activity of God. The members of the churches should be filled
with the

_____ _____ . see //

/　　Christians
//　　Holy Spirit
///　　visible
&　　invisible
&&　　Bible
&&&　　churches, congregations or SIMILAR WORDS
$　　multiply
$$　　visible

123. God wills the multiplication of the number of _____

                                          see /

124. Four aspects of our faithfulness to God are:

_____

_____

_____

_____

                                          see &&

      Church growth requires faithfulness in relating to the world.
A Church that is so separated from the world that mutual comprehension and communication are impossible can not grow. Nevertheless, the Church needs to be separate and holy enough to please
God. It is convenient to mention here that the teaching of our
Lord in Mark 7:15 and other passages is that worldliness consists
principally in the values and the spirit of the world. A Christian, even though he has no vices, can still be guided by values
and attitudes which demonstrate more the spirit of the world than
of Christ. Christians, like their Lord, have to remain in the
world but not be of it. Sometimes this is the most difficult
problem: to maintain a pure testimony in the midst of a needy
world. Christ was incarnated. He identified with the world that
God had created and with the men that He had come to redeem.
The Church, by means of its members, must enter into all the
legitimate activities of the world. It should show that it is
possible to be an evangelical and a respected and appreciated
member of the community at the same time.

125. The Church should not isolate itself. It must maintain contact with the

    _____. see ///

126. It is only through normal means of communication that it is
possible to proclaim the

    _____. see &

127. If the Church can not communicate with the people that
surround it in terms that they can understand, it will be hard
to win new

    _____. see //

/ churches or SIMILAR WORDS

// members or SIMILAR WORDS

/// world or SIMILAR WORDS

& gospel or SIMILAR WORDS

&& proclaim the gospel, find the lost, gather and nourish, multiply churches

128. It is only through the expansion among those from outside that the Church is able to

_____ .   see &

129. In an effort to identify with the world the Church must be careful not to lose its identity as the people of
                    see $ _____ .

130. In the incarnation Christ assumed _____ nature.
                                        see /

131. But He never ceased to be _____ .   see &&

132. The Scriptures say that Jesus suffered every kind of temptation without

_____ .   see $$

133. The Church also has to avoid corruption. It must maintain its

_____ .   see &&&

134. Participation in almost all aspects of our culture is possible for

_____ .   see ///

135. The Church must express its faithfulness to God by _____ to the world.   see $$$

136. Christ identified with our condition in the _____ .
                                                  see //

137. The five aspects of faithfulness to God which produce church growth are:

_____

_____

_____

_____

see the list on page 1-18

/ human
// incarnation
/// evangelicals, believers, Christians
& grow, expand
&& God, divine
&&& holiness, purity or SIMILAR WORDS
$ God
$$ sinning, sin
$$$ relating

Three types of factors operate in the Church which are important for its growth. They are spiritual, social and personal. This study emphasizes the social factors because the Church is a social organism. To a certain degree it is directed by the principles which govern other social entities. Religious change is a type of social change although spiritual factors are involved. Therefore we will emphasize certain social or sociological factors in this study. There are many other good books which treat more specifically the religious or spiritual factors in the life of the Church. Church growth depends on social factors, but it is not a mere sociological process. The spiritual dimension must be added. We must always in this study operate within the framework of a biblical and evangelical faith. The extension of the Church throughout the world can not be considered in merely human terms. We are not talking about the ramifications of human organization. Churches which multiply throughout the world are evidence of God's power.

138. Although the Church is an institution established by God, it is similar in certain ways to other
               see /   _____ institutions.

139. Therefore we may apply to the Church some of the sociological findings, that is of the science of
               see &   _____ .

140. Entrance into the visible Church is an example of religious and
            _____ change.   see ///

141. But a man enters the invisible Church through the work of

            _____ .   see &&

142. Therefore church growth is not just the result of _____ effort.   see //

143. Like all science, sociological knowledge was given by _____.
               see &&&

144. Studying social movements will help us to understand the success of the Jehova's Witnesses and other
               see $ _____ .

SIMILAR WORDS

/   human or human
//   social
&   sociology
&&   God, the Holy Spirit
&&&   God
$ sects

145. It is difficult to believe that the entrance of many people in false religions is because of

see & _____ factors.

146. The Church of Christ, like other organizations, grows due to

_____ as well as spiritual factors.   see /

147. We must also consider the personal factor. The state of a congregation depends in part on the capabilities and the zeal of its

_____. see ///

148. If we apply human knowledge besides depending on God's power, we can expect that, in comparison with other groups, the Church will grow

_____. see &&&

---

149. The three types of factors that influence the growth of the Church are

see // _____, _____ and _____.

Review and Reflection

We have now examined some examples of the worldwide growth of the Church and particularly what God is doing in Latin America. We have also seen that growth is what God wants and that it reflects faithfulness to God. We will end this lesson with a brief review of some of the points mentioned and also with the application to the experience and situation of the student. In the questions that follow put an "X" in the space in front of the most correct answer.

150. With regard to the actual growth of the Church

_____a) There is more growth now than ever.

_____b) There are fewer congregations now than ever.

_____c) There is little growth in these days.   see &&

/ social
// spiritual, social,
 personal
/// pastor OR SIMILAR WORDS
& spiritual
&& a
&&& more

151. The expansion of the Church has taken place

_____a) Only in "Christian" countries.

_____b) Only in non-Christian countries.

_____c) In "Christian" and non-Christian countries.   see //

152. In general terms, we can say that

_____a) The Church always grows everywhere.

_____b) Obstacles can destroy God's work forever.

_____c) In spite of difficulties the worldwide Church grows.
                                                    see &&

153. Christians labor toward this goal in order to please

_____a) God.

_____b) Themselves.

_____c) Satan.   see ///

154. With relation to the proclamation of the gospel and its results, churches multiply

_____a) Wherever the gospel is preached.

_____b) Wherever men listen to the gospel.

_____c) Wherever men listen to and accept the gospel. see &

155. The salvation offered by God depends completely on

_____a) The grace and mercy of God.

_____b) The preaching of the gospel.

_____c) The response of the person.

_____d) All the elements a,b,c.   see /

156. Considering growth as a reflection of faithfulness to God we see that it is God's will that

_____a) The sheep be sought.

_____b) The sheep be sought and found.

_____c) The sheep be forgotten.   see /

157. Referring to the parable of the Prodigal Son, the servant of God should be satisfied when

_____a) He knows where the prodigal is.

_____b) The prodigal realizes his condition.

_____c) The prodigal returns to his Father.   see &

158. The illustration of sheep is not entirely adequate to show the human condition because

_____a) It is not necessary to look for people.

_____b) People never need physical help.

_____c) No one can be saved against his will.   see //

159. In order for a person to be restored (reconciled with God) he must

_____a) Attend a church some time.

_____b) Sign a decision card.

_____c) Become a believing member of a church.   see &&

160. As a result of not being gathered and fed in a church, a person who professes faith in Christ

_____a) Has to remain faithful to God regardless.

_____b) Can harden his heart against a Christianity that doesn't satisfy.

_____c) Contributes to the growth of the Church.   see ///

161. Feeding refers to what new, and old, members receive or experience in our churches. The life of a new believer should be full of

_____a) Many rules for every aspect of the Christian life.

_____b) The Holy Spirit.

_____c) Spiritual pride.   see ///

162. The Kingdom of God is equal to

_____a) Our denomination.

_____b) All the denominations.

_____c) No human organization.   see &&

163. There is a certain tension in the Christian life because of the need to be in the world without being of it. Let us examine this problem of relating and keeping separate at the same time. In order to maintain his relationship with the people that surround him, the Christian should

_____a) Avoid friendships with non-Christians.

_____b) Prove himself to be a responsible member of the community.

_____c) Participate in all the activities of his neighbors even though they may be of a questionable nature.   see //

164. Separation from the world means

_____a) Rejecting the world's values.

_____b) Deprecating the world's knowledge.

_____c) Attacking human institutions.   see &

165. The Gospels reveal that Jesus

_____a) Was a friend of sinners.

_____b) Kept Himself free from sin.

_____c) Avoided men for fear of contamination.   see /

166. It is regrettable, but true, that many persons who make a profession of faith in evangelistic campaigns or on other occasions do so without the sincerity or the knowledge necessary for a lasting decision. Nevertheless, there are some who sincerely seek Christ, but never reach a mature faith. It could be that these people afterwards are not ready to pay the price of being disciples of Christ. It could also be that the Church and its members must share the blame for not providing the instruction and the fellowship that these inquirers need. Indicate some ways in which the Church or individual Christians can help such people.

167. Although there are certain political conditions in which to confess Christ openly would be suicide, and although there are other circumstances, of which we will speak later, in which a man should not abandon his family or people in order to join a church, the biblical evidence indicates that the normal Christian life includes affiliation with a congregation of men of like faith. Name some of the advantages or values of such an association.

168. It has been said that the Church must struggle to maintain always and simultaneously its identity and its universality. That is, it must demonstrate its distinctively Christian character. But at the same time it must offer its fellowship and faith to all men who seek to unite with it. Explain how you personally could maintain open the lines of communication with the world without being contaminated or compromised.

2

EXAMPLES OF GROWTH

Before the student becomes involved in the theory of church growth he should have the experience of examining various cases of rapid and slow growth. It will be possible to refer to these examples again later as illustrations of the principles that are presented. By comparing the Churches mentioned we will be able to consider some criteria that will serve to judge any Church, including that of the student.

The Evangelical Church of Peru

In Peru at the beginning of this century people were hungry for something to read. The government at that time provided for the free distribution of any periodical published within the country. John Ritchie, a missionary, decided that it would be better to publish a newspaper than to distribute tracts. Therefore, in 1911, he began to publish "El Heraldo" and send it to everyone whose address he could find. Many of those who received the newspaper wrote in asking for Bibles, spiritual advice or a visit.

1. One of the most productive means of evangelism in Peru was the distribution of _____. see /

/ literature

2.   John Ritchie published "El Heraldo" which was a _____ .
            see /

3.   In comparison with tracts, the newspaper appeared _____
(more/less) like Protestant propaganda.   see &&&&

4.   Ritchie took advantage of the government provision for the free
            _____ of newspapers.   see $

5.   Judging by the number of responses, it seems that "El Heraldo" stirred up
            _____ interest.   see //

6.   Some readers, wanting to know more about the gospel, asked for a copy of the
            _____ .   see $$

7.   Others requested a visit from the publisher of the paper whose name was
            _____ .   see &&

        John Ritchie took advantage of these contacts to enter towns
as the guest of the person with whom he had corresponded. He
didn't try to organize formal services, but rather talked of
common themes such as the lost sheep and sowing and harvest.
During his visit of two or three days the missionary taught the
Bible to all who were interested. He always tried to use a Bible
text in his answer to questions so that the people would want to
buy and read the Word of God. Ritchie helped the people, giving
instructions concerning hygiene, agriculture, etc. In this way
he showed his interest and friendship toward the people to whom
he preached.

8.   Ritchie took advantage of contacts made through the distribution of the
            _____ .   see ///

9.   He answered the invitations and entered the communities as the
_____ of some resident there.   see $$$

10. He taught in simple terms. He spoke of seedtime and harvest
because many of his listeners were
            _____ .   see &

/   newspaper
//   much, or SIMILAR WORDS
/// newspaper
&   farmers
&&   Ritchie
&&&& less
$ distribution
$$ Bible
$$$ guest

11. He always quoted many Scripture texts so that the people would recognize the value and authority of the

                 see &   _____ .

12. Ritchie advised the people about certain practical matters to show his interest in his listeners. He wanted to be accepted as their

          _____ .   see $$

13. He only sold the most precious thing, which was the _____ .

                       see /

      When he concluded his visits Ritchie urged the believers or those interested to read the Bible and seek the help of other literature to grow in the faith. He declared that it wasn't necessary to have a teacher from outside. Those interested would name a committee to take charge of meetings. He suggested that every night when they finished their work they read a Bible portion and pray together. From these groups were born many congregations.

14. The believers should depend on the _____ as their spiritual guide.   see $

15. Leadership for the group was from _____ . see &&

16. With regard to worship, a committee could assume responsibility for the

             _____ .   see //

17. The financial help from outside which the group received was

    _____ .   see $$$

18. There was no need of a trained leader. Since the Bible was available, the group only needed someone who knew how to

                  see &&&   _____ .

19. Ritchie believed that through reading the Bible the group would arrive at an adequate understanding of

             see ///   _____ .

20. As time went by many of these groups became _____ .

           see %

/ Bible

// services, meetings

/// Christianity, the gospel, Christ

& Bible

&& the group itself or SIMILAR WORDS

&&& read Bible

$ friend or SIMILAR WORDS

$$ none or SIMILAR WORDS

% churches, congregations

In 1918 delegates of the churches held a conference and in 1920 began annual meetings for business and inspiration. After the meeting in 1922 the leaders began to evangelize in many towns throughout the region. In 1929 there were already sixty churches of some twenty members each. These groups were not uniform in spiritual maturity or organization. This family of churches established by Ritchie and his followers, later called the Evangelical Church of Peru, grew in number until it reached sixty congregations with 1400 members in 1930.

21. Ritchie began to publish "El Heraldo" in 1911. The need for a conference of church leaders was felt in 1918 after

_____

years of work.   see /

22. The groups or congregations saw the need to identify with a larger entity than their local group. They recognized that their congregation was part of the

_____. see &&&

23. The inspirational value of the meetings is seen by the fact that after the conference in 1922 the leaders dedicated themselves to the work of

_____ . see &

24. If the sixty congregations in 1929 had an average membership of twenty, the total number of members for the denomination would be

_____ (60 X 20).   see ///

25. A year later the total was 1400. The Church had added _____ members in one year. (1400 less 1200) see $

26. The Church had added a new member for every _____ old members.   (1200
                                                                                 ────
                                                                                 200)   see &&

27. This increase represents a rate of growth of 17 per cent. In comparison with the percentages of growth of the Churches in some of the countries we have studied in the first chapter, this was

_____ growth.   see //

/   seven
// good, rapid
/// 1200
&   evangelism
&& six
&&& Universal Church or SIMILAR WORDS
$ 200

Five districts were formed, each one supervised by a Peruvian worker. The churches did not depend on foreign funds. They supported themselves and contributed to the salaries of the five workers. Each congregation was directed by a Peruvian layman who donated his time. The elders of the congregation were responsible for discipline and also administered the ordinances in addition to the regular services. In some cases the elders knew very little, but this system had the advantage of being indigenous and stimulated interest and devotion on the part of the laymen.

28. To supervise the five districts the Evangelical Church of Peru named those who knew the situation best. They were workers of

_____ nationality.   see ///

29. The churches depended for their support on _____.
see &

30. The congregations contributed also to the support of the five

_____.   see /

31. With the exception of the five workers the whole movement was directed by

_____.   see //

32. Even baptism was administered by _____.   see &&

33. This system demanded more _____ on the part of the laymen.   see $

34. The only ones who earned a salary were the _____.
see &&&

/   workers, supervisors
//   laymen
///   Peruvian
&   themselves or SIMILAR WORDS
&&   elders or local leaders
&&&   workers, supervisors
$ participation or SIMILAR WORDS

35. Ritchie only entered those towns where a person with whom he had had correspondence or other contact invited him. This policy is in contrast with the way in which many other missionaries have operated. What could be the advantages of entering a town by invitation or where there is someone who sponsors the missionary or pastor?

The Foursquare Gospel Church in Ecuador

The Foursquare Gospel Church in Ecuador presents a very different but also good kind of growth. In 1962 the Foursquare Church had a congregation of some thirty members in Guayaquil, Ecuador. In that year an evangelistic campaign was organized in a soccer field. In spite of the prayers of the congregation it appeared that the campaign would be a failure. A short time before the campaign the other denominations in the city announced that they would not cooperate. The Foursquare church did not have trained counselors, nor seats, nor choir, nor special musicians. But at the last moment the director of a local radio station in Guayaquil offered to transmit the services at cost.

On the first night of the campaign one thousand persons appeared in the stadium. After the evangelistic message the evangelist prayed for the healing of some of the people present. The news of their healing spread over the radio. On the second night attendance was five thousand, the third night ten thousand and at the end of the week the gospel was being preached to twenty thousand. People came from all over the country.

36. Using the experience in Guayaquil as a model we can reach some general conclusions about evangelistic campaigns. Apparently the success of a campaign depends on

_____a) An adequate location.

_____b) Great musical talent to attract the people.

_____c) Much propaganda before the campaign.

_____d) None of these factors.   see /

37. The best propaganda for a campaign may be

_____a) Announcements in the churches.

_____b) The testimony of those who have attended.

_____c) Leaflets dropped from a plane.   see ///

38. For a campaign in a city such as Guayaquil (population 600,000) the attendance may be expected to

_____a) Increase night after night.

_____b) Be the greatest the first night.

_____c) Be more or less the same every night.   see &

39. In order to carry out a big campaign, one requisite is

_____a) A large denomination that sponsors it.

_____b) The cooperation of all the denominations.

_____c) Any number of believers.   see //

40. The most important preparation for a campaign is

_____a) Prayer.

_____b) The formation of committees.

_____c) Good physical arrangements.   see //

41. Possibly that which attracts more attention of the unconverted is

_____a) A large number of conversions.

_____b) A large number of healings.

_____c) A large number of posters.   see &

　　　At the end of the six weeks of campaign, a baptismal service was held which 30,000 attended. 1500 persons were baptized in an inlet in Guayaquil. During the campaign itself instruction was given to the baptismal candidates. It was noted that at 9:00 p.m. when the evangelist began his message people were still coming. Therefore those in charge decided to begin the service a little later, while an associate evangelist taught about the Christian life from 8:30 to 8:50 every night. Those who attended regularly received more instruction during the weeks of the campaign than many other candidates receive in other systems of preparation for baptism that last longer. (Weld, 1968:62).

42. The Foursquare was criticized for having baptized so many people in so little time. Many doubted that the preparation and stability of these persons were adequate. But those who were baptized were

_____a) All those who had attended the campaign.

_____b) All those who had received instruction for several weeks during the campaign.

_____c) All those who heard of the campaign.   see /

43. Instruction concerning the Christian life was given

_____a) Every night.

_____b) Several months after the campaign.

_____c) By someone who had nothing to do with the campaign.
　　　　　　　　　　　　　　　　　　　　　　　　　see ///

44. The first time that an invitation was given to go forward 2,000 persons responded. Therefore, the number of decisions on one night was

_____ than the total of those baptized. see /

45. If a believer received instruction concerning the Christian life twenty minutes every night for twenty-four days, he would have received

_____ hours of instruction.

(20 minutes = 1/3 hour, 24/3 =   )   see ///

46. In addition to the instruction he listened to _____.

see //

47. Later we will consider the instruction given before and after baptism. Nevertheless, we should think in a preliminary way about this ordinance of the Lord. What does baptism mean for an evangelical? When should it be administered in the life of a Christian? Should it mark the beginning or the end of the formal instruction that church members receive? Converts are more ready to receive instruction during a campaign or several months afterwards?

/ greater
// the evangelistic messages or SIMILAR WORDS
/// eight

The most serious problem at the end of the campaign was what to do with all the new converts. The Foursquare Church before had just a small meeting place. Therefore it opened eight new churches. But who would serve as pastors? In the first congregation there were ten Sunday School teachers. With this experience they were the best qualified to pastor the new congregations. The recent converts were ready to listen to anyone who knew a little more about Christian doctrine and conduct than they did. These "pastors" grew in maturity as their congregations grew in number. They continued in their secular work until the congregation decided to support them in a full time pastorate.

48. Before the campaign the Foursquare Church had thirty members. The number of baptized new members was
see /   _____.

49. If only 1200 remained faithful, each one of the eight new congregations would have an average of
(1200/8)   see &&&   _____ members.

50. The tithes and offerings of more than 100 members should provide the funds necessary to pay the salary of a
see $ _____.

51. The new pastors had had experience in one of the pastoral ministries which is
_____.   see //

52. The pastors only had to know more than _____.
see &&

53. The decision to have a full time pastor in a certain congregation was taken by
_____.   see &

54. All the administration of each church depended on the resources of the
_____.   see ///

/   1500
// teaching, instruction or SIMILAR WORDS
/// local church or SIMILAR WORDS
&   the congregation or SIMILAR WORDS
&& the rest or SIMILAR WORDS
&&& 150
$ pastor, worker

55. In view of the experience in Guayaquil and that of the student in other places, give your opinion of the relative value of short campaigns in which much is spent on propaganda beforehand or of long campaigns with less propaganda.

The Adventist Church in Peru

In chapter I reference was made to the success of the Adventists among the Aymara Indians. We will now examine in greater detail the Adventist work among the Aymaras of Peru because the case illustrates well the influence of certain social factors. In 1907 an Aymara speaking Indian, Mr. Camacho, returned from Chile, where he had been educated in a Methodist school. He went to his town on the shore of Lake Titicaca in Peru and opened a school for the people there. The Roman Catholic Church kept a tight rein on the Aymaras and the community was persecuted for this attempt at independence. Therefore Mr. Camacho asked the evangelical missionary in Arequipa to send someone to live in the town and help the Indians. But there was no one to send.

56. The Aymaras live in the Andean countries of Bolivia and ____.
see /

57. The Adventist work illustrates how certain religious and

_____ factors operate.   see //

/ // Peru social

58. Mr. Camacho was an evangelical because he was educated in a

_____ .   see &&&

59. He wanted to help his people that spoke _____ . see /

60. In order that his people could improve their lot Mr. Camacho founded a

_____ .   see $

61. This institution constituted a threat to the authority of the

_____ .   see &&

62. Persecuted by the Catholics Mr. Camacho sought the help of

_____ .   see //

63. Because of other commitments the evangelicals in Arequipa

_____ his request.   see $$

A short time afterward an Adventist colporter visited the town and soon an Adventist missionary couple came to live there from 1907 to 1911. The fame of the missionary spread and he was asked to establish schools and churches through the region. After the establishment of one center in 1910 the movement grew until in 1922 there were ten centers, each one responsible for several schools and churches. In that year there were 1000 members. In 1930 the membership had risen to 4376 baptized members in Peru and 1600 more in the adjacent region of Bolivia among those of the same race and language (Hamilton, 1962:46-47).

64. Because a member of the community had become an evangelical, the Aymaras were (more/less)
          see &   _____ open to the gospel.

65. By returning to his town and establishing a school there Mr. Camacho showed his interest in

_____ .   see ///

66. For this reason the members of the community thought that it was a good thing to be an

_____ .   see $$$

/   Aymara
//   Protestants, evangelicals
///   his people or SIMILAR WORDS
&   more
&&   Roman Catholic Church
&&&   Methodist school or SIMILAR WORDS
$ school
$$ refused or SIMILAR WORDS
$$$ evangelical

67. Their responsiveness to the evangelical faith was increased also because of the _____ by the Roman Catholic Church.   see //

68. Ignored by other evangelical groups the Aymaras decided to become _____ .   see $

69. This (the Adventists) was the only group that visited them when they were ready to change their

    see &&&   _____ .

70. The Adventist missionary was successful, in part because he lived _____ .   see /

71. One missionary could do little in a movement so large. The responsibility for carrying forward the work belonged to the

_____ .   see &&

72. The Adventist faith spread as far as Bolivia, to other people of the same _____ .   see ///

73. With respect to cultural and political boundaries, it is easier for the gospel to cross the

    see &   _____ ones.

The Church in Aracaju, Brazil

In 1964 the leaders of the Evangelical Church in Aracaju, Brazil, made plans for a year long campaign which would reach the whole city. They divided the city into sectors and assigned a sector to each congregation. Every church employed the following methods:

1) They organized prayer cells to pray for the revival of Christians and a harvest of souls.
2) The pastors preached about the condemnation of the lost and the blessings of those that repent and accept Christ as their Savior and Lord.

SIMILAR WORDS

/ in the midst of the people or
// persecution
/// culture, language
& political
&& laymen,
&&& believers religion
$ Adventists

3) They held open air services with the cooperation of some of the groups. They invited evangelists from other cities.

4) They distributed hundreds of thousands of tracts and Scripture portions.

5) The Christians went in pairs to visit every home in the city to invite the people to the meetings and to offer to teach them the way of the Lord.

74. This movement in Aracaju is very similar to the programs of Evangelism in Depth. The evangelistic work in Aracaju was not the result of a spontaneous movement. Everything was done according to a

_____ .   see /

75. The goal was to reach _____ the city.   see $

76. In order to cover all the territory the city was divided into

_____ .   see ///

77. Each sector was the responsibility of a _____. see &

78. An important element in the preparation was _____.
                              see &&&

79. The first evangelistic method was the organization of prayer

_____ .   see $$

80. The second was the proclamation of the _____.
                                     see //

81. The pastors indicated the necessity of accepting _____.
                              see $$$

82. In third place services were organized outside the church in the

_____ .   see %

83. The evangelistic message was based on the teachings of the

_____ .   see &&

/ plan
/// gospel sectors
& church, congregation
&& Bible
&&& prayer all
$$ cells, meetings
$$$ Christ
% open air

84. The fourth method of evangelism was the _____ of Scripture portions.   see &&

85. In order to reach the unconverted people it is necessary for Christians to move out of the

_____.   see ///

86. The evangelicals also visited the homes of _____.
see &

87. The fifth evangelistic method was _____.
see //

88. With the combination of these methods the churches tried to reach

_____.   see /

---

89. The five methods or phases of evangelism employed in Aracaju, Brazil were:

•_____•

•_____•

•_____•

•_____•

---

see the list on pages 2-13, 2-14

All the evangelical churches from the Assemblies of God to the United Presbyterians cooperated in this campaign. They were increasingly encouraged on seeing the results. Men, women, boys and girls were won to Christianity every week. There was confession of sin. Resentments between some persons were resolved. Separated families were reunited. Classes were begun to instruct the new Christians in all the churches.

After the campaign and the instruction and baptism of the converts won during the year of special efforts, it was discovered that the total membership of the churches in the city had doubled from 1200 to 2400 baptized members (McGavran, 1970:26).

/ the whole city
/// visitation
/// homes, churches
& all or SIMILAR WORDS
&& distribution

90. Perhaps one of the reasons for the success of the campaign was the cooperation of

_____ .   see $

91. The results of the campaign were seen in the lives of individuals. Some confessed their

_____ .   see &

92. Another evidence of God's work was the reconciliation of persons who were

_____ .   see /

93. In order to preserve the fruits of the campaign it was necessary for the converts to identify with one of the
see ///   _____.

94. One step toward this identification is the rite of _____.
see //

95. In preparation for this step all the churches offered _____.
see &&

96. The pastors and other believers were _____
with the success of the campaign.   see &&&

97. Taking into consideration all the aspects of evangelism mentioned above, which depended for their success more on the average church member than on the pastor?

/   resentful
//   baptism
///   churches
&   sins
&&   classes,
        instruction
&&&   satisfied
        OR SIMILAR
        WORDS
$ all the churches
        OR SIMILAR WORDS

The Presbyterian Church in Brazil

During the years 1917 to 1954 the Brazil Plan of the Presbyterian Church was in effect. According to this plan the field was divided between the Presbyterian Church of Brazil and the mission. The Church received all the established and self-supporting congregations. Its responsibility was to develop these churches and work in the densely populated coastal sector while the missionaries were to penetrate the interior of the country.

98. The National Church was in charge of

_____a) The congregations which needed mission support.

_____b) Some areas of concentrations of people.

_____c) The interior of the country.   see /

99. The Church and the mission

_____a) Cooperated.

_____b) Had the same work.

_____c) Were in competition.   see ///

100. With regard to the division of labor, the national Church

_____a) Received the area of less opportunity.

_____b) Had more possibilities for evangelism.

_____c) Had no base on which to build its work. see //

In those years the concept of mission was not that of the pioneers who struggled to plant churches in responsive areas. In 1917 the mission of the foreign workers was that of "penetration." The interior was a difficult area in which to plant churches. It seemed easier and perhaps more necessary to help the people toward social reform, teach them better agricultural methods, and organize mission stations in strategic points throughout the region. Some churches were organized. No one was against it and some prayed that it might continue. However, no one thought of measuring the success of the work in terms of church growth. Unfortunately, there are no membership figures available for the Church during that period.

101. In this period (1917-1954) the concept of mission was

_____a) Plant churches everywhere.

_____b) Plant churches in areas responsive to the gospel.

_____c) Penetrate the society in preparation for evangelism.
see //

102. Emphasis, although perhaps not conscious, was given to

_____a) Establishing churches.

_____b) Material benefits for the people.

_____c) Religious reform.   see /

103. The success of the mission and its work was evaluated by

_____a) The number of people baptized according to annual reports.

_____b) The number of congregations established.

_____c) Subjective concepts which did not need data. see &

104. The problem with the concept of the "work of penetration" is that

_____a) Preparation is never needed for evangelism.

_____b) No one knew when to begin to harvest.

_____c) The Church should not get involved in social matters.
see ///

Many talked of the Brazil Plan, but no one analyzed its results in terms of conversions and congregations. In some cases institutions dominated the work, absorbing the resources of personnel and finances. Although we can appreciate the faithful labors of many servants of God and the fruits which have remained, it is possible that other methods and the concentration of resources in other regions would have produced more (Read, 1965:60-62).

105. In some sectors the Brazil Plan failed because

_____a) No one analyzed the results.

_____b) The institutions used up the resources that should have been used for evangelism.

_____c) There were no faithful servants of God.   see //

106. It is very possible that there could have been better results if they had

_____a) Given emphasis to difficult sectors of the region.

_____b) Given greater resources to the institutions.

_____c) Used other methods.   see /

The Ecuadorian Church

During the first fifty years of the Evangelical Church in Ecuador (1896-1946) evangelistic progress was very slow. From 1900 to 1925 there was an average of twenty missionaries and five national workers in the country, but in 1925 the Church had fewer than 150 members. From 1925 to 1945 an average of forty-five missionaries and ten national workers were faithfully proclaiming the Word of God, but the number of members only rose to some 1000 baptized. Really the number of believers for years of missionary service was not very different from that in Colombia, Peru or Venezuela during the same period. But comparing the results with those of other Latin American countries there is reason to ask if there were no more fruitful methods or no more responsive areas indicated by the Holy Spirit.

107. During the first fifty years

_____a) The Church grew rapidly.

_____b) The Church showed great stability.

_____c) The Church grew slowly.   see ///

108. The work was directed mainly by

_____a) Missionaries.

_____b) National workers.

_____c) Angels.   see //

109. The limited success of the first years was due to the fact that

_____a) No one preached the Word of God.

_____b) Reasons which are not shown here.

_____c) There were too many national workers.   see ///

110. In comparison with the evangelistic work in other parts

_____a) That of Ecuador compares favorably with the majority of
the Latin American countries.

_____b) Ecuador had more or less the same number of baptisms per
year of missionary service as in the River Plate republics.

_____c) There is reason to ask if it would not have been possible
to produce greater results during the whole period. see /

These examples of church growth demonstrate the complexity
of the processes by which God multiplies His churches. We need
to know much more. For some countries studies have already been
made of the history of the growth of the Church and the reasons
for greater or less growth have been analyzed. For other countries the facts are still very obscure. Perhaps there are stories
of the work, but these are full of biographical references instead of figures of the concrete results of the work. In addition to the inspiration which biographies offer, we need the objective analysis which the other type of study furnishes.

111. The specific cases that we have studied indicate that

_____a) Church growth is a simple process.

_____b) We need to know more about how the Church grows.

_____c) We understand perfectly the reasons for the results
shown.   see &

112. With regard to the study of growth in various countries

_____a) More or less the same information is known about all the countries.

_____b) There is no need to make special studies of growth.

_____c) For some countries the facts are not very clear. see //

113. The class or classes of literature that we need are

_____a) Critical studies of the processes of growth.

_____b) Inspirational and promotional writing.

_____c) Both types of presentation of the work.   see /

114. As a review of this analysis of the Churches studied, write a resumé in your own words of the factors which promoted or hindered church growth.

A Comparison of the Churches According to Certain Characteristi

We have seen examples of rapid and slow growth. There are other criteria that can be applied to the study of the Church besides its size and rate of expansion. These other considerations have to do with its stability and its capacity to extend itself spontaneously. We might say that they refer more to the quality than the quantity of the members. Nevertheless it is impossible to separate the two characteristics. A church that produces mature members has to grow. The five criteria that will be applied to this study of the Church are:

Dependence on others.
Decisions made individually or in groups.
The proportion of the total population.
The rate of growth.
Indigeneity.

The first way of comparing churches is with respect to their dependence on the mission or on outside help. Of the cases which we have considered, the Ecuadorian Church was that which depended most on missions. The majority of the pastors and workers were foreigners. They dominated the Church. The few national believers could not sustain the evangelistic efforts, pay pastors or provide funds for renting or constructing church buildings. On the other hand, the Peruvian Evangelical Church did not depend on outside help with the exception of a percentage of the salaries of the five superintendents. Each congregation was responsible for its place of worship and pastoral care. All the programs were dependent on local funds. While it is true that the Church was begun by a missionary whose salary came from England, once the congregations were established they were not directly dependent on him or on others.

115. We are interested not only in the number of church members but also in their

_____ . see //

116. A congregation of well instructed Christians has _____
possibilities for growth.   see /

117. The Church expands if the local members sense that the respons
bility for the work is

_____ . see ///

/ greater quality
// theirs or
/// SIMILAR WORDS

118. The kind of Church that is needed is one that can extend itself without the need of a push from outside. Such a Church can realize natural or

_____ growth.   see &

119. The Ecuadorian Church was closely tied to various missions. It was

_____ on them for funds.   see ///

120. Also the major part of the pastoral and evangelistic work was done by the

_____ .   see $

121. On the other hand the Peruvian Evangelical Church was sustained by

_____ .   see &&

122. The Peruvian congregations paid part of the salary of the five

_____ .   see $$

123. In the Presbyterian Church in Brazil the work of penetration was the responsibility of the

_____ .   see //

124. The institutions in Brazil were dependent on _____ funds.   see &&&

125. Nevertheless, the mission handed over to the Church the congregations that could

_____ themselves.   see /

126. These churches were no longer dependent on the _____ .
                                              see %

127. The first criterion of the quality of the church is

_____ .   see $$$

The most important thing about this study is not the historical facts or theories but the application to the situation and ministry of the student himself. Answer the following questions for your own congregation or denomination.

/   sustain, support
//   missionaries
///   dependent
&   spontaneous
&&   its members or SIMILAR WORDS
&&&   foreign or SIMILAR WORDS
$ missionaries
$$ superintendent
$$$ dependence on others
%   mission

128. Who pays the pastor's salary? Who handles the funds?

129. Where do the funds come from for church construction?

130. Who determines church policies? Who assigns pastors?

131. What other types of dependency can you mention?

The second criterion of the study of the Church has to do with the way in which the believers entered the church. Did they make individual decisions, defying their relatives and friends? Were there decisions by smaller or larger groups to follow Christ? Often we have snatched individuals from their place in society unnecessarily instead of leaving them where they could have the opportunity of sharing the gospel. We want to know, therefore, if the decisions were made individually or in groups.

We don't have the facts to judge the cases mentioned above. Nevertheless we may suppose (without being far off) that the majority of the decisions made in Guayaquil, as in other campaigns, were individual. Among the multitude of unknown people there were men and women who decided for Christ. But when they got home they encountered opposition. However, in Peru, there were communities that decided, after joint conversation and consideration, to become Adventists. Later we will have opportunity to examine the motives and the advantages and disadvantages in more detail. It is sufficient for now to say that in decisions made by families or whole communities there is not the same social conflict over a change of religion. The family or the community decides to support instead of oppose the new religion of the individual. For this reason it is important to know if the decisions were made individually or in groups.

132. It is important to know how persons became Christians and members of the

_____ .   see &

133. Often the enemies of a Christian are those of his own _____ .

see ///

134. If a man makes his decision for Christ in spite of the opposition of his parents it is

_____ likely that they will

make the same decision.   see $

135. If someone decides against the group, a barrier is raised and the Christian may lose the opportunity to

_____ the

gospel to the group.   see &&

136. It is important to know if the decisions to follow Christ were made individually or in

_____ .   see /

137. It is supposed that the majority of the decisions made in evangelistic campaigns are

_____ .   see //

138. But among the Aymaras of Peru, evangelical Christianity was accepted, at least nominally, by some

_____ .   see &&&

/   groups
/// individual
     house or
     SIMILAR
     WORDS
&   church
&&   communicate
     or SIMILAR
     WORDS
&&& groups
$ less or
     SIMILAR
     WORDS

139. In this case the friends and parents of the Christian would be
_____ of the gospel. see /

140. In order to have an idea of the possible conflict between Christians and their families it is necessary to know the way in which the Christians entered the church, that is
_____
or _____ .   see &

141. Ritchie entered a town only when he was _____ .
see ///

142. He probably spoke with all the members of the _____ .
see &&&

143. When he left the town Ritchie placed the respnsibility for continuing the work in the hands of a
see //   _____ .

144. The second criterion of the quality of a church is that of the
_____
see &&

145. In the student's congregation, how many whole families are there?
_____

146. How many members come from families in which no one else is an evangelical?
_____

147. Are more families united or divided by the gospel?_____

The third criterion is the proportion of the total population that is evangelical. If a high percentage of the total population is evangelical, it is probable that the faith has reached all levels of society, although not in equal measure. Therefore it will have more influence. Many will think of the faith as a real option for themselves since so many others have accepted it. History gives us examples of evangelical communities which had ethical standards very superior to those of the rest of the population. Therefore it is important not only to know the proportion of Christians in the total population, but also the proportion in the local situation.

/ — in favor or SIMILAR WORDS

// — commit- tee, group

/// — in- vited

& — indivi- dually, groups

&& — way in which the decisions were made, indivi- dually or in groups or SIMILAR WORDS

&&& — family, community

148. The second criterion asked if the believers had made their decision alone or in

_____ . see /

149. Now we want to know the proportion of the Christian community in the total

_____ . see $

150. It is more likely that a high percentage of the community will be Christian if the decisions were made

see &   _____ .

151. A low percentage of evangelicals has _____ opportunity of changing the society.   see //

152. If in Brazil there were 10% evangelicals and in Venezuela 1%. the Church with greater influence over its country's culture would be that of

_____ . see &&&

153. It is easier to become an evangelical when _____ have already done so.   see $$

154. The goal of the Church (in theory) should be to win _____ per cent of the population.   see ///

155. The third criterion of the Church is _____

_____ . see &&

     The fourth criterion is the rate of church growth. In Chapter I we noted the growth rates of the Churches in the Latin American countries. Ecuador had the highest rate, partly because the number of evangelicals was so small. An increase of 1000 members in Ecuador means an important change of percentage for the Church there. But a thousand members represent a very small per cent in Brazil. In a congregation or a section of the Church we can see more dramatic changes. For example the Foursquare Church in Ecuador experienced a very high rate of growth in 1962. If the number of evangelicals doubles in one year the percentage of growth is 100. This was the experience of the Church in Aracaju, Brazil. The annual growth rate is one of the best measures of the vitality of the Church.

/   groups
//   less, little
/// 100
&   in groups
&&   the proportion of the total
     population or SIMILAR WORDS
&&& Brazil
$ population
$$ many, others

156. The third criterion considers evangelicals as a proportion of the

_____ .   see &

157. Now the number of those who join the Church in a year is compared with the total number of

_____ . see $$

158. According to the data of the churches which were presented in Chapter I we would expect a smaller Church to have a

rate of growth.   see /   _____

159. The growth rate for a Church in any country is an average. Some congregations which make up the Church grow more and others

_____ than the average.   see &&&

160. An increase of 5000 members in Costa Rica represents a (higher/lower)

_____ percentage than the entrance of
5000 members in the Church of Mexico.   see //

161. If every member of the Church won another during a year the number of Christians would be

_____ times as great. see $

162. This would be _____ per cent growth. see &&

163. The fourth criterion of the Church is the _____ .
                                        see ///

Now calculate the growth rate of your church.

164. How many members did the church have on January 1, 1971? _____

165. How many members did the church have on January 1, 1970? _____

166. The increase was _____ . (You must subtract.)

The rate of growth is calculated by dividing the increase in membership, in this case the figure in question 166, by the number of members at the beginning of the period, in this case, the figure in question 165.

/   higher or SIMILAR WORDS
//   higher growth rate or SIMILAR WORDS
/// total population
&   100
&&   less
&&& two
$ old members
$$

Examples:

	1971	120 members		1971	220 members
	1970	100 members		1970	150 members
		20 difference			70 difference

$$\frac{20}{100} = 20\%$$ $$\frac{70}{150} \cong 47\%$$

167. Calculate the percentage of growth of your church during 1970.

The fifth and last criterion in this study of the Church is its indigeneity. If the forms of worship and the Church structures are natural to the region, it is more likely that it will attract the people. If the missionaries have imposed on the Church some aspects of their culture, thinking that these things were Christian essentials, they have raised cultural barriers for many. The evangelical faith is identified in that case as the religion of foreigners. We have already seen the case of the ethnic churches in certain countries that minister only to a certain cultural group without touching the majority of the population. It is important that Christianity be an integral part of any culture and not an expression of a foreign culture. For this reason an important criterion of the Church is indigeneity.

168. Christianity

_____a) Is a distinct culture.

_____b) Is not a part of any culture.

_____c) Must express itself in each culture.   see /

169. The man who seeks God will find Him more easily in a church that expresses its faith according to

_____a) A foreign culture.

_____b) The culture of the region.

_____c) A combination of the two cultures.   see //

c c
—/ /

170. An indigenous church is one that

_____a) Practices the customs of the missionary.

_____b) Practices the customs of its region.

_____c) Practices the customs of the nation's capital. see //

171. Of the Churches which have been considered in this lesson, the most indigenous would be the

_____a) Peruvian Evangelical Church.

_____b) Presbyterian Church of Brazil.

_____c) Ecuadorian Church.   see /

172. An important criterion in the study of the Church is

_____a) Indigeneity.

_____b) Conformity to other Churches.

_____c) The form of worship.   see ///

173. Some indications that a Church is indigenous are the originality of the hymns that are sung, the style of the building and the order of worship. What other indications can you suggest?

---

174. As a review of this section, write below the five criteria in a study of the Church.

see the list on page 2-22

3

THE MISSION

OF THE CHURCH

In the first two chapters we discovered the complexity of church growth and we examined some of the forms that it assumes. In many parts of the world the Church is growing rapidly. But this growth is not uniform and the Church needs to expand more. Nevertheless, it is said that the Church, like its Lord, must die in order to redeem the world. Are those who say this right? What does the Bible say? The present chapter treats this theme: the Mission of the Church. It is a very important theme because if the goal is not well defined, the discussion of methods is valueless. If we don't know where we are going it is impossible to know what route to take, nor if we have arrived. This chapter attempts to define the mission or purpose of the Church and presents biblical proofs to support the position taken. In this way a base is provided to consider the facts of growth and the other topics which follow.

God's Plan for the World

What is the mission or purpose of the Church? We must first recognize that the Church is the Body of Christ. The mission of the Church therefore is the mission of God. It is subject to its Lord and must submit to the divine will. In saying that the Church is the Body of Christ we must not forget that not it but the Holy Spirit is the continuation of the presence of Christ on earth. The Church, the human agency of the divine will, learns this will through the Holy Spirit. The Church depends in part on the definitive revelation of the Scriptures and in part must listen to the voice of the Spirit through the circumstances in which it lives.

1. The mission of the Church is not human but _____.
                                see /

2. The Church is the Body of _____ .   see &&

3. Nevertheless, the presence of Christ is experienced through
the person of the
                    _____ .   see $

4. It is the Holy Spirit that directs the activities of the
    _____ .   see //

5. The Church is directed also by the inspired message of the
    _____ .   see &&&

6. Only in submission to God can the Church carry out the
    _____ that God has given it.   see &

7. The Church receives its mission from _____ . see ///

      God loves the world. He loves it so much that He sent His
Son to redeem it. In His mercy the Father makes the sun to shine
on the good and the bad and sends rain to the just and unjust.
But while God provides physical life to all, He is most interested in their spiritual welfare. Man was created for communion
with God and the heavenly Father wants the persons who have wandered from Him in sin to be reconciled with Him. God is satisfied when men come to Him in faith.

      One of the basic characteristics of the Church's mission
therefore is that, through it, men are converted and enter the
kingdom of God and in this way the Church grows. Our Lord was
not satisfied with feeding the multitudes and healing the sick.
He gave His life as a ransom for many and sent His disciples
to evangelize the nations.

/   divine
//   Church
///   God
&   purpose, mission
&&   Christ
&&&   Bible
$ Holy Spirit

8.   God loves

_____a) All men.

_____b) Some men.

_____c) No men.   see &

9.   God is interested most in the

_____a) Spiritual welfare of men.

_____b) Material welfare of men.

_____c) Social welfare of men.   see /

10.   The most important thing for God is

_____a) The transformation of society.

_____b) The evolution of man.

_____c) The redemption of man.   see &&

11.   Men should be reconciled first with

_____a) God.

_____b) Other men.

_____c) Science.   see ///

12.   The Church as the Body of Christ should reflect His ministry.
Based on your study of the life and ministry of Christ, answer
the following questions. The purpose of Christ was to

_____a) Correct the evils of society.

_____b) Establish a political kingdom.

_____c) Establish the Kingdom of God.   see //

a c c a c
/ // /// & &&

13. In His ministry of healing the sick, Jesus

_____a) Healed all the sick people in Palestine.

_____b) Sought opportunities to heal the sick.

_____c) Sometimes avoided opportunities to heal.   see /

14. Jesus said that He had come to

_____a) Feed the multitudes.

_____b) Seek that which was lost.

_____c) Entertain the people.   see &&

    The Word of God is subject to human interpretation. Conse-
quently men have interpreted in various ways God's purpose for
the Church. For some the mission of the Church includes God's
whole plan for mankind. It includes all the activities and the
aspects of life. In Latin America there are many needs - economic, social, educational and religious. There are many good
activities in which the Church and its members can participate.
The problems consists in choosing between the possibilities. Sometimes we must leave the good in order to do the best. Resources
must be proportioned out wisely. For example, it is a good thing
for Sao Paulo to have enough water to water all the flowers, to
have schools for all the children and to have such knowledge of
Jesus Christ that anyone can put his faith intelligently in Him.
The three things are good, but we must put them in order of importance.

15. There are diverse opinions regarding the _____ of
the Church.   see ///

16. God has established an institution on earth through which
He seeks to reconcile men with Himself. Some men think that
all God's plan should be carried out by means of the
                         see &   _____.

17. The Church has to decide in which activities it should invest its
        _____.   see //

/ c
/// resources
purpose,
mission
Church
& b
&&

18. There are many ways of trying to satisfy the needs of _____.

see /

19. The Church must establish priorities. This means that is has to decide which activities are the most

see //   _____.

20. One of the reasons for the complexity of church growth is that its activities are diverse. In the example of Sao Paulo three activities - social, educational and religious - are mentioned. Put these three activities in their order of importance and indicate why you chose this order.

21. Enumerate the activities of the Church in your city or sector and classify them as social, educational or religious.

          There should not be a conflict between evangelism and the social program of the Church. Both are important, but the right proportion must be maintained. Social service can not substituted for salvation. Nor can we expect that salvation will automatically produce all the services that the Church can offer. In this world of rapid change it is necessary to adjust constantly the proportion of services that the Church offers in order to meet the needs of the people and plant churches. We must always keep in mind that the divine purpose is the salvation of men.

/ men, people
// important

The transformation of society is another goal that we must consider along with the multiplication of Christian cells "from every nation, from all tribes and peoples and tongues..." Corruption in society offends Christians. Social injustice and the oppression of minority groups are clearly against the will of God. Christians recognize these conditions and work to better the conditions of the needy. But there is a difference in the relative importance between the effort to christianize the social order and evangelism. Some Christians have come to believe that the conditions are intolerable and have given themselves completely to the elimination of the evils of our society. They believe that they can not evangelize until they have corrected social evils. Others maintain that the social order is a fruit of new life in Christ and that therefore evangelism takes priority. In addition to the biblical basis for this second position there are some practical considerations. The Evangelical Church in almost all the Latin American countries represents a very small percentage of the total population. It is not an important social or political force. Therefore if the Church wants to change Latin society, the best way is to concentrate now on the multiplication of Churches and the transformation of individuals, in order to arrive at the point at which it will be an important minority in the society.

22. The relationship between social service and evangelism is very important and warrants our constant attention. The social program of the Church should

_____a) Compete with evangelism.

_____b) Contribute to evangelism.

_____c) Be independent of evangelism.   see /

23. With regard to its relative importance

_____a) Service is more important.

_____b) Salvation is more important.

_____c) They are of equal importance.   see //

24. Our actions as well as our words testify to our faith.

_____a) Social service is sufficient testimony.

_____b) There has to be verbal testimony.

_____c) Our actions don't need explanation.   see /

25. In setting priorities the Church should be guided by

_____a) God's revealed will.

_____b) Other human institutions.

_____c) What men ask for.   see &

26. Because of its social concern the Church should

_____a) Convert itself into a political power.

_____b) Avoid the corrupting influence of politics.

_____c) Proclaim the social implications of the gospel. see //

27. No one denies the need for social change. Nevertheless, we should make clear the matter of priority in time and importance. With regard to time

_____a) It is necessary to do social work so that people will believe the gospel.

_____b) It is necessary to change the individual first so that there can be a basis for social change.

_____c) The Church should not get involved in social causes until it is very strong.   see ///

28. With regard to the relative importance

_____a) The Church should evangelize and secondarily do what it can to better social conditions.

_____b) The Church should christianize the society and later evangelize those that are interested.

_____c) The Church should dedicate equal resources to the two aspects of its ministry.   see &&

29. In order to transform the society, the Church

_____a) Should form a political party.

_____b) Should grow greatly.

_____c) Should dedicate itself to social work.   see /

      Up to this point we have spoken of the mission of the Church in rather broad terms. Now let us define it in more concrete terms. <u>The mission of the Church is to proclaim the gospel of Jesus Christ and persuade men to become His disciples and responsible members of His Church.</u> This definition is so important that the student should memorize it. In broad terms the mission of the Church includes good works, social action and evangelism. We must arrive at a balanced program between these elements. But we must put the most important things into effect first. We should examine this definition with regard to faithfulness to God. Later we can examine the theological and biblical bases of various positions concerning the purpose of the Church.

30. In chapter I we learned that church growth reflects faithfulness to God. This faithfulness takes five forms. The faithfulness is expressed first in seeing that others hear the message of salvation. The servant of God has to _____

the gospel.   see &&&

31. He must proclaim _____ of Jesus Christ and persuade men to become His disciples and responsible members of His Church.   see ///

32. The minister of the gospel can not be indifferent to results. The faithful servant desires the
                    see &   _____ of the lost.

33. It is not sufficient to present the gospel. One must use arguments or other methods to
                _____ men.   see //

34. According to its mission the Church has to _____

_____ and _____ to become His disciples and responsible members of His Church.   see &&

/ b persuade
/// the gospel
/// salvation, redemption
& proclaim the gospel of Jesus Christ, persuade men
&& proclaim, persuade men
&&& proclaim, preach

35. The goal is man's salvation. The process by which the Holy Spirit works a change in the person that results in his salvation is called

_____. see //

36. The mission of the Church is _____

_____

to become His disciples and responsible members of His Church.
see &&&

37. Converts should not be left alone without spiritual nourishment. The pastor should

_____ and _____

the sheep.   see &

38. Believers should learn from the life and ministry of _____
see ///

39. We want men to be followers of _____ of Christ.
see /

40. Salvation is the first step for the Christian. The Church has to take him beyond an immature faith. The mission of the Church includes (according to our definition)

_____

•——•

•——•

see page 3-8

41. Christian workers try to organize groups of believers into

_____ see $

42. The normal Christian life includes participation as a

_____ of a church.   see &&

/ disciples
// conversion
/// Christ
& gather, feed
&& member
&&& proclaim the gospel of Jesus Christ and persuade men
$ churches, congregations

43. Adding this element to our definition of the mission of the Church we see that it is

_____

_____

_____ responsible _____ of His Church .

see page 3-8

44. The Church should not isolate itself but rather _____ with the world.   see ///

45. This teaching means that the Christian has a certain responsibility toward others. His faith should be expressed in all his relations and actions in the

_____ . see /

46. The Christian should sense some _____ for meeting the world's needs.   see //

47. In relation to the several aspects suggested in the definition of the Church's mission, write below the five aspects of faithfulness to God which result in church growth. (See the list on page 1-18 to check your answer.)

```
48.   The definition of the Church's mission is so important that
it should be memorized.  Write it below. (See page 3-8 to check
your answer.)




```

/ world
// responsibility
OR SIMILAR
WORDS
/// relate OR
SIMILAR WORDS

Search Theology

The world and especially Latin America today responds to the gospel as never before. Nevertheless, there are very many Christians that are still dedicated to a theology of searching or sowing. By "theology" we mean that this is their way of interpreting the revelation and mission of God. These persons think that the essential thing for the Church is to preach the gospel in all the world and leave the results to God.

This type of thinking emphasizes the truth that the conversion of souls is the work of God. It is God who works in hearts and it is He who gives the fruit. Nevertheless, if we consider only this facet of the truth we are likely to fall into the error of an impersonal and irresponsible evangelism. There is no one so carefree as the evangelist who travels from one spot to another without worrying about whether he is leaving any permanent and real results of his preaching. How many of us have preached in the open air or have given out tracts without really expecting any concrete results of our work? In this way we believed that we fulfilled our duty to evangelize.

Much evangelism doesn't try to understand the way its audience thinks or feels. Nor does it try to adapt its message to be more persuasive. Search theology implies that the mere fact of preaching the gospel enables us to forget about the lost. If the sinner "does not turn from his way; he shall die in his iniquity, but you will have saved your life." (Ezk.33:9). Carried to an extreme, the preaching would benefit more the preacher by clearing his conscience than it would benefit the sinner who walks in darkness and has not been convinced of the truth of the gospel.

49. The first aspect of the mission of the Church is _____

_____ see //

50. This act corresponds to _____ the sheep. see /

51. The pastor who does no more than look for the lost has a ministry which is

_____ see ///

/   seeking,
    searching for
// preach the
    gospel OR
    SIMILAR WORDS
/// incomplete OR
    SIMILAR WORDS

52. Nevertheless, there are many persons who believe that the proclamation alone fulfills the _____ of God for the Church.   see ///

53. The results, they say, are the responsibility of _____
                          see &&

54. But this does not take into consideration our duty after or beyond proclamation which is
                see &   _____ men to be converted.

55. It is too easy to preach to a crowd without worrying about the
          _____ that make up the crowd.   see %

56. A preacher who does not care if souls are lost has a false concept of
                _____ .   see &&&

57. It seems that _____ theology is incomplete. see/

    Where has this theology come from? In the first place it arose because of the hostility to the gospel which resulted in the barren fields. In many parts of Latin America there has been opposition of all kinds - fanaticism, violence, hardness of heart. The Church has needed a theology that would sustain it during the long years in which there were only a handful of Christians. Therefore it accepted the idea that the validity of the mission and the work of the Church did not depend on results. The search or the proclamation was accepted as the will of God and this became the goal of evangelistic work.

58. Search theology was born in the adverse _____ which the Church encountered.   see $

59. In Latin America missionary work turned out to be _____.
                          see //

60. After several years of work there were _____ evangelicals.   see $$

61. The Church needed a _____ that would explain the facts.
                                see $$$

/ search
// hard, difficult or SIMILAR WORDS
/// mission
& persuade
&& God
&&& the gospel, Christianity or SIMILAR WORDS
$ conditions or SIMILAR WORDS
$$ few or SIMILAR WORDS
$$$ theology, theory, reason
% individuals or SIMILAR WORDS

62. Therefore it declared that the evangelistic success of the Church is not measured by the

_____ .   see //

63. Missionaries said that to carry out God's will it was sufficient to

_____ .   see &&

64. The proclamation of the gospel, instead of being a means towards the divine goal, came to be an

see &   _____ in itself.

In the second place, the missionaries found many things to do. Although the people were not interested in the gospel, they asked for schools, hospitals, agricultural experts and technicians of various kinds. As a result the missionaries chose to construct schools and clinics thinking that perhaps later they would be able to build churches. They could not point to many conversions, but at least they were relatively successful because the number of medical treatments and of students rose every year. In order to avoid failure they changed their objectives so that they would coincide with the results. They dedicated themselves to the work of preparing for the gospel. And today some of them are still preparing for the work that they could do if they did not do so many other things.

65. The people did not want to listen to spiritual things, but they were ready to receive schools, clinics and other

benefits.   see &&&

66. The missionary program was determined by the will of _____ .
see ///

67. Besides evangelism the missionaries found _____ to do.   see $$

68. The missionaries thought that their good works prepared the people for the

_____ .   see /

69. Nevertheless, their activities gave the people the impression that the things of least importance and urgency were

see $ _____ .

/   gospel
///   results
&   people
&&   end proclaim the gospel or SIMILAR WORDS
&&&   social, material
$ spiritual
$$ much, many things

70. After founding institutions it was impossible to hold back from them the resources necessary for the work of
see $$ _____.

71. Therefore the missionaries explained that what they did was the
_____ of the Church.   see $

In the third place, in many areas, such as Grand Colombia, the Church grew slowly. The missions could not cite the number of conversions or baptisms to justify their work. Instead of changing their methods they changed their goals. The Church conformed to slow growth and convinced itself that this was normal. Under such conditions the Church embraced a theology of mission that accepted mere searching or proclamation as the fulfillment of God's command. It was not necessary to take into consideration the results.

There are those who say that no one should brag about numbers. They are interested, they say, in quality, not in quantity. The pastors departing to search for lost sheep agree that they will not measure their success in terms of the number of sheep found.

72. The Churches that are most willing to give figures of conversions and baptisms are those that have grown
see &&   _____.

73. The Churches that grew slowly maintained that the figures were of
_____ importance.   see ///

74. Because of their own experience, the Churches came to believe that it was normal for the Church to grow
see &   _____.

75. They declared that the only responsibility toward the lost was that of
_____.   see //

76. The pastor should not measure his success by the _____ of persons that are converted.   see &&&

77. Of greatest importance is the _____ of Christians.
see /

/ quality
// proclamation, preaching, searching
/// little or SIMILAR WORDS
& slowly or SIMILAR WORDS
&& more, much, or SIMILAR WORDS
&&& number
$ mission
$$ evangelism

78. Before going any farther it would be good to meditate on the following question: Should the number of conversions influence the direction and the intensity of the search?

Those who maintain search theology answer negatively the above question. It is possible only to list briefly their arguments. Some believe that in this dispensation, before the milenium, God is calling from among the gentiles a limited number of persons for His Church. The missionary or pastor can do nothing to change the purposes of God. In the fulfillment of time the milenium will come. The mission of the Church today is to preach the gospel to every creature. We can not know who will be saved and who will be lost.

79. According to the dispensationalist argument the number of gentiles converted is

_____ .   see //

80. An attempt to win more persons would be contrary to the will of

_____ .   see /

81. Therefore the Church should _____ to all and leave their conversion to God.   see ///

82. The error of the dispensationalist argument is to assume that

_____a) The purposes of God never change.

_____b) The number of gentiles called will be small.

_____c) We can not know who will be saved.   see &

/ God
// limited or SIMILAR WORDS
/// preach
& b

Others who have studied psychology believe that it is easy to justify our conduct and hide mixed motives. They believe that winning souls to Christ, establishing the Church or extending the Kingdom of God are expressions of imperialism or of spiritual pride or superiority. They believe that evangelism is an attempt to impose our will upon the rest. Therefore they say that the true Christian proclaims Christ without seeking results for his own glory. We must avoid trying to dominate other persons.

83. Students of psychology say that we preach our religion to glorify

_____ . see ///

84. Every person must be completely free to _____ his religion.   see &&

85. Persuasion violates the _____ of the individual.
see //

86. They say that we try to impose our ideas because we want to
_____ the other.   see /

87. Which of the following declarations would not be that of those who analyze psychologically Christians and their motives?

_____a) We should not try to change others.

_____b) Church extension is human ambition.

_____c) Psychological techniques should be applied to evangelism.

_____d) Preaching that only Christ saves shows spiritual pride.

_____e) Missions are a form of imperialism.   see &

Some Christians deprecate numbers because they consider every soul of infinite worth. Christ died for every man. Therefore any soul merits all the missionary effort from the Day of Pentecost to the present. They insist that the Church which wins fifty souls in fifty years pleases God as much as the Church which wins fifty thousand.

/   dominate, or SIMILAR WORDS
//   liberty, dignity or SIMILAR WORDS
/// ourselves
&   c
&&   choose or SIMILAR WORDS

89. According to those who focus their attention on the salvation of the individual

_____a) God wants us to be faithful in preaching the Word.

_____b) God wants the greatest number of men to be saved.

_____c) It doesn't matter whether men are saved.   see //

We should be thankful for the sincere persons who have labored faithfully seeking the lost with one of the theologies already mentioned. But we believe that God wants more than a search. He wants His sheep to be found. Let us consider the evidence for this belief.

The Biblical Evidence

There are four classes of biblical evidence that can be cited to demonstrate that search theology is not biblical theology. These are:

The teachings of Jesus and the apostles
The parables of Jesus
The nature of God
The practice of the New Testament Church

In the first place we note the explicit teachings of Jesus and the apostles. In Matthew 9:37-38 our Lord indicates the necessity of sending workers into the harvest. It is obvious that their mission is not to search, but to reap. Seeing the receptivity of a particular segment of the population our Lord recognized the need of harvesters. Study these two verses in Matthew in order to answer the following questions.

90. The harvest belongs to _____. see /

91. The one who sends the workers is _____. see &&

92. The implication is that the workers should _____.
                              see &&&

93. The persons whom God calls and sends are the _____.
                              see ///

94. The number of workers in the time of Christ was _____.
                              see &

/   God
a
///   workers insuffi-cient or SIMILAR WORDS
&   God
&&   God
&&&   harvest or SIMILAR WORDS

95. The mission of the workers is to _____. see &

96. One of the biblical evidences that the Church should not only search is contained in the words of
see // _____.

   The question has already been raised: Should the number of persons found influence the direction and intensity of the search? The Scriptures answer this question. In Matthew 10:14 Christ says: "And if any one will not receive you or listen to your words, shake off the dust from your feet as you leave that house or town." Acts 13:51 indicates that Barnabas and Paul followed these instructions, at least on that occasion. Probably this was the practice of the New Testament Church. The disciples did not pressure those who were opposed to the good news of salvation, but rather went on to those who were ready to receive the message. The Christians sought those whom they could win.

   These words of Jesus and this practice of the Apostolic Church can not be applied always everywhere. There are many examples of evangelistic work that had little fruit and suddenly a great harvest resulted. But we should always apply the positive aspect of the teaching: win those who are winnable while they are winnable.

97. It appears that the apostles did not waste efforts on hostile fields. They did not remain long where the gospel was

_____. see $

98. They sought those that were _____ to respond to the gospel.   see &&

99. The receptivity of peoples is one of the factors which should determine the place where one should
see /// _____.

100. The principle of leaving hostile areas should be applied in
_____ cases. see &&&

101. The receptivity of peoples can change. Therefore we should always attend those peoples which now are
see / _____.

/   receptive or SIMILAR WORDS
// Jesus and the apostles
/// search, preach, evangelize
&   harvest
&& ready or SIMILAR WORDS
&&& some
$ rejected or SIMILAR WORDS

102. The scriptural teachings and our own experience teach us
that the receptivity of a people can

_____ . see ///

103. If the crop is not harvested when it is ripe, what can happen to it?

_____ . see /

104. We must harvest souls when they are _____ . see //

105. Considering the case of those who reject the gospel, what
reasons are there for not continuing to preach to them?

106. Do you believe that this practice should be applied to individuals or to whole populations? Why?

107. In view of the examples of a harvest after several years
of evangelistic effort, when should we decide that it is better
not to continue preaching to a given people?

/ It rots or SIMILAR WORDS

// ready or SIMILAR WORDS

/// change or SIMILAR WORDS

The Great Commission is evidence of great value. On that solemn occasion our Lord specifically ordered His disciples: Make disciples of all the nations. The New Testament does not teach that a Christian can witness without having the goal of conversion in mind. When Paul proclaimed Christ in Corinth, the Bible says that "he argued in the synagogue every sabbath, and persuaded Jews and Greeks." In view of his desire to save Jews, expressed in Romans 9:1-3, it is hard to believe that Paul witnessed of Christ without trying to persuade the Jews to become Christians.

108. According to the examples given, the preaching of the gospel is

_____a) Something for the first century only.

_____b) The goal of the Church.

_____c) A means of fulfilling the mission of the Church. see //

109. The Lord's command requires that His disciples

_____a) Win souls.

_____b) Add members to the Church.

_____c) Produce other disciples.   see ///

110. The purpose of Paul was fulfilled when the Jews

_____a) Accepted the message.

_____b) Listened to the message.

_____c) Forgot the message.   see /

111. If our mission is not that of only proclaiming the gospel, but also of persuading men to accept it, what should the servant of God know about those that he wants to convert into disciples?

a c c

///

112. In order to make disciples is more contact with the people required than for preaching? Why do you believe so?

In addition to the explicit teachings of Jesus and the disciples, we find another type of evidence in the more symbolic and less direct teaching of our Lord. His parables give emphasis to finding. The woman that is mentioned in Luke 15 not only looks, but seeks "diligently until she finds it" (the lost coin). The shepherd is not satisfied to return without the lost sheep, but goes "after the one which is lost, until he finds it." In the parable of the great feast, the Lord does not praise the servant that brings him the news that the guests have found excuses. He sends him to look for others to fill the house. In these three parables the emphasis falls on finding the lost. Witnessing is not an end in itself, but the means for finding the lost.

113. Examine the three parables: Luke 14:15-24; 15:1-19. What additional observations or applications can you make in regard to the pastor's responsibility?

The third class of evidence refers to the very nature of God. He shows Himself as the God that seeks and saves. He found Israel in Egypt and redeemed His people. Our Lord came to seek and to save that which was lost. The lost are always persons. They are persons that can be counted. According to the various ways in which God has revealed Himself, the proclamation of the gospel is not the final goal. The goal is the salvation of people. The preaching of the gospel is the means and should not be confused with the goal which is the reconciliation of man with God.

114. God revealed Himself in Egypt and on Calvary as a God that redeems His people. The liberation of the Israelites can be considered as a type of the liberation of men from sin. In Egypt Moses and Aaron

_____a) Were satisfied with preaching to Pharaoh.

_____b) Did various things to persuade him.

_____c) Persisted until they freed the people.   see /

115. In view of this type of redemption a pastor

_____a) Only has to preach Christ.

_____b) Should use methods of persuasion.

_____c) Must win all the people.   see ///

116. The goal of the Church is

_____a) Man's salvation.

_____b) The preaching of salvation in Christ.

_____c) The development of persuasive methods.   see //

The fourth class of evidence is that of the New Testament Church which went where the people responded, believing that this was the will of God. For some years witnessing was limited to the Jews and the Church multiplied among them. But we see again that the Church won the winnable while they were receptive. If, on the Day of Pentecost, Peter had said that Christians did not need to keep the law, in an effort to win the gentiles in Jerusalem, very few Jews would have entered the Church. Therefore in the wisdom of God the disciples were inspired to direct themselves first toward the Jews and later toward the gentiles who had relations with the Jews and attended the synagogue, and finally to the whole Graeco-Roman world. This was not the apostles' plan but that of the Holy Spirit. The Primitive Church permitted the number of persons baptized to determine the direction and intensity of the evangelistic work.

117. The historical evidence in Acts is very important because
the same principles should be applied today if we want the same
blessing of God on our ministry. At first the Church preached
only to the Jews because

_____a) God loves the Jews more.

_____b) They were more receptive to the gospel.

_____c) There were no gentiles in Palestine.   see ///

118. The greatest number of Jews in Palestine were converted

_____a) In the first years of the Church.

_____b) After the destruction of Jerusalem.

_____c) After the faith spread to the gentiles.   see /

119. The Apostles were guided by

_____a) Personal interests.

_____b) Anthropological principles.

_____c) The Holy Spirit.   see //

120. Did the Church make a mistake in accepting as Christians in
one place those that believed that they should keep the Mosaic law
and accepting gentiles who did not keep this law in another?
Should this problem have been resolved first? Explain your
answer.

a c b
/ / /

121. We have already seen four types of evidence that prove that God's purpose is not fulfilled by merely searching. The first type of evidence is found in the definitive teachings of

see /   _____.

122. In the second place we have the examples of finding in the

_____ .   see ///

123. The examples of redemption in the Old and New Testaments reveal that searching alone is not in agreement with God's

_____ .   see &

124. The fourth class of evidence is found in that which Acts teaches us about the practice of the

see //   _____ .

125. Summarize below the four types of evidence that demonstrate that search theology is not sufficient.

._____.

._____.

._____.

._____.

see the list on page 3-17

In view of all this evidence we must believe that the mission of the Church is to search and find deliberately. The evidence indicates that for God the number of the redeemed is important. God Himself desires that multitudes be reconciled with Him. The Church that our Savior bought with His blood is composed of redeemed sinners that are commissioned to beseech others on behalf of Christ: be reconciled to God.

126. God desires the _____ of men.   see &&&

127. Leading men to a relation of forgiveness and communion with God is part of the

_____ of the Church.   see &&

/   Jesus
//   Primitive Church
/// parables
&   nature
&&   mission or SIMILAR WORDS
&&& salvation, redemption

128. After finding salvation men have the responsibility of

_____ .   see /

129. God wants _____ to find salvation in Christ.
see //

130. Therefore, the mission of the Church is not only to look for the lost, but also to

_____ .   see &

The whitened fields and laborers that bring sheaves from certain fields have theological significance. Christians do not enter the whitened fields of their own accord. They don't gather the sheaves for their own benefit; they take them to the storehouse of the Lord. God gives the growth. God prepares the harvest. God rewards the laborers. Certainly God is more pleased if Christ is proclaimed where men are reconciled to Him than where they are not. This is a harvest theology.

131. The faithful worker does not please himself but rather seeks

_____ .   see $$

132. Great harvests are evidence that _____ is working.
see ///

133. It is God that makes the Church _____ .   see &&&

134. It seems that God's purpose is to give emphasis to places where

_____ .   see $

135. The search is only a means. What God wants is the _____ of souls.   see &&

136. Is search theology false therefore? By no means, but it is incomplete. It is necessary for some men and some situations. It is false only if it is considered the only theology of mission for the Church and applicable in every circumstance. It can never be the intention of a servant of God to search without hope of finding. Sometimes the search remains fruitless and in this case Christ consoles His servant. But Christ came to seek

/ saving others or SIMILAR WORDS

// all, everyone

/// God

& find them or SIMILAR WORDS

&& salvation or SIMILAR WORDS

&&& grow, increase

$ there are abundant harvests or SIMILAR WORDS

$$ God's glory or SIMILAR WORDS

and to save the lost and this is the mission of the Church also. In certain circumstances search theology and harvest theology coincide. Mention these circumstances.

Perhaps we have oversimplified the mission of the Church in this discussion. It is very complex with many aspects, all of them important. But among these activities which are good and approved by God there is one of supreme importance. That is the multiplication of churches among the responsive peoples of the world.

137. God's mission in the world includes _____ things.
see &

138. Nevertheless, of greatest importance is the _____ of the Church. see //

139. This expansion occurs in societies which are_____ to the gospel.   see /

140. The Church should multiply where_____.
see ///

When he faces all the needs of the world in which he lives, the Christian does not have to depend on his wisdom or will. His way is shown through God's revelation. Jesus said: "Seek first his kingdom and his righteousness, and all these things shall be yours as well." Man's basic need is spiritual. Even in order to reach secondary goals, the first step is to lead men to faith in Jesus Christ. When multitudes are converted we will better be able to change the social order. The Church should fight to improve social, economic and educational conditions, but while it is doing so it must not lose sight of the principal goal. In another chapter more will be said about the social responsibilities of the Church. It is sufficient to indicate here that the whole man must be redeemed.

/ open, receptive

// growth, expansion

/// people are won OR SIMILAR WORDS

& many

141. The Christian finds God's will revealed in the _____.
      see /

142. There we read that the most important things are _____.
      see &&&

143. As far as the needs of the world, the Christian can not ignore them and do nothing. He has the responsibility to do

_____ see //

144. Nevertheless, it must not be forgotten that what men need
most is

_____. see &&

145. With relation to other ministries, evangelism comes _____.
      see ///

146. As a secondary goal the Church should try to change the

_____. see &

Examples of Little Growth

It is to be hoped that the readers are in agreement with
what has been said so far. However many of God's servants have
not concerned themselves with church growth. The emphasis of
this course on church growth is necessary because great ingatherings do not occur automatically. In many parts of the world
little growth has been seen. It will be useful to mention a few
examples, principally from Latin America.

In Sinaloa, Mexico, the Congregational Church, now the
United Church of Christ, had worked for more than fifty years.
During that period missionaries had served with dedication and
sincerity. However, in 1962 the Church barely had 300 members
in nine static congregations.

In Chile, where the pentecostal denominations in the last
forty years have grown from nothing to 200,000 members, a North
American mission with thirty missionaries had labored for thirty
years and in 1955 had fewer than 300 members in its congregations.

/   Bible
//   what he can
     OR SIMILAR
     WORDS
/// first
&   society
&&   salvation
&&& spiritual OR
     SIMILAR WORDS

In 1850 the Baptist, Methodist, Moravian and Presbyterian Churches in Jamaica had a total of 54,000 members among the various groups. During the following one hundred years these Churches increased their membership to 60,000. For a whole century, aided by missionaries and funds from England, they added only 6,000 members, or 15 members per year per denomination. Meanwhile the island's population rose from 400,000 to 1,700,000. The members of these four denominations made up 13.50 per cent of the total population in 1850 and 3.50 per cent in 1950.

147. We have emphasized the need to promote church growth because, unfortunately, there are areas of Latin America where the Church

_____. see //

148. The static churches had the services of faithful _____.
see /

149. We know that the stagnation did not occur because the people were hostile to the gospel because at the same time in these countries there were
see /// _____.

Many examples of little growth can be found. Anyone can do nothing if that is his goal. But in the cases studied we have found missionaries, pastors and laymen that believed that they were faithfully carrying out the mission of the Church. However their groups continued static while other Churches, among similar peoples grew greatly. The tragedy is that the Churches with little growth could have had better results. Without more details it is impossible to determine all the reasons for failure, but let us consider some factors.

150. Some factors that have to do with the success of the Church are: economic resources, adequate methods, personnel, doctrine, dedicated workers, definite objectives and population changes. In your opinion, in the Churches that didn't take advantage of their opportunities, what was lacking?

/ missionaries, pastors

// doesn't grow OR SIMILAR WORDS

/// other groups that grew in the same place OR SIMILAR WORDS

Almost all denominations could cite cases of little growth
in one country or another. For example, a few years ago the
leaders of the Foursquare Gospel Church made a study of the
growth of ten younger Churches. They found a Church of 25,000
members that grew rapidly, three Churches of about 10,000 each
that grew more or less rapidly and six static Churches of fewer
than 2,000 members each.

In some cases lack of growth or slow growth is irremediable.
It is because of the hardness of heart of those who hear the gospel or for political or social conditions. This would be the
case in some Mohammedan countries. In most cases, however, slow
growth is caused by mistaken practices. Lack of growth is an
unnecessary characteristic of many Churches.

151. If you were the Secretary of Mission of the Foursquare
Church, what would you do about the differences in growth in
the countries where your Church does missionary work?

The urgency of church growth is intensified by the fact
that we live in a world open to the gospel. A comparison with
conditions of a hundred years ago shows the great receptivity
at present. But the whole world is not open. The Church does
not advance today in Arabia. On the other hand, here in Latin
America there are opportunities to present the gospel as never
before.

152. A century ago_____ countries were open to the gospel.   see /

153. One of the great regions of the world which presently ex-
periences rapid expansion of the Church is
                              see ///   _____.

154. It is urgent that the Evangelical Church evangelize the
world
_____.see //

fewer
now
Latin
America

/
//
///

155. Does the fact that many respond to the gospel today mean that we will have the same opportunities ten or twenty years from now? Will the responsive fields always be the same? Explain your answer.

In some countries the number of peoples which respond to the gospel is remarkable. Let us consider one more example. In the first years of this century thousands of Italians immigrated to Brazil. Many were dissatisfied with the Roman Church. The first generation and many of the second spoke Italian. They were ready to hear the gospel, but the Methodists, Presbyterians, Lutherans and Baptists were busy working among the Brazilians who spoke Portuguese. The leaders of the Churches didn't know Italian and didn't see the opportunity among these immigrants.

Nevertheless, an Italian layman, converted in Chicago, without financial backing moved to Brazil and began to preach to his countrymen. The Church which he established held services in Italian until 1936. In 1965 its membership was 400,000. Many whitened fields exist which are never found by missionaries and Church leaders.

156. Who is responsible for taking advantage of evangelistic opportunities that exist? Explain your answer.

Latin America offers almost limitless opportunities for evangelism. Its peoples are not responsive by accident. We can see that God is working in history. His providence and His Holy Spirit have prepared the hearts of thousands and even millions of persons. The fields are already white for the harvest. If we do not reap others will. Listen to what they say:

Colombia, also, is a country of varied climate that invites, not only the tourists, but those that are impelled by the spirit of God to go and spread the "good news" where the people anxiously await it. A few years ago it was common for missionaries to find violent hostility, fomented by influential priests. Nevertheless, today attitudes have changed so radically that missionaries frequently answer the door bell of the mission house and find someone who seeks help in studying the Bible.

Here is a country where, for decades, the people were discouraged from reading the Bible. But now it can easily be found in bookstores and elsewhere. In just a few years local Witnesses and missionaries have distributed 37,000 Bibles. And the people want to understand this Book of books. This is clearly indicated by the demand for aids in studying the Bible. While the Watch Tower Society office in Colombia sent 20,000 copies of the book "Let God Be True" in eight years, the most recent publication "Things in Which It Is Impossible for God to Lie" has had the phenomenal distribution of 22,270 copies in just ten months. (Atalaya, 15 Nov., 1968 pp 699-700).

Many sectors of the population in Colombia and other countries are open to the gospel now and we must reach them while there is time. The need is urgent. The Jehovah's Witnesses are one of the fastest growing religious organizations in the world. Why are we left behind? Is it because they have a better message and God is blessing them? Of course not. They use better methods. They have cheap and abundant literature. Every day they visit in homes. In comparison we are lazy. We are not motivated. We are disobedient to God. May God forgive us and help us to work intelligently and fervently for the growth of His Church.

157. According to your experience and the text, what are some of the reasons for the rapid growth of sects in many parts?

158. Which of the characteristics or methods of the sects could
we use?

4

IGNORANCE OF GROWTH

In lesson III we examined the evidence that convinces us
that God does want the Church to grow. But how can we know if
the Church is growing? What are the facts that we need? This
lesson tries to answer these questions and explain why in the
past the necessary emphasis has not been given to church growth.
After presenting the facts we must interpret them, the subject
of another chapter. In this lesson we will mention some factors
which have hidden the facts of growth. In particular we must
examine some theological positions that contribute to the lack
of information. It will also be necessary to determine what
facts we need and how to obtain them.

The Darkness that Hides Church Growth

If the question is raised - Is the Evangelical Church growing well in your country? - some will say yes. But few know if
it really grows rapidly or is barely increasing. If one asks
about percentages of growth in the Church no one knows. Why is
so little known about church growth? Does the lack of data mean
that we do nothing to promote the extension of the Church?
Aren't we interested in whether the Church grows?

If we have a school we keep all kinds of records of the
graduates. If we sponsor a clinic we keep a list of treatments
and cures. If we are evangelists it is possible that we know
how many tracts have been given out, how many Bibles have been
sold, how many miles we have traveled and how many services we
have conducted, but nothing is said about results. A lot of
missionary literature gives the impression that results are not
important because they are never mentioned.

4-1

1. In order to measure the evangelistic success of the Church we must measure the

    _____. see /

2. We have fewer specific facts about evangelistic work than about other
    see & _____ sponsored by the Church.

3. Possibly the lack of attention to evangelistic results has been produced by

    _____ theology.   see ///

4. Often our knowledge of the Church and its growth is vague. In order to know how much it has grown one can

    _____a) Guess at the increase.

    _____b) Count baptisms in local churches.

    _____c) Focus on Sunday School attendance.   see &&

5. Little is known about growth because

    _____a) There is no way to get the facts.

    _____b) The facts are not important.

    _____c) The facts have not been recorded.   see &&&

6. The facts of the evangelistic work

    _____a) Are not important.

    _____b) Are as important as those of educational work.

    _____c) Are invisible.   see //

7. Most available figures on evangelism have to do with

    _____a) Wasted funds.

    _____b) Efforts realized.

    _____c) The results.   see $

/ results
/// b search
   & activities
      OR SIMILAR
      WORDS
   && b
   &&& c
   $ b

8. The argument of this section is that the Church

_____a) Should eliminate social programs.

_____b) Should be responsible for resources invested.

_____c) Should work harder.   see /

9. What does the declaration that an evangelistic campaign was successful mean? Are you in agreement with the general opinion?

10. How is the success of a pastor measured? Why is it said that one pastor is better than another? Are common criteria just? Why?

11. Many factors have combined to hide growth that has occurred and to obstruct plans for obtaining greater results. One of the unfortunate effects of our lack of information is that we are unable to make

_____ that would promote growth. see //

12. Many missionaries and pastors continue in their programs and activities year after year without measuring the success of their efforts. When they are satisfied with what they have done the tendency is to continue
                    see ///   _____.

/ b
// plans
/// doing the
same thing
OR SIMILAR
WORDS

Sometimes it is said that a school, a clinic, or literature distribution contributes to the Church. How do we know that it is so? Have we compared the membership of a church where there is an evangelical school with that of a church that does not have one? If we spent the same funds in evangelism that are now spent on the school would the church expand more rapidly? No one knows because studies have not been made. The facts needed to reach concrete conclusions are not available. Without this information we are in the dark. We can't make intelligent plans or policy changes.

13. Sometimes we must determine the validity of a certain institution or investment through

_____ of various projects.   see &

14. Often a plan continues in effect for many years because

_____a) It is impossible to change it.

_____b) It is difficult to carry it out.

_____c) We see no reason for changing it.   see //

15. We know that a school contributes to the church

_____a) Because they always do.

_____b) If its contribution can be proved.

_____c) If the believers want a school.   see ///

16. Plans should be based on

_____a) Concrete data.

_____b) Tradition.

_____c) Public opinion.   see /

17. The student should imagine that his church is considering opening a clinic to help its evangelistic program. How can it know if it is worthwhile to do so?

|

/ // /// &   the   study, compar-
a c   b   ison

One reason for not knowing how the Church grows is that exact data on membership do not exist. Nor is there uniformity in the way statistics are gathered. It is impossible, for example to compare figures from an Episcopal church which include baptized children as members with those of a Baptist church which accepts only adults as members. Lack of uniformity in data impairs comparisons of churches and even of the same congregation at various periods, if the manner of gathering figures has changed. We can't rely on the few figures that we have. In the graphs included in this study we have used the best data available knowing that they are not exact.

18. The best measure of the churches is the number of _____.
                                        see /

19. In order to make valid comparisons it is important that all the churches use the same
                    see /// _____ to count its members.

20. We must always use the same method to count church membership. In order for comparisons to be valid there must be

_____ in the gathering of data.   see &

21. Nevertheless, human imperfection must be recognized in all our activities. The data are never

                    _____. see //

22. The comparison of data from various periods helps us to discover if a church is
                    _____. see &&

The Causes of Darkness

Three very common non-theological causes for lack of information are:

1. Administrative practices.
2. Ignorance in regard to cultural differences.
3. The use of inexact terms.

/ baptized
members

// perfect,
exact

/// measure
& uniformity,
precision

&& growing

Administrators of missions and Churches sometimes proceed as if it didn't matter if the Church grew. The budget does not take into account results. If there is an increase in funds, they are prorated and everyone receives equally. Certainly there are many difficulties, and personal factors enter into this matter. One pastor receives more help because he has been in the work longer or has influence. It is believed that old fields must be preserved at all cost since so much has already been invested in them that they can not be abandoned now. In order to be good stewards we must invest the Lord's funds where they will do the most for His glory.

23. We are stewards and therefore the funds that are used in the churches belong in the first place to
see /// _____.

24. Church funds should be assigned according to

_____a) Reports from the churches.

_____b) Evidence of results.

_____c) The whim of administrators.   see &

25. In the absence of concrete data Church administrators usually distribute funds

_____a) For greatest growth.

_____b) Equally for everyone.

_____c) In the best way.   see /

26. The Church's resources should be invested according to

_____a) The interests of the directors.

_____b) The opportunities for growth.

_____c) Popular vote.   see //

27. Certain financial practices and other aspects of the

_____ of the Church are obstacles for growth.
see &&

/ b
/// b God
& b administra-
&& tion

28. If two fields have received the same funds but one has grown more than the other, should we give more to the field with limited growth so that it will produce the same or should we give more to the receptive field to take advantage of opportunities which exist? Why do you think so?

29. Another obstacle for the Church is that our ideas are culturally conditioned. We learn from our environment. We are products of our

_____. see /

30. Often we don't consider the fact that we belong to a sub-culture of the society and that there are other sub-cultures which are different from ours. We don't all share the same

_____. see ///

31. These divisions or distinctions within a general culture are called

_____. see $

32. Only in general terms do Latin Americans share the

_____ culture. see &&&

33. The majority of the missionaries who have come to Latin America are from Europe and
                        see & _____.

34. Sometimes they have erred by imposing in Latin America, as if they were Christian essentials, elements of their own

_____. see //

35. We should expect that many of their ideas would be

_____ from those of the areas to which they have come.   see &&

/ culture
// culture
/// culture
& North America
&& different
&&& same, Latin American
$ sub-cultures

36. We must distinguish between aspects of a particular culture and the universal teachings of _____. see &&

37. Sometimes Latin American leaders have ignored cultural differences also. They have thought that what worked in Cali should be applied in Cordoba, Cuenca, Cuernavaca and Cochabamba. But we must remember that every situation is see $ _____.

38. Some people have criticized the "myth" of a Latin American culture. In the Americas there are see // _____.

39. The culture exercises its influence over our _____. see &&&

40. Christianity is not a culture, but rather an integral and integrating part of every _____. see $$

41. The first obstacle for growth has to do with certain practices in the _____ of the Church. see &

42. The second obstacle is that our strategy and practices are determined in part by our _____. see /

43. The gospel is one and the same for all men. Men everywhere have the same basic spiritual need. Therefore the gospel is for _____. see $$$

44. But even spiritual needs are expressed in different ways according to the _____ of the individual. see %

45. In order to satisfy the needs in various cultures and subcultures the gospel must be see /// _____.

46. Social and political conditions vary from one place to another and from year to year in the same place. Sometimes men are not aware that what they need most is see %% _____.

/ culture
// many cultures
/// expressed in different ways OR SIMILAR WORDS
& administration
&& Christianity
&&& thinking OR SIMILAR WORDS
$ different
$$ unique culture
$$$ everyone
% culture
%% salvation

47. If a Church wants to establish a congregation in a certain place it can not copy completely the methods used in other parts. It can't ignore

_____, see /

48. The two obstacles to understanding church growth that we have found so far are:

_____

_____
see //

49. Mention the distinct sub-cultures in your area or province.

50. Describe the aspects of church services which are culturally determined. What could be changed without losing the essence of Christian worship?

51. Another cause of confusion is the vague terminology that is used to speak of the Church and its activities. For example, what does it mean to you that a Church has a "work" in a certain area?

/ cultural differences
// church administration, ignorance of cultural differences OR SIMILAR WORDS

52. This could mean that some Christians have regular services there. It could be that a building has been rented, but that there are no believers yet. Perhaps it means that some laymen from another church visit the town to hand out tracts once a month. All these circumstances can be represented by the term

_____. see /

53. The same vagueness is seen in the use of the word "evangelize." If we say that a town has been evangelized no one knows if a church has been organized, if some Christians have visited all the homes in the town or if the gospel has been preached once in the park. According to your own concept, when has a town been evangelized? Why do you believe so?

What elements of the mission of the Church should be included in evangelism?

54. The third obstacle for the understanding of information about the Church is the use of

_____ terms. see //

The very natural desire of the pastor to look good sometimes produces some distortion of the facts. If a pastor is asked about the work under his responsibility, he will generally say something good, unless he can blame others for his problems. Perhaps he has visited five new towns, or there is a very good spirit among the members of the church, or a young man has been gloriously converted. This is great. But let us think not only

/ work
// vague, inexact

about a few striking incidents, but also about statistics and the general condition of the church. Sometimes it is possible to hide the facts behind a few stories. In our reports as in our sermons we should remember that illustrations are not valid unless they represent basic scriptural or historical truth.

A certain holy optimism is necessary to believe that God is going to work in our lives and churches. Promotion and enthusiasm are important. But in addition to promoting the work we must examine the facts carefully. In addition to capturing the imagination of the people and raising their hopes, we must be stewards who submit exact reports of the results obtained from the resources invested under our responsibility.

55. In order to justify what has been done, pastors sometimes tell

_____. see //

56. The pastor is the key person in the extension of the gospel. Which of the following declarations is correct?

_____a) If the church does not grow it is always the pastor's fault.

_____b) The pastor should be a pessimist.

_____c) The pastor should analyze his situation.   see /

57. Part of the pastor's responsibility is to clarify the situation that actually exists in his church, avoiding the use of

_____. see ///

58. So far we have seen the non-theological obstacles to our comprehension of church growth. These three are:

_____

_____

_____

see the list on page 4-6

/ c
// anecdotes, stories or SIMILAR WORDS
/// vague terms or SIMILAR WORDS

In addition to the factors already mentioned there are certain theological currents which add to the confusion. Three of these theological obstacles are:

1. The idea that the Church is only an instrument.
2. Universalism.
3. Service as sufficient testimony.

In lesson III we learned that some men consider that the Church's mission includes all of God's plan for the world. Literature produced by certain organizations expresses this point of view. It is impossible to examine these theologies here. We can only indicate some of the consequences.

59. We have examined some cultural and personal obstacles. Now it is time to investigate

see // _____ obstacles.

60. Certain missiologists, that is, students of the Church's mission, say that the Church is only an instrument. It has no value in itself but is only the means of producing a better world. Consequently it can not be the goal of God's servant to build the

_____ . see &

61. This concept is _____ to the ideas expressed in this book. see ///

62. These missiologists affirm that God loves the world (John 3:16), not the Church. He is not interested in the

_____

of the Church. see /

63. They say that the Church's mission is to extend the Kingdom of justice and peace among all men, whether or not they are Christians. Certainly this teaching includes the truth that God loves

_____ men. see &&&

64. But we can't accept the declaration that a church that gives itself exclusively to social concerns, seeking the betterment of society, fulfills in this way

see && _____ .

/ growth
// theological
/// contrary, opposed
& Church
&& God's mission
&&& or SIMILAR WORDS
&&&& all

65. Some say that it is egotistical to establish a church composed only of those that believe in Jesus Christ and accept the Bible as their rule of faith and practice. We agree that the Church in Latin America needs to show more social passion. But at the same time we repeat that the basic need of man is

see &&   _____.

66. The idea that the Church is only the agent of social action for God produces lack of interest in

_____. see ///

67. If the Church does not commit itself fully to these ends, some radicals are ready to abandon it and look for another

_____ to change the society.   see &&&

68. The first theological obstacle to church growth is the belief that it is

_____ . see //

69. According to this theory the Church's mission is to

_____a) Convert the world.

_____b) Separate itself from the world.

_____c) Transform the world.   see &

70. These persons believe that the best church is one that

_____a) Grows fastest.

_____b) Maintains its Christian identity.

_____c) Submerges itself in the world.   see /

/   c
//   only an instrument
     or SIMILAR WORDS
/// evangelization,
     church growth
&   c
&&   salvation,
     spiritual or
     SIMILAR WORDS
&&& means or
     SIMILAR WORDS

71. This group believes that persons should be helped

_____a) After they are converted.

_____b) So that they will be converted.

_____c) Without regard to their conversion. see /

72. What should our attitude be toward good works?

73. Should good works contribute to evangelism? Explain your answer.

74. Is there danger of "buying" nominal Christians? How can this danger be avoided?

75. Should we help other Christians first? Why?

o

‾

Another group of theologians is concerned with our attitude toward non-Christian religions. Some believers, guided more by tolerant ideals than by the Bible, believe that God has revealed much in other religions and that the Christian attitude should be to learn from them also. They say that through dialogue we can together seek the truth. The fact that the Bible opposes this point of view doesn't matter to them. They quote verses such as Acts 14:17; 17:27, 28; Romans 2:14; 8:2-9 out of context but they never mention John 14:6 or Acts 4:12. Of course no one needs to be saved if he is not lost to begin with.

76. This group of theologians has universalistic tendencies. That is, they believe that

_____ will be saved. see //

77. They affirm that religious intolerance is a non-Christian attitude. Which of the following phrases do you believe is most correct?

_____a) Other religions contain some elements of truth.

_____b) Other religions contain all the truth.

_____c) Other religions contain no truth.   see &

79. Which of the following declarations best reflects evange- lical Christianity?

_____a) Christians should unite with others in seeking univer- sal truth.

_____b) My Church teaches the whole truth.

_____c) Christianity contains the truth necessary for man's salvation.   see /

79. We must accept other persons without necessarily accepting their religious ideas. Chose the best answer.

_____a) Sincerity is more important than orthodoxy.

_____b) We should accept persons of other religions assum- ing that they are sincere.

_____c) No sincere person could fall into the error of other religions.   see ///

c a d b a
& /// // /

80. According to your understanding of the biblical message

_____a) All who have not accepted Christ will be condemned.

_____b) God will save everyone in one way or another.

_____c) It is impossible to know who will be saved.   see /

81. Read Acts 14:17; 17:27, 28 and Romans 2:14. What is the argument that is based on these passages without considering the rest of the biblical evidence?

82. What is the second theological error that hinders the Church?
_____, see &

    A third group of persons declares that service in the name (although the name is not mentioned) of Christ is sufficient testimony. Christians should orient others toward a better life. The Church should offer disinterested service to all the needy. It is clear that in Latin America with so many needs and with so few evangelicals resources are limited and can not produce great changes. However, social service has become the principal concern of missions in some parts.

83. The third theological concept emphasizes _____.
                                            see //

84. This group would say that we should serve and not preach. In the following list mark the declarations which you believe are correct. You should base your answers on a biblical faith according to the explanation above. (The list continues on the next page.)

_____a) God accepts the good works of non-Christians.

_____b) Our actions, after conversion to Christianity, are much better.

_____c) The Christian's motives for doing good works are different.   see ///

/   a   service
///   c   universal-
=   ism or
&   SIMILAR
            WORDS

_____d) God accepts our deeds because our motive is right.

_____e) Everybody will recognize the motive for our actions.

_____f) A Christian's actions can be perverted by sin.

_____g) Christians don't have time for good works.

_____h) Good works are the most important thing we can do.

_____i) Good works always lead to salvation.

_____j) Everything we do shows that we are Christians. see &

The necessity of serving others as much as possible is not denied. But we do reject the idea that service alone is sufficient. The Latin American Church needs to examine its conscience in regard to the social implications of the gospel. But we insist on certain priorities. The conversion of many persons will not resolve automatically all the problems that Latin American society must face. However, the transformation of individuals forms the indispensable basis for a genuine transformation of the society. Social, economic and educational assistance are good, but they can not save.

85. The Latin American Church should concern itself _____
with the conditions that surround it.   see //

86. The evils of society will not disappear automatically through the conversion of
_____ .   see &&

87. Nevertheless, the only acceptable base for the transformation of social structures is
_____ . see ///

88. The gospel of Christ has something to say about conditions both
_____ and _____ . see /

/ spiritual, social or SIMILAR WORDS

// more

/// conversion or SIMILAR WORDS

& d, f

&& individuals or SIMILAR WORDS

89. The three theological concepts that hinder church growth are:

_____

_____

_____

see the list on page 4-11

90. Is it necessary to chose between evangelism and service? What should be the relation between these two activities of the Church?

91. Erroneous concepts, whether theological or non-theological, produce certain results of ignorance and confusion with respect to church growth. Winning men becomes less important than proclaiming the gospel. In an earlier lesson we called this type of thinking that doesn't take into consideration results

theology.   see ///   _____

92. Another result is that every activity receives equal emphasis and value. The church, the school and the experimental farm are considered of equal importance and treated as ends in themselves. The necessary priority is not given to
                    see /   _____.

93. The third result is that this error reinforces work which doesn't produce churches and holds back work where many churches spring up. It hinders the wise investment of
                    see //   _____.

/   evangelism or
    SIMILAR WORDS
//   resources
/// search

44814

95. When there is no basis for distributing funds due to ignorance of results and relative possibilities, equal distribution is made to everyone. Consequently there is a lack of spiritual care for believers in churches that

see & _____.

96. Let us suppose that a Church established evangelistic work among the Aymaras and the Quechuas of Bolivia. It assigned eight missionaries to each cultural group. Among the Aymaras 20,000 were converted while the number of Quechuas converted to the gospel was 2000. The policy of maintaining the same number of missionaries in the two sectors would result in lack of spiritual care for the

_____. see ///

Those of us who believe that one of the principal purposes of the Church is that of proclaiming Christ and persuading men to become His disciples and responsible members of His Church, should fight against that darkness that covers the Church's activities. Perhaps it will be necessary to designate one of the pastors of each denomination to study the situation for a time and make plans to improve the methods and policies of the Church. This would be a wise investment. In any event, we must insist on data from the congregations in order to be able to make more intelligent decisions. The processes by which God blesses and increases churches are complex, but He will help us to understand them for His greater honor and glory.

97. The desire of the authors of this book is that the Church

_____. see &&

98. In order to make intelligent decisions Church leaders must

_____ the situation. see /

99. Objective investigation will result in new _____.

see &&&

100. The purpose of objective study is not only to understand what has happened, but also to

see // _____ for the future.

/ study or SIMILAR WORDS
// plan or SIMILAR WORDS
/// Aymaras
& grow faster or SIMILAR WORDS
&& grow
&&& understanding or SIMILAR WORDS

101. In your denomination or congregation who would be the most likely person to study the situation of the Church in his area?

102. How could he be freed from other responsibilities in order to make the study that is needed?

We have considered some causes of the darkness that hides the facts of church growth. There are certain theological factors and others which are more personal and cultural. Many of the current concepts impede the evangelization of the nations. They seem to be reasonable, but they hurt the work. They confuse matters and take away the desire to win men to Christ. Debate replaces action. We must recognize these harmful ideas in order to counteract their influence.

103. Can we say that it doesn't matter what people say about the Church? Why?

_____. see //

104. In lesson III two factors were mentioned which helped to produce search theology. They were hostility and difficulty in the work and the slow progress that was registered. Existing conditions and results determined the theology and policy of the missionary work. The sad thing about it all is that when conditions changed, missionaries and pastors did not change their

_____. see /

105. Those that experienced slow growth came to believe that this was normal for the Church. They even criticized rapid growth, denying its value, spirituality or stability. But their theology was based on history and not on the authority of the

_____. see ///

Some fear the problems that could arise with rapid growth. They express themselves as follows:

We do sound work and are not interested in short cuts.
The oak takes decades to grow; a pumpkin grows in a single summer.

/ thinking, practice OR SIMILAR WORDS

// ideas detract from the work OR SIMILAR WORDS

/// Bible

God, in His time, will produce a healthy church.
Soundness of growth and not speed should be the goal.

106. Examine the declarations above and write below the qualities mentioned or implied in genuine missionary work according
to this type of thinking

_____. see //

        All these concepts take for granted that slow growth is
necessarily healthy and that the longer it takes for the work
the higher quality will be the product. Nothing in the Bible or
in the history of the New Testament Church supports this position.   These ideas come from man's imagination, not from the Bible.

107. One of the fundamental reasons for rejecting rapid growth is
that these men never

_____. see &

108. They believe that if one works long enough in a sector that
the Church has to

_____. see ///

109. The error of the concept that the length of time employed
to produce growth determines the value is that of supposing that
the Church grows in a geographic region while really it grows in
a sector of mankind. The Church grows only through the conversion
of

_____. see &&

110. The size of a church does not depend on the number of years
that a church building has been on a certain corner but on the
number of

_____. see /

111. If a pastor labors for many years in a poor section of a
large city, should we expect that he will organize a large and
stable church? Why? Will those converted be there after five
years?

_____.
                                            see &&&

/   members,
     conversions

//   slow, stable,
     healthy, solid
     OR SIMILAR WORDS

/// grow

&   experienced it
     OR SIMILAR WORDS

&&   persons OR
     SIMILAR WORDS

&&& No. Many who live
     in these areas
     move frequently
     OR SIMILAR WORDS

The concepts which impede growth have arisen where missions have suffered not only slow growth, but failure and defeat. It is always difficult and painful to admit defeat. The workers try to convince themselves that God didn't want growth after all. The concept of the small remnant is very attractive. Didn't our Lord say that many are called, but few chosen?

112. When men try to explain why the Church doesn't grow it is easy to say that it wasn't the purpose of

_____. see //

113. They believe that the responsibility for results rests with

_____. see /

114. From their study of the Old Testament they conclude that not everyone will be saved, but that God will call out for Himself a

_____. see &&

The glorification of smallness implies that a small group is holy. Slow growth is considered good growth. Sayings such as the following influence the thinking of the Church.

The small minority that suffers for its faith is the true Church.
The persecuted Church, the Church under the cross, is the true Church.
The power of a small group of men, with God, should not be despised.

115. According to this type of thinking the best church is a

_____ one. see ///

116. They maintain that a conflict exists between the Church and the world. Therefore those outside the Church are considered

_____. see &&&

117. With this attitude it is more _____ to win people from outside the church community. see &

/ God, others
// God
/// small
& difficult
&& remnant
&&& enemies OR SIMILAR WORDS

Under certain circumstances, for certain Churches, and in
certain cases, these concepts are valid. Our Lord said that his
disciples were as leaven - a little leaven in the dough. But
the force of this figure is precisely that leaven makes the
dough to grow excessively. The virtue of leaven is not its smallness but its capacity to grow. The minority, if it is to be
creative, must not only originate productive ideas but also convince the majority to accept them. It must grow.

118. What is the purpose of yeast in making bread? _____

_____, see /

119. If the Church wants to propagate its ideas and standards in
the whole society it can not remain a

_____. see ///

120. In order to transform the society the Church must _____,
see &

121. Search in chapters 2 to 9 of Acts for verses which support
rapid or slow growth.

122. Perhaps some pastors talk so much of the little flock because for them it means

_____ responsibility. see &&

Even if we were convinced that God wanted only a small remnant, how could we determine the size of the remnant? If the
flock should be 1000 or 10,000 or 100,000? If there are 100,000
chosen and our churches only have reached 1000, shouldn't we
seek the 99,000 that are still lacking?

123. We shouldn't cease to evangelize because we don't know how
many

_____. see //

/ to make it rise or SIMILAR WORDS
// are lacking or SIMILAR WORDS
/// minority
& grow
&& less, little

124. If our goal is that one out of every ten persons in a population of 1,000,000 enter the Church we must win
see ///
_____.

125. All Christians agree that we should be concerned that the Church be a genuine Church. We don't need nominal Christians but genuine disciples of Christ. But we find in the Bible that Jesus and the apostles preached not only to individuals but also to
_____. see //

126. Based on your experience in the churches which you have visited, write below the advantages and the disadvantages of a small congregation.

The Facts That We Need

Numerical data are essential for understanding church growth. The Church is made up of persons. It is possible to count persons and there is nothing spiritual about not doing so. The census is a measure of the spirituality of the Church.

127. Each cipher in the statistics of the Church represents a

_____. see &

128. Every church has a certain _____ of members. see /

/ number
// multitudes, crowds, groups
/// 100,000
& person, individual

129. The spiritual vigor of a church is measured in part by the way in which the number of members

_____ . see ///

130. Therefore the census is one way of determining the _____ of a church.   see $$$

131. In order to describe church growth we need _____ .
see $$

Some people deprecate church statistics. They cite II Samuel 24:1-10 to affirm that David sinned in numbering the people. But they overlook the many chapters in Numbers in which God requires the exact enumeration of all the people of Israel and of each tribe (Numbers 1:2, 3). Nor do they pay attention to the emphasis which Luke gives to numbers in Acts. God's approval of numbering the people depends on the motive.

132. The census mentioned in II Samuel was for the glory of

_____ .   see /

133. The census in Numbers was for the glory of _____ .
see &&

134. The census in Numbers was _____ by God.   see &

135. Therefore we see that God's approval of a census depends on the

_____ for making it.   see //

137. In biblical terms we must say that the use of numbers is consistent with God's wisdom. In practical terms it is as nec-essary as honesty in finances. The Christian steward must be ready to render

_____ .   see &&&

137. Write below the figures or references to numbers given in

Acts 2:14_____   Acts 4:4_____   Acts 5:14_____
see $

/   David
//   motive
///   increases or
        SIMILAR WORDS
&   approved,
        ordered
&&   God
&&&   reports, accounts
$ 3000; 5000
$$ great number
$$ figures, data
$$$ vigor, vitality

It is certain that no one has ever been saved by statistics, but neither can the thermometer or X-rays heal. Nevertheless, they are of great value to the doctor in determining the condition of the patient. In the same way church growth data can not in themselves lead someone to Christ. But they can be very valuable to the Church that wants to know where, when and how to carry out its evangelistic work so that great increase of membership will result in the churches.

138. Data have values and limitations. Like methods, they are means and not ends. Figures of membership, baptisms, etc.

_____a) Guarantee wise use of resources.

_____b) Hinder wise use of resources.

_____c) Permit wise use of resources.   see //

139. The data help us to

_____a) Determine evangelistic success.

_____b) Resolve the problems of evangelism.

_____c) Save the persons counted.   see &

The first figure that we need is the denominational total of members in a country. Generally this figure is in the files of the Church or mission. If the membership total for each year is found we can make comparisons and determine how much the Church has increased during each period. There will be periods of great growth, little growth, stagnation, and even decrease. In order to obtain uniformity year after year it is better to use always the number of baptized members.

140. In order to get a national perspective we need the figures of the (Church/church)

_____ .   see ///

141. Probably the period between one report and another will be

_____ .   see /

142. The commonest and most useful figure for membership is that of

_____ .   see &&

/ one year
/// c Church
& a baptized members

143. Who in your denomination will have the information about membership totals? As part of your homework in this lesson, write to him asking for the figures of national totals for every year.

144. If the total for January 1969 is subtracted from the total in January 1970, the number that remains is the increase or loss during

_____ .   see &&&

145. We should expect that the differences between periods should be

_____ . (distinct/ the same) see /

     After saying that we should try for denominational totals it is necessary to warn you that sometimes these figures fool us. We must use them carefully. Of greater value are the totals of <u>homogeneous</u> units (homo - same, genus - order). These are groups that are identified as separate units because of culture, language or other geographical or political factors. For example, in Ecuador the Gospel Missionary Union works among homogeneous units that speak Spanish, Quechua and Jivaro.

146. The first figure asked for was that of the _____ .
                                           see &

147. Now we want to examine totals of more local units which are called

_____ units.   see //

148. In a Church that has work in Spanish, Quechua and Jivaro there are at least

_____ homogeneous units.   see ///

149. A group that is distinguished from others by cultural differences is a

_____ unit.   see &&

     Now let us examine some examples that demonstrate the danger of depending only on denominational totals. In 1965 and 1966 the Christian and Missionary Alliance experienced considerable growth in Ecuador, but this growth as a denomination was the same as the increase among the members of the Yumbo tribe in the eastern

/ distinct
// homogeneous
/// three
& Church, denomination
&& homogeneous
&&& 1969

jungles and among churches in the province of Guayas. This indicates that the Alliance did not grow in the rest of the country.

We could cite another example of the Foursquare Church in
Guayaquil, Ecuador. Between 1966 and 1968 the membership of the
several churches of that city increased approximately 350. But
during this period the central church added 400 members to its
rolls. Therefore the net result for the other Foursquare churches in the city was a decrease in membership.

Let's see one more example, this time of the Evangelical
Covenant Church in Ecuador. In 1965 the total membership in the
country was 173 and in 1968, 317. This would lead us to believe
that all was well in the Covenant. But looking more closely at
the individual congregations we see something else. In 1965 the
congregation in Ambato had seven members and that of Guayaquil
fourteen. By 1968 the Ambato church had climbed to forty-two,
but the Guayaquil church had only sixteen members. The figures
indicate that something was wrong in Guayaquil even though the
denominational statistics present a good picture for the country
as a whole.

150. The denominational total doesn't indicate what is happening
in the
_____.   see /

151. The fact that a congregation increases signifies for another
congregation
_____.   see //

Now we leave the theory to pass to the practice. The student should obtain membership figures for his congregation for
each year. The pastor or secretary of the church should have
these figures. The student should also try to obtain the figures
for other churches of his denomination or of his city or area.
Make a list like the one at the bottom of the page.

In Lesson V we will learn to interpret these figures and
also to construct graphs which will show what has happened in
the churches through the years. We will return to this matter
of figures in Lessons VI and VIII also. Meanwhile the student
should make an effort to obtain the greatest number of exact
figures that he can.

1967	15
1968	25
1969	42
1970	59
1971	72

/ churches, congregations OR SIMILAR WORDS
// nothing OR SIMILAR WORDS

5

GRAPHS OF GROWTH

In this lesson we will discover the way to collect and interpret the data that we need to understand church growth. In the preceeding lessons we have studied the need to determine the reasons for growth and the theological bases that demonstrate that God wants His Church to grow numerically. In Lesson IV we explained the data on which we will base our study. Now we have to use these figures for a practical analysis of Churches and congregations. Through the study of this lesson the student will learn the importance of graphs and how they can indicate to us changes in church growth.

The Value of Graphs

After determining church growth data we must interpret them. Why does the Church grow in one place and not in another? It is not enough to keep statistics. The goal is to understand growth processes. Behind the figures we must discover the reason for them, the factors which God has used to multiply His churches and the conditions in which the Church did or did not grow.

1. Besides discovering data of growth we must interpret them. The goal of our study is to

_____a) Obtain church growth data.

_____b) Determine when the Church grew more.

_____c) Determine why the Church grew more in certain periods.

see /

ɔ

2.   Our study is not just of historical interest.   We should also learn

_____a) How certain congregations grew.

_____b) What are the general conditions in which churches grew.

_____c) Why a certain congregation grew.   see /

3.   The objective of this study in general terms is that of

_____a) Promoting growth in the church of the student.

_____b) Presenting to the student certain interesting cases of growth.

_____c) Giving the student a formula for evangelization that will work in any kind of conditions.   see &

The reasons for growth are complex and there is always danger in oversimplifying them.   Those who work in evangelical radio stations say that radio is of great help in evangelism because it enters into every home.   However, we must remember that only certain programs have value for certain persons.   Literature has been used greatly by God, but only when it has been prepared especially for a specific class of readers.   Many believe that radio and literature are impersonal methods of evangelism and that they only serve as preparation for personal contact in which an individual is led to conversion and church membership.   In this case these means would be among various factors that operate in the conversion of men to Christianity.

4.   We can not say that the Church grew for one reason or another because the reasons are

_____ .   see ///

5.   The two most widely used means for reaching the masses are

_____ and _____ .   see //

6.   How many of your non-evangelical friends listen to evangelical radio programs?

_____

/   b
//   radio,
     literature
/// complex
&   a

7. Do you know someone who was converted by listening to evangelical radio programs without having had personal contact with believers?

_____

8. If the answer above was no, does this mean that radio is worthless? Why? or why not?

9. The value of radio or literature in evangelism depends on its orientation to reach

_____ . see &

Another factor in the extension of Christianity has been revival. We will consider revivals in greater detail in Lesson VII. We all hope for revival. Nevertheless, without denying its value, we must realize that it does not always extend the Church. We should also add that genuine revivals are so rare that Christians can not wait for them to see many people come to Christ and His Church.

10. Revivals, that is, movements of the Holy Spirit that result in the transformation of believers, are

_____a) Good.

_____b) Common.

_____c) Good and common.

_____d) Unnecessary.   see //

11. Revivals contribute to church growth because they

_____a) Automatically solve all the Church's problems.

_____b) Can empower the believers for evangelization.

_____c) Eliminate the need to evangelize.   see /

/ b

// a

/// No, it prepares people for personal contacts or SIMILAR WORDS

& certain people or classes of people OR SIMILAR WORDS

In view of the variety of factors and the relative value of each, the only valid way of determining the relation between cause and effect is to find out the chronological order of the factors and their results. For example, if the churches experience a considerable rise in membership after a revival there is reason to believe that the increase was a product of the revival.

12. If quantities of literature are distributed continuously and there is a sudden increase in church membership, we can not say for certain that literature distribution was the
                              see /   _____.

13. Possibly the growth has no relation to a certain _____.
                              see &

14. It is also possible that the growth was due to the method or factor in effect (before/after)
                    see //   _____ growth occurred.

15. It is necessary, therefore, to know when growth occurred before we can say
_____. see &&

16. Therefore in our study we need something to show us

_____. see ///

What we need is the graph of growth. Columns of church membership contain hidden information. But when these figures are transformed into a graph they reveal to us their secrets. In order to understand church growth and explain it to others we have to construct graphs. On the following page you will find a column of figures and a graph. Which captures your attention first? Which indicates most clearly what has happened?

/ cause
// before when growth occurred or SIMILAR WORDS
/// factor
& what was the cause or SIMILAR WORDS
&&

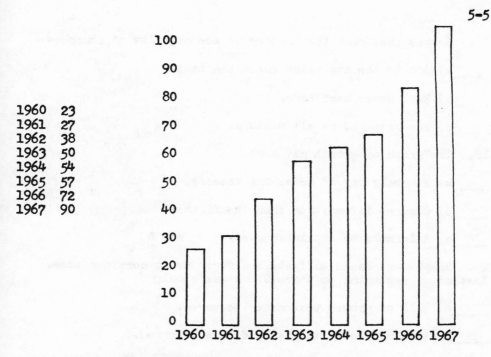

1960	23
1961	27
1962	38
1963	50
1964	54
1965	57
1966	72
1967	90

Probably few students have seen graphs of their churches or denominations. Consequently they have a rather vague idea of their denomination's progress or that of the evangelical movement in general. If our goal is church growth we must use the means to measure our success. All thinking about church growth must be based on graphs of growth because without accurate knowledge we can be mistaken. Sometimes we talk about what should have happened without knowing precisely what did occur. It is possible to look for the cause of growth which never occurred. The plans of the Church should be based on facts, not on hopes or guesses.

17. With regard to the relationship between the columns of figures and the graphs

_____a) The graph reveals much more.

_____b) The graph has nothing to do with the figures.

_____c) The columns of figures reveal enough.   see /

18. Graphs that show the history of the majority of churches

_____a) Add to the confusion about the facts.

_____b) Have never been made.

_____c) Are prepared by all pastors.   see /

19. The graph of growth gives us

_____a) The only way of measuring success.

_____b) Clearer information than the figures.

_____c) A formula to obtain success.   see &

20. Graphs are based on facts and force us to consider them. Instead of depending on impressions one should

_____a) Talk of growth that never occurred.

_____b) Talk of growth that should have occurred.

_____c) Know exactly what occurred.   see //

21. Church plans and policies should be based on

_____a) The wishes of pastors.

_____b) The horoscope.

_____c) Statistics of growth.   see &&

22. Church growth is guaranteed by the installation of

_____a) A new building.

_____b) A new pastor.

_____c) A new program.

_____d) None of these.   see ///

Later in this lesson we will have practice in constructing some graphs. But first we should think about their use. It will be helpful to study some examples before talking about the

theory. Graphs, like figures, are used in every area of life:
education, finance, science, etc. There are various types.
Some are formed by columns whose height represents a certain
quantity or size. This is the type of graph that was presented
earlier. An even commoner form is the line graph. On squared
paper points are located which represent the data to be indicated. Later a line is traced to join these points and indicate the continuity, in this case, of church growth. Line
graphs are those used most in this study.

23. The first step in the use of graphs is to learn to _____.
                                        see //

24. Many graphs are found in magazines and books that have to
do with

    _____ . see &

25. In the most common type of graph points are joined by a

    _____ . see /

26. The graph on a preceding page represents numbers by means
of

    _____ . see ///

/ line
// use them
/// columns
& education,
  finance,
  many aspects
  of life OR
  SIMILAR WORDS

The Disciples of Christ in Puerto Rico

Sometimes changes are seen so clearly in the graph that it is almost impossible to ignore them. The graph below represents the growth of the Church of the Disciples of Christ in Puerto Rico between the years 1900 to 1955. The solid line indicates the number of members. The dotted line indicates the funds invested in establishing and helping the Church. The actual amount of funds is not important.

The Disciples of Christ in Puerto Rico

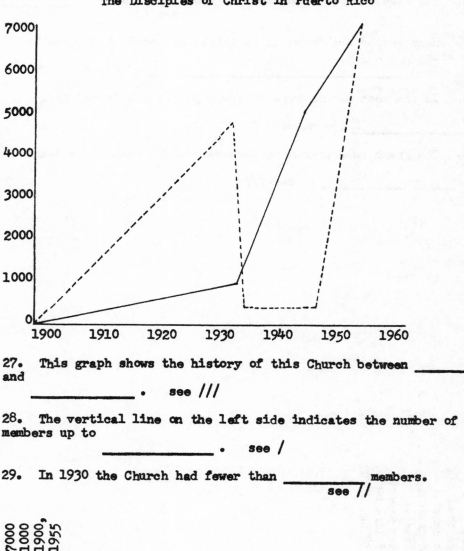

27. This graph shows the history of this Church between _____ and

_____ . see ///

28. The vertical line on the left side indicates the number of members up to

_____ . see /

29. In 1930 the Church had fewer than _____ members.
see //

7000
1000
1900,
1955

/ // /// /

30. More rapid growth began in the year _____ . see $

31. After _____ growth was slower.   see &&&

32. In 1955 total membership was _____ . see /

33. In 1943 total membership was _____ . see $$

34. During the years from 1932 to 1955 growth was _____
more rapid than that before 1932.   see %

35. Between 1932 and 1943 the Church increased by _____
members.   see ///

36. The funds decreased after _____ . see &&

37. The continued to drop until _____ . see %%

38. They remained at this level until _____ . see $$$

39. The most rapid growth of the Church occurred during the
years from

_____ to _____ . see //

40. The Church grew most when the level of funds was _____ .
see &

41. Do these figures prove that the way to stimulate church
growth is to reduce the funds that the Church receives? Why?

see %%%

   As we have seen in the graph, during the years of the economic recession in the United States, mission funds were drasti-
cally reduced and did not reach their former level until World
War II. The question is: Why after thirty years, did the
Church begin to expand rapidly and what relation does this expansion have to the lack of mission funds? Is it possible that
withholding funds from the United States caused the sudden growth?
The evidence proves that the lack of financial support had no-

/   7000
// 1932, 1943
/// 3800
&   low
&& 1928
&&& 1943
$ 1932
$$ 4800
$$$ 1943
%   much
%% 1932
%%% No. Other
    factors could
    have made
    the differ-
    ence or
    SIMILAR
    WORDS

thing to do with growth. In Puerto Rico during the recession financial aid was withheld also from the Baptist, Methodist and Presbyterian missions. But in these Churches the number of members decreased. Therefore we can eliminate lack of financial aid as the cause of growth and we must look for the real cause among other factors.

42. The graph of the Disciples of Christ proves that

_____a) Withdrawal of funds produces growth.

_____b) Withdrawal of funds hinders growth.

_____c) The Church can grow with little financial aid.   see ///

43. The relationship between two facts (in this case lack of funds and growth)

_____a) Is always that of cause and effect.

_____b) Can be coincidence, that is unrelated factors.

_____c) Never is that of cause and effect.   see /

44. The value of a comparative study of two or more Churches is that

_____a) It is possible to study the effect of certain factors in various cases.

_____b) Finances can be eliminated from the Church.

_____c) There is no value at all.   see //

    It happened that during 1932 the Church of the Disciples of Christ experienced a touch of pentecostal fire. A genuine revival took hold of the Church. Its pastors were filled with the Holy Spirit. Men and women repented of their sins. Many were freed of their vices and in their place experienced and manifested the fruits of the Holy Spirit. Some of the leaders opposed these manifestations. But at last they recognized that they were of God. This church, like that mentioned in Acts 9:31 "had peace and was built up; and walking in the fear of the Lord and in the comfort of the Holy Spirit it was multiplied."

News of the new power available through faith to the common man spread through the communities and among the relatives of the believers. For several years hundreds were converted each year. Laymen went out to preach and to teach. Ordinary members organized Sunday Schools, Bible studies and prayer meetings in their homes and in shacks and rented quarters during those years. Some of these groups and meetings became churches. Without the graph of growth no one would have been able thirty years later to say when the growth occurred and why.

45. It has already been stated that revival does not always bring growth. Nevertheless in this case it was a very important factor in growth. Make a list of the proofs that this was a genuine revival.   see //

46. Revival is something few have experienced and almost no one understands. For this reason sometimes it is not recognized as a revival. Some of the leaders opposed the movement because

_____a) They couldn't control it.

_____b) The Christians followed immoral practices.

_____c) The Christians followed practices contrary to the Bible.
                                          see ///

47. Under the impulse of the Holy Spirit, during the revival the evangelicals adopted methods of evangelism that

_____a) Can not be practiced except during a revival.

_____b) Any Christian guided by the Holy Spirit can put into practice.

_____c) Never have been used before or after.   see /

/ b
// full of the Holy Spirit, repentance, changed lives, fruits and gifts of the Holy Spirit or SIMILAR WORDS
/// a

48. The graph identifies revival as the cause of growth because

_____a) Revivals are always seen in growth graphs.

_____b) The graph tells us to look for non-economic factors in
the years 1932-33.

_____c) The graph has no value in this case.   see //

49. Which of the activities of the Disciples of Christ could
your church use today?

The graph reveals not only periods of rapid growth, but
also periods of stagnation. Two reasons why churches cease to
grow are a change in personnel or policy and the evangelization
of all of a responsive element of the population. Often after
a rapid advance a church enters a period called consolidation.
This is a time in which the church is busy with other things
than evangelism. Sometimes progress terminates in consolidation
because the Church has reached all those who are open to the
gospel in a given sector.

50. If many Italians enter the churches in Buenos Aires, it is
possible that these churches cease to grow when they have
reached all those who speak

_____.   see /

51. In a population where some elements are responsive and others
are hostile the Church will cease to grow when

_____ ,   see &   _____

52. There are other reasons also that the Church decides to
consolidate instead of

_____.   see ///

Italian

b
evangelize

it has reached all
the receptive elements
or SIMILAR WORDS

/
///
&

53. Another reason is the change of personnel or policy. If a pastor arrives who doesn't promote evangelism it is probable that the church

_____ . see ///

54. We see therefore that the cause of stagnation in a church may be a change of

_____ .   see &&

55. A church will not evangelize much if its pastor prefers to do

_____ .   see /

---

56. Write below two reasons why stagnation is produced in a church after a period of good growth.

---

see //

57. No one is aware of stagnation because everyone is working faithfully and therefore the necessary remedies are not applied. Much activity in the church does not guarantee

see &   _____ .

Some Ecuadorian Churches

In the graph that follows we can see the history of a congregation in Ecuador. For a period of ten years (1956-1966) this congregation maintained more or less the same level. Since nobody called attention to the situation nothing was done to correct it. No one sought the reasons for success in the first years nor the causes of the interruption of the church's progress. The leaders responsible for the church never faced the facts presented graphically.

/ other things or SIMILAR WORDS

// For having reached all the responsive element of the people,

/// for a change in personnel or policy or SIMILAR WORDS

& will not grow

&& growth or SIMILAR WORDS

&& personnel, policy

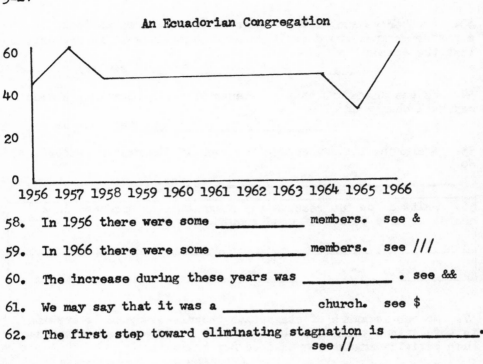

An Ecuadorian Congregation

58. In 1956 there were some _____ members. see &

59. In 1966 there were some _____ members. see ///

60. The increase during these years was _____ . see &&

61. We may say that it was a _____ church. see $

62. The first step toward eliminating stagnation is _____ .
    see //

63. Seeing the success at the beginning of the period, it is possible to believe that the church could have continued to

_____ .   see &&&

64. In order to break out of stagnation it is always possible to
    _____ the program.   see /

    It is important to make graphs of every congregation and every region. Graphs based on the denominational total of members hide more than they reveal. In the graph that follows it can be noted that although the denomination is growing well there is much difference between the two congregations indicated. If the problem is not studied in detail one would believe that all the churches were enjoying the blessing of God, who gives the growth.

/   change, better or SIMILAR WORDS
// recognize it OR SIMILAR WORDS
/// 60
&   60
&& 0, nothing
&&& grow
$ static

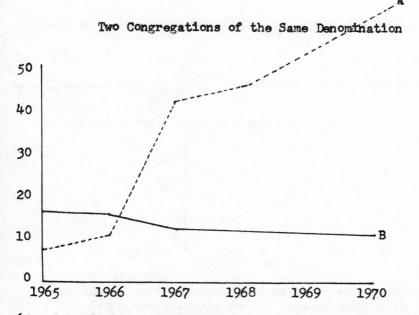

Two Congregations of the Same Denomination

65. One of the most effective ways of using graphs is in comparing two or more congregations or denominations. In the graph above the contrast is noted. It is important to prepare graphs of

_____a) Each congregation and region.

_____b) Each nation and continent.

_____c) Each meeting and activity.   see //

66. Graphs of denominational totals of membership

_____a) Are the only useful graphs.

_____b) Don't indicate the differences between congregations.

_____c) Reveal all that is necessary to know.   see /

67. Since the congregations compared in the graph are of the same denomination, it is reasonable to believe that the differences between them are because of

_____a) Doctrine.

_____b) Local policy.

_____c) Resources.   see ///

b a b

\\\

68. It would be interesting to find out what happened in church A in

_____ .   see &

69. Why does this period interest us? _____
                                    see ///

70. If you were a member of congregation B, what would you do?

Graph Construction

In the preceding pages we have examined some graphs and considered their usefulness. Now we are going to construct some simple graphs. The basic structure consists of two perpendicular lines. The vertical line indicates the number of members or other category desired. The horizontal line indicates time, usually in years. A scale or proportion is chosen which is convenient to show the data. If the graph covers a period of five years we must leave enough room between years so that the horizontal line extends from one side of the page to the other. See the example below:

| 1965 | 1966 | 1967 | 1968 | 1969 | 1970 |

In the same way choose divisions for the vertical line which will fit in the available space.

71. The number of members is indicated on the left along the

_____ line.   see &&

72. Years are shown at the bottom of the graph or along the

_____ line.   see /

73. On the horizontal line the _____ are shown.
                                                  see //

/   horizontal
// years
/// because it
    began to
    grow OR
    SIMILAR
    WORDS
&   1966
&& vertical

74. On the vertical _____ are indicated. see /

75. In order to show 2000 members we must see the _____
line.   see $

76. To find the year 1965 we must look along the _____
line.   see &&

77. Time is indicated along the _____ line. see ///

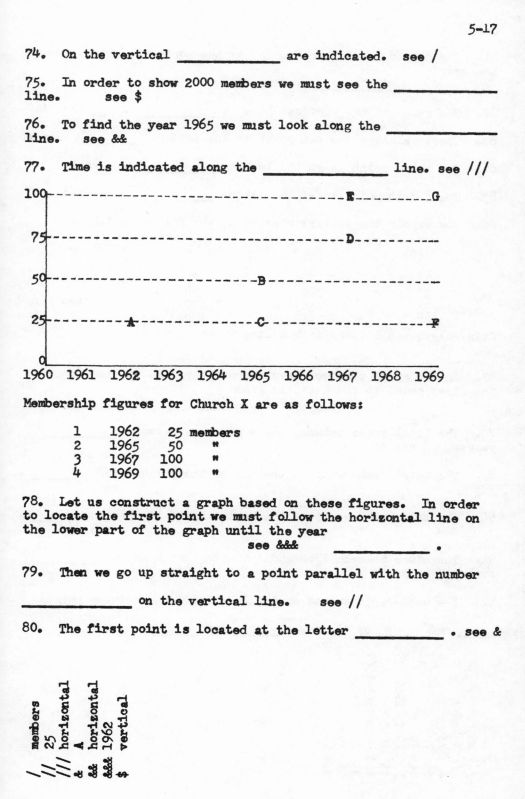

Membership figures for Church X are as follows:

1	1962	25 members
2	1965	50 "
3	1967	100 "
4	1969	100 "

78. Let us construct a graph based on these figures. In order
to locate the first point we must follow the horizontal line on
the lower part of the graph until the year
                    see &&&   _____ .

79. Then we go up straight to a point parallel with the number

_____ on the vertical line.   see //

80. The first point is located at the letter _____ . see &

/   members
// 25
/// horizontal
&   A
&& horizontal
&&& 1962
$ vertical

81. The second point corresponds, on the horizontal line, to the year

_____ .   see $$

82. The value of the vertical line is _____ . see &&&

83. These values place the point at the letter _____ . see /

84. The third point is at the letter _____ . see %

85. The fourth point is at the letter _____ . see %%%

86. Now supply the letters missing in the following table:

Point	Year	Members	Letter
1°	1962	25	
2°	1965	50	
3°	1967	100	see ///
4°	1969	100	

Join only these letters with a line

87. In the graph that you have drawn the period of time (from the first point to the last) is from

see $ _____ to _____ .

88. The total space between these years represents _____ years.   see &&

89. The total membership at the end of the period was _____ .
see %%

90. The total membership at the beginning of the period was _____ .
see //

91. Therefore between 1962 and 1969 the church added _____ members.   see &

92. The most rapid growth during the period was between points

_____ and _____ or the years _____ and _____ .   see $$$

/ B
/// 25
/// A–B–E–G
& 75
&& 7
&&& 50
$ 1962, 1969
$$ 1965
$$$ B–E, 1965–1967
% E
%% 100
%%% G

93. There was a period of stagnation between the years _____ and _____ .   see /

Membership of Church X, 1900-1970

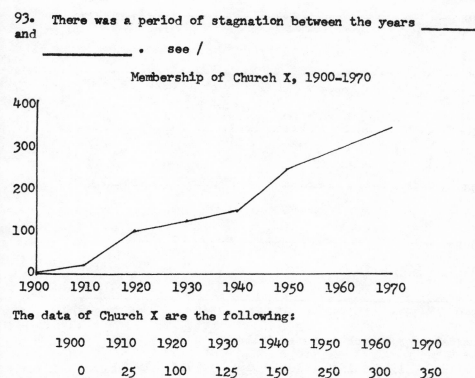

The data of Church X are the following:

1900	1910	1920	1930	1940	1950	1960	1970
0	25	100	125	150	250	300	350

Using the data of Church X above the student should construct the same graph that appears above. But he should do so looking at the data and not at the graph. Locate each point and trace the line between them in pencil. Later you can compare your graph with that above to see if they are the same. The important thing is not to produce the graph perfectly the first time, but rather to learn the method, because to produce the next graph there will be no model to follow.

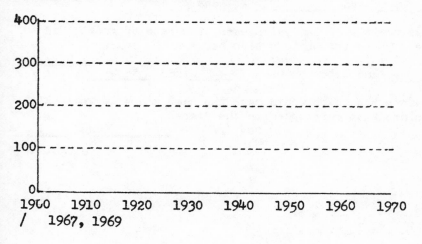

/   1967, 1969

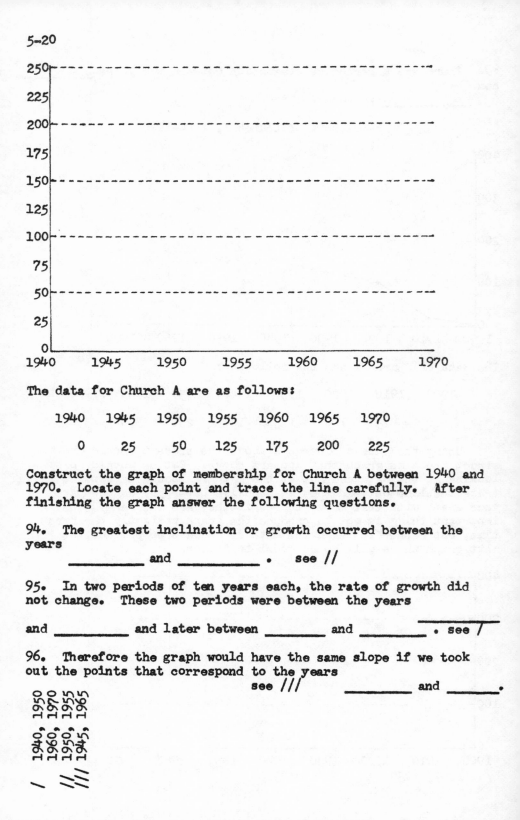

The data for Church A are as follows:

1940	1945	1950	1955	1960	1965	1970
0	25	50	125	175	200	225

Construct the graph of membership for Church A between 1940 and 1970. Locate each point and trace the line carefully. After finishing the graph answer the following questions.

94. The greatest inclination or growth occurred between the years

_____ and _____ .   see //

95. In two periods of ten years each, the rate of growth did not change. These two periods were between the years

and _____ and later between _____ and _____ . see /

96. Therefore the graph would have the same slope if we took out the points that correspond to the years

see ///   _____ and _____ .

```
     0  0  0  5
     5  7  5  5
/    9  9  9  9
     1, 1, 1, 1,
//   0  0  0  5
///  4  6  5  4
     9  9  9  9
     1  1  1  1
```

/   1940, 1950
//   1960, 1970
/// 1950, 1955
     1945, 1965

97. There are three changes of the slope of growth. These changes occurred in the years
     see &&   _____, _____ and _____.

98. The most rapid growth is seen during the years _____ to
     _____. see /

The data concerning Church B are:

1960	1961	1962	1963	1964	1965	1966	1967	1968	1969	1970
0	10	20	40	45	50	60	75	90	90	100

Construct the graph based on these figures. The first step will be to indicate values along the axes, that is, the horizontal and vertical lines.

99. The years are shown along the _____ line. see ///

100. The membership is shown on the _____ line.   see &

101. Locate each point carefully. There are _____ points.
     see //

/ 1950
  1955
// eleven
/// horizontal
& vertical
&& 1950,
   1955
   1960

102. Trace the line between the points. How many changes of slope are there?

_____ see /

103. These changes occur after the years _____, _____, _____

_____, _____ and _____ . see &&

104. The most rapid growth took place during (year) _____ (The figures are for January of each year)   see &

105. The Church stood still during the year _____ . see &&&

Now on the sheet of squared paper that follows construct the graph of your own church. If you have obtained the figures for more than one congregation you may trace two or more lines in the same framework. If you have not been able to obtain the figures or if they exist for only a few years you can use the figures that follow to construct a graph. If you are in doubt as to the way to procede you should review the steps that were given in preparing the graphs of Church A and B. The figures for congregation X are as follows:

1965	1966	1967	1968	1969	1970	1971
5	20	40	45	53	70	85

In the graph that you construct note the periods of rapid and slow growth. Use only one side of the squared paper because there will be another assignment for the other side.

Graphs serve not only to analyze the progress of a congregation but also to compare various denominations. In the same way that it is possible to compare two congregations represented on the same graph we can also compare two denominations. On the page that follows the squared paper there is a graph of "Membership of some Ecuadorian Churches, 1947-1968." Study this graph to answer the following questions.

106. Which Church has more members? _____ . see ///

107. Which Church has the fewest members? _____ see //

/ 6
// Evangelical Covenant
/// Foursquare
& 1962
&& 1962, 1963, 1965, 1966, 1968
&&& 1969 1968

Membership of some Ecuadorian Churches

1947 - 1968

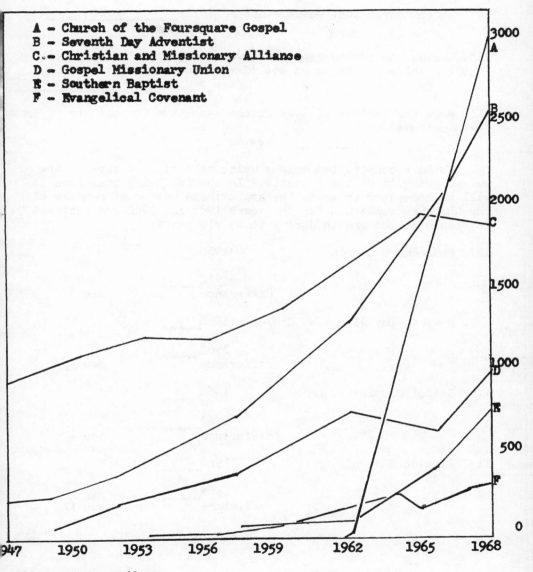

A - Church of the Foursquare Gospel
B - Seventh Day Adventist
C - Christian and Missionary Alliance
D - Gospel Missionary Union
E - Southern Baptist
F - Evangelical Covenant

Source: Weld, 1968:71.

108. Which Church grew most rapidly in the last five years shown on the graph?

_____ see $$

109. Which Church lost members after 1965? _____

see &&&

110. During the period represented on the graph, how many denominations suffered losses at one time or another?

see / _____

111. Were the periods of loss at the same time for all the denominations?

_____ see &&

     We have constructed graphs using columns of figures. Now we are going to do the opposite. In the following questions it will be necessary to write the approximate number of members of the Churches mentioned for the years 1968 and 1962 and subtract to determine the growth during those six years.

112. Foursquare Church   1968_____

                                    1962_____
                         difference_____   see $

113. Seventh Day Adventist Church 1968_____

                                    1962_____
                         difference_____   see ///

114. Gospel Missionary Union   1968_____

                                    1962_____
                         difference_____   see &

115. Baptist Church   1968_____

                                    1962_____
                         difference_____   see //

/ three
// 760-90-670
/// 2580-1220-1360
& 990-700-290
&& no
&&& Christian and Missionary Alliance
$ 3000-30-2970
$$ Foursquare

We have one more exercise before leaving the study of graphs. Those who study this book will not only be leaders in their congregations, but also will be interested in the progress of their denomination and the Church in their country. We have already seen a graph that represents the Ecuadorian Churches during 1947 to 1968. On the unused side of the squared paper draw a graph of some Colombian Churches during the same period, that is, from 1949 to 1968. If we were to include all the denominations the graph would be too cluttered and confusing. We have had to select denominations that represent certain sectors of the Church and also those whose figures do not present extremes that would make the construction of the graph more difficult.

The figures are as follows:

	1949	1952	1957	1960	1966	1968
Christian and Missionary Alliance	1278	1078	1145	1711	2274	2637
Assemblies of God	20	40	40	175	488	1120
Mennonite Brethren	0	100	100	92	350	488
Lutheran Church	200	200	582	372	890	977
Presbyterian Church	1636	1500	1328	1684	1882	2363
Wesleyan Mission	20	30	30	205	387	373

116. The first observation that should be made is that the intervals between the years are

_____. see /

117. Therefore the points will not be equally distant along the

_____line. see ///

118. On the vertical line we must leave space for more than

_____ members. see //

119. It will also be necessary to approximate the points because the numbers of members do not coincide with the values along the

_____ line. see &

/ different
// 2637
/// horizontal
& vertical

Taking into consideration these observations, construct the graph and later answer the questions that follow. If the student has constructed the graph precisely he will be able to approximate the answers to these questions. The figures are from January of each year.

120. The Christian and Missionary Alliance reached a total of 1500 members in the year

_____. see &&&

121. With two exceptions the Churches had difficulty during the violence in Colombia and began to gain members after the year

see / ___.

122. The two exceptions were _____ and _____.

see $

123. The Church which grew the most after 1966 was the _____

_____. see &&

124. The Church which grew the least after 1966 was the _____

_____. see ///

125. The Lutheran Church crossed the line of 500 members in the years

_____, _____ and _____. see $$

126. The only Church that never registered a loss was the

_____. see //

127. The Assemblies of God and the Wesleyan Mission had the same number of members (where the lines cross) in the year

_____. see &

/ 1957
// Assemblies of God
/// Wesleyan Mission 1961
& Assemblies of God
&& Assemblies of God 1959
&&& Lutheran Church
$ Assemblies of God
$$ 1955, 1958, 1961

6

N SEARCH OF THE REASONS FOR GROWTH

In lesson IV we talked of the data needed to know what real growth occurred and when. In lesson V we saw that the best way to use these data is the construction of graphs based on them. In this way a glance will tell us what happened in a congregation or denomination. It indicates to us the periods or years in which the church grew normally and also when it did not. With this information we can look for the cause of growth or the lack of it.

In lesson VI we will hunt for these causes or reasons. In the first place, we must examine the classes of growth. Afterwards some factors that combine to extend the Church are presented. The New Testament example always serves as our guide and we must study it again and again from various points of view. The last part of the lesson has to do with certain general rules for growth. But it is necessary to repeat that the greatest value of this study is not historical but practical. The student must analyze his own congregation and determine the factors which have led to its present condition.

Classes of Growth

There are three basic classes of growth - biological, transfer and conversion. Biological growth is that which produces Christians of the second and successive generations. In Latin America there are many small groups that are made up of little more than one family. The children are evangelicals because their parents are. We will see more of this type of growth. It is certain that biological growth is also a type of conversion growth. Birth into an evangelical family does not guarantee faith. The children of evangelicals must be genuinely converted if they are to be added to the Church. Nevertheless, there is some value in preserving this distinction to indicate to us the way in which these converts have come into the Church.

1.   Biological growth occurs among children whose _____ are evangelicals.   see /

2.   In an evangelical community that consists of a single extended family, probably the young people are evangelicals because
_____. see &&&

3.   In the future the Church in Latin America will experience (more/less)
_____ biological growth.   see ///

4.   These children become genuine Christians only when they
_____. see &

5.   Personal faith in Christ is not the natural result of having been born in a
_____ home.   see //

6.   The first class of growth takes place within the Christian community and is called
_____ growth.   see $

Biological growth is very slow. The Church grows through the excess of births over deaths. Generally the proportion of biological growth of the Church is less than that of the total population because almost inevitably some of the children of evangelicals do not follow the faith of their parents. Biological growth will never be sufficient because the non-Christian sectors of the world population grow more rapidly than do the "Christian" peoples.

7.   Biological growth will never fill the churches because it is
_____. see &&

8.   The Christian community would extend more if all the evangelical couples had more
_____. see $$

/   parents
//   Christian
///   more
&   are converted
        OR SIMILAR WORDS
&&   slow
&&&   their parents are
        OR SIMILAR WORDS
$ biological
$$ children OR
        SIMILAR WORDS

9. Some children of evangelicals don't continue in _____.
                                                    see $

10. Probably the majority of the members of the student's
church were born into the
                    _____ faith. see &&&

11. Here we have evidence that the Church doesn't grow through
physical but rather through
            see /   _____ reproduction.

12. _____(type) growth is inadequate. see &&

        The second class of growth is by transfer. This is impor-
tant and every church should try to help spiritually its members
that move to other places until they join another congregation.
If the distances are great this care can be very difficult.
But at least the pastor and other members should urge the believer to seek another church, although of another denomination,
the first Sunday that he is in his new home. If a member is
absent from his church for three months or more it is advisable
to remove his name from the list of active members. Members
should be aware of this policy so that they will realize that
if they don't seek another church in their new area they will
end up without belonging to any congregation. This procedure
will also help the church to maintain realistic figures of membership and will force the member that moves to become a responsible member of the Christian community where he lives.

13. When a believer moves from one place to another his old
church should try to
                    _____. see &

14. Instead of keeping his membership in the congregation
where he used to attend it is better for him to look for

_____.   see //

15. Instead of waiting until he is well installed in his new
home a believer should seek a local church as
                                            _____
as possible.   see ///

/   spiritual or
    SIMILAR WORDS
// another church
/// soon
&   help him
&& spiritually OR
    SIMILAR WORDS
&&& biological
    Catholic or
    SIMILAR WORDS
$ their parents'
    faith OR
    SIMILAR WORDS

16. After an absence of three months from his former church he should no longer be considered a

_____ .   see &&

17. It is important for the believer to join a church where he

_____ .   see ///

18. In the definition of the Church's mission in Chapter III it was said that a Christian should be a

_____

of a church.   see &

19. When a church loses a member, another church should _____ .
                                                    see &&&

20. This process is called the _____ of members. see /

Growth by transfer suffers the same limitations as biological growth. The Church will never grow this way. In our age of urbanization churches in large cities can gain by the addition of Christians who have come from rural areas. But at the same time the membership of rural churches drops. And many Christians are lost along the way from one church to another. The Church must make an effort to promote the transfer of members who have moved, not in order to grow, but just to help keep the members that it has.

21. Generally through the transfer of members

_____a) Urban churches gain members.

_____b) Rural churches gain members.

_____c) There is no change.   see //

22. When one of his church members moves to another area the pastor should

_____a) Forget him.

_____b) Ask him to return since he is still considered a member in his old church.

_____c) Tell him about another church he should attend in the new area in which he will live.   see $

/   transfer
a
/// lives, is
or
SIMILAR
WORDS
&   respon-
sible
member
&&   member
&&& gain him
or
SIMILAR
WORDS
$ c

23. Unfortunately the transfer of members from one place to another often results in

_____a) A net gain in Church members.

_____b) A net loss in Church members.

_____c) No change in total membership.   see //

24. To be sure not to lose an active believer the pastor or his old church should inform of his move the

_____a) Civil officials of the place where the believer goes.

_____b) Evangelical pastor of the place where the believer goes.

_____c) Catholic priest of the place where the believer goes.   see /

25. The two kinds of growth that we have considered so far are

_____ and _____ .   see ///

The third kind of growth is by conversion. This occurs when persons place their faith intelligently in Christ. As a consequence of this conversion the normal Christian life includes baptism and church membership. This is the only way in which the good news of salvation can reach even the most remote parts of the earth. The goal of the Church is to have a congregation in every community and every sub-culture. When this happens we can be more or less sure that the gospel has been preached to every creature. In order to reach this goal the Church must grow greatly.

26. The most important kind of growth is _____ .
                                        see &

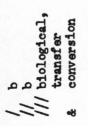

/ b
// b
/// biological,
    transfer
& conversion

27. In this study "conversion" refers to the moment in which a person

_____a) Listens to the gospel.

_____b) Places his faith in Christ.

_____c) Is baptized.

_____d) Becomes a member of a church.   see &&

28. The goal and realistic hope of the Church should be to

_____a) Preach once to every creature.

_____b) Establish a church in every community.

_____c) Win the whole world for Christ.   see ///

29. In order to reach this goal the Church must _____.
                                        see &

---

30. The three kinds of growth are:

_____, _____ and _____ see /

It has been said that in order to have uniformity in the reports of membership only baptized members should be counted. To have an even more accurate picture of the Church we should distinguish between baptisms within the Christian community, that is of children of evangelicals, and baptisms from the world. The case of a large Asian Church demonstrates the truth of this. This Church reported 4000 baptisms annually. For some smaller Latin American Church this figure is quite impressive. But this number is seen in a different light when we discover that the Church has a membership of 200,000. If the population increases at an annual rate of 2 per cent, that is for every hundred persons two more are born, this Church should experience biological growth of 4000 yearly. It can be seen, therefore, that the Church is barely baptizing the majority of the children of its members. Really it is a static Church.

31. Biological growth is really one type of growth by _____.
                                        see //

/ biological, transfer, conversion

// conversion

/// b

& grow greatly OR SIMILAR WORDS

&& b

32. It is important to know if converts come from evangelical families or from the

_____ .   see //

33. Biological growth is necessary, but this kind of growth will never extend the Church

_____ .   see &&

34. Let us suppose that the student's denomination has 3000 members. The total population of his country increases 3 per cent yearly. This means that for every hundred persons the annual increase is

_____ .   see ///

35. Remembering that your Church has 3000 (30 x 100) members, how many children will be born to the members every year? (30 x 3)

_____ .   see &&&

36. Suppose that all the children of the Christians are converted and join the Church. After a year, just through biological growth the Church will have
            (3000 + 90)   _____ members. see /

37. If after a year the Church has 3100 members, this means that it is winning very

_____ new members.   see &

If we compare the number of baptisms from the world with the growth of the Church we can see that solid growth occurs only when a good number of persons from non-evangelical families are converted and baptized. There is nothing that produces growth except baptisms from the world, when these persons are instructed and guided toward becoming stable and active Christians.

38. How many were baptized in the student's church last year?

39. How many of the baptized members are children of evangelicals?

40. In order to reach the average rate of growth for Latin American Churches a Church must baptize at least three times more persons from non-evangelical families than its own children. By this criterion your Church

_____ .

/ 3090
/// world
/// 3
& few or SIMILAR WORDS
&& rapidly or SIMILAR WORDS
&&& 90

41. What are some of the advantages and disadvantages of evangelicals who come from Christian families?

An analysis of families within the Church helps us to understand the way in which it grows. The stability of a congregation depends partly on the number of complete families or at least couples that it contains. In many parts of Latin America it has been noted that if the wife is converted first it is less likely that the husband will soon follow her. But if the husband is converted first, in the majority of the cases, the wife will follow her husband in the evangelical faith. Therefore if there is a high percentage of women whose husbands are not evangelicals in your congregations, more emphasis should be given to the evangelization of the men.

42. The most stable unit of the church is the _____.
see //

43. In Latin America it is better if the first member of the family that is won is the
_____ . see /

44. The possibility exists that single evangelicals will win their boy or girl friends. But the other possibility also exists that they
_____ . see ///

Again it is the student's turn to apply the theory to his local situation. If he has not obtained a list of the members of his church he should do so. In order to answer the following questions he may need the help of the pastor, the members of the church board, the Sunday School superintendent and the presidents of the young people and women's groups. The work that this involves depends, of course, on the size of the congregation.

/ father
// family
/// will leave the church OR SIMILAR WORDS

45. How many complete families or couples belong to the church?

_____

46. How many single adults are there? _____

47. How many persons are there whose spouse is not an evangelical?

_____

48. How many young people are there who have boy or girl friends who are not evangelicals?

_____

49. Are there more men or women on the membership list? _____

50. Considering the information above, does the church seem very stable? Why or why not?

51. What has been done or can be done to reach other members of the families of evangelicals?

52. Do the members of the church belong to receptive areas of the population or are they there because some special effort has been made to reach persons of that type?

53. Would it be possible to reach more people by changing methods or emphases?

54. What has been done to reach the men of your community or city? What more could be done?

Finding the Reasons for Growth

Where should one look to find the causes of church growth? The study of graphs has demonstrated that one should seek the factors that operated when the Church began to grow rapidly. But what should we expect to find? Some say that the answer is simple. Evangelistic campaigns win men to Christ and permit new churches to be established. But we must recognize that the results are not always permanent. The student will be able to remember some campaign in which there were many decisions. Nevertheless, for lack of a good system of follow-up many of those who made decisions never found their way into the local churches and the net gain for the Church was minimal.

55. One can learn where to seek the causes of growth through the study of

_____ .   see /

56. Our study indicates that the causes of growth are

_____a) Complex.

_____b) Simple.

_____c) Impossible to determine.   see ///

57. Evangelistic campaigns

_____a) Always produce many lasting results.

_____b) Sometimes produce many lasting results.

_____c) Never produce many lasting results.   see //

graphs
b
a
/ // /

58. From the church growth point of view, the value of an evangelistic campaign is that

_____a) Many people attend the meetings.

_____b) Many people make decisions of faith.

_____c) Many people join local churches.   see &

     The study of many cases of growth in various countries brings us to the conclusion that there are many factors and certain combinations of these factors that can give the desired results, that is, church growth. The best source of information concerning the reasons why a church has a continual increase of members should be the pastor. He was there. He saw what happened, the influences that operated among the people. Unfortunately, many pastors have the tendency to attribute everything to spiritual factors. Basically it is the Holy Spirit who changes hearts and renews men. God is a God of order and we can even say that there is a certain economy in the miraculous, so that God employs social forces to carry out His purposes.

59. The easiest way to explain growth is to say that it has been the work of
                   _____ .   see /

60. The person who knows best what has happened in his congregation is the
                   _____ .   see ///

61. Probably growth occurred because of

_____a) Purely spiritual reasons.

_____b) God's manifestation in signs and wonders.

_____c) Purely social reasons.

_____d) A combination of social and spiritual factors. see //

God
/ d
/// pastor
// c
&

62. Generally the Church expands because

_____a) God does miracles.

_____b) Men employ wise methods.

_____c) God operates through men.   see //

   An example, even though it is not from Latin America,
will illustrate this point. One of the reasons for the entrance
of thousands and hundreds of thousands of persons in the Church
in Indonesia in recent years has been the political situation.
The government welcomed Christianity as an anti-communist force.
Becoming a member of the Christian church is one of the easiest
ways of demonstrating that a person is not a communist. Undoubtedly some "conversions" are superficial. We will consider
this aspect of the problem later. What interests us now is knowing that in the midst of instability and uncertainty, many responded to the positive message of the gospel. The combination
of some religious and political factors resulted in this remarkable movement to Christianity.

63. The political situation in Indonesia

_____a) Was the only reason for growth.

_____b) Was one of the reasons for growth.

_____c) Didn't have anything to do with the growth.   see &

64. In view of what happened there we must conclude that

_____a) The Church should not accept the help of the state.

_____b) The Church should take advantage of every opportunity.

_____c) The Church should try to become the official religion.
                       see /

65. Generally men are more ready to listen to the gospel when

_____a) They are insecure and uncertain.

_____b) It is presented as something purely spiritual.

_____c) They are satisfied with their way of life.   see ///

66. The act of joining a Christian church should indicate

_____ a) Loyalty to Christ.

_____ b) Political neutrality.

_____ c) Rejection of communism.   see &&

     If in our Christian service we always have mixed motives how much more will there be complex reasons for the decision to become Christians. Nevertheless, after some time, we think only of the spiritual motives. For this reason it is better to ask recent converts about why they became Christians. The older members have already been indoctrinated to speak in spiritual terms with others in the church. They don't want anyone to question their motives for becoming Christians. For a recent convert it is still natural to say that he came to the church because his girl friend attended there.

67. It is better to ask about the motives for conversion of those who have been in the Church for
                                      _____ time. see &

68. The older members almost always give an answer in

_____ terms.   see //

69. Some church members will not answer frankly because they fear that they will be criticized for
                       _____ motives.   see ///

70. The answers of greatest value come from those who have been members for (20 years/2years/2months)
               see &&&   _____.

71. We must distinguish between the decision to attend a church and the more important decision of
             see /   _____.

/ conversion
// spiritual
/// religious OR
    unworthy OR
    SIMILAR WORDS
&& a
&& little
&&& 2 months

In addition to the investigations among recent converts, it is also worthwhile to ask non-Christians why they have decided against the Christian faith. If you have their confidence, they can reveal important factors that influence their decision. If it is discovered that their reasons are not religious we can seek to eliminate the obstacles without compromising the gospel.

72. Non-Christians also have made a _____. see &&&

73. Behind that decision there are certain _____ .
see /

74. It could be that these reasons are not spiritual but

_____ . see &&

75. It is impossible to take away from the gospel message the scandal of the
see // _____ . (If you need help, see I Cor. 1:18)

76. On the other hand we should try to find a way to eliminate

_____ obstacles. see $

It is also valuable to ask recent converts about their parents and friends that are interested in the gospel. Sometimes there is a problem that can be resolved by a mature Christian so that these people will come to a definite decision for Christ. In any case these questions will lead us to other persons that God is preparing for His harvest. It will also tell us something about the receptivity of that sector of the population. In addition these questions will awaken in the recent convert a sense of the importance of testifying to his family and friends.

77. If someone has entered recently in the church for social reasons probably some members of his family are

in the gospel   see /// _____

78. The conversion of two or three persons in one sector of the people may indicate that the sector is

_____ to the
gospel.   see &

/ reasons, causes
// cross
/// interested
& receptive, open
&& social OR SIMILAR WORDS
&&& decision
$ non-theo-logical OR SIMILAR WORDS

79. The person who can best testify to those people is

_____ . see //

80. The church should not be satisfied with a single conversion
if there is a possibility of winning
                    see &&&   _____ .

     Many declarations concerning church growth are due to the
desire to justify what has been done. Instead of admitting defeat we prefer to say that we have consolidated our position.
If it is not possible to talk of the number of converts we exalt
their quality. Sometimes an erroneous scale of values is constructed. According to this scale people are judged according
to certain categories or professions. Those who insist in the
value of a single soul are right, but not entirely right. We
must remember that God is no respecter of persons (James 2). In
Lesson XI we will study the consequences of such a teaching.
Now it will be sufficient to refute the argument in favor of the
quality versus the quantity of converts.

81. Some pastors and workers emphasize the quality of their converts because, in regard to quantity, they have won
                         see /   _____.

82. Many arguments against rapid church growth have the purpose
of
     _____ . see &&

     Not everything can be explained by a difference in methods.
Sometimes a new technique arises to guarantee the success of the
church. Another book is published that has all the answers. Before believing that a method has produced good results all the
cases in which the method has been used should be examined. It
could be that this method has coincided with another factor which
was the real cause of evangelistic success.

83. It is dangerous to say that the growth of the Church is only
the result of a new
                    _____ . see &

84. It could be that another factor or factors were the real

_____ . see ///

/   few
//   the recent
     convert OR
     SIMILAR
     WORDS
/// cause OR
     SIMILAR
     WORDS
&   method
&&   justifying
     what has
     been done
     OR SIMILAR
     WORDS
&&& many OR
     SIMILAR
     WORDS

In the same way there is room for a little holy and healthy scepticism with regard to theological explanations. For example, theological conservatism does not guarantee growth. Nor can it be said that one denomination or group has a monopoly on the Holy Spirit. The gospel is the same even if it produces much fruit in one place and little in another. The amount of growth depends, like a cooking recipe, on the correct combination of various ingredients.

85. Some cults have experienced much growth. This tells us that growth does not depend on

_____ theology. see &&

86. This growth is purely human and only resembles the growth of the

_____ . see ///

87. Nevertheless, these false movements show us that growth does not depend on

_____ reasons. see &

88. Another bit of evidence that contradicts theological explanations of church growth is the fact that often two denominations equally orthodox don't grow

_____ . see //

89. The success of the Church does not depend on a single factor but on

_____ . see /

Differences in rates of growth are found not only between denominations but also between congregations. It is interesting to study the history of every pastor and worker. The human factor is the most important in the multiplication of churches. God never changes, but men present infinite variety. It is possible to discover that when a certain pastor arrives the church begins to grow. But when another pastor serves the same congregation it stops growing. This fact is explained by differences in methods, of policy, of gifts and of dedication. Denominational leaders must find the way to resolve this problem. Overlooking ministerial failures is not good Christian stewardship.

/ a combination of factors OR SIMILAR WORDS
// in the same way OR SIMILAR WORDS
/// Church
& theological OR SIMILAR WORDS
&& orthodox OR SIMILAR WORDS

90.   Jesus Christ is the same yesterday, today and forever, but

_____ aren't.   see //

91.   Since pastors are different, there will also be differences
in the

_____ of their ministries.   see /

92.   If a church were seeking a pastor, how could it know (although not infallibly) that a certain pastor would make the
church prosper?

93.   Mention some of the factors that explain the success of
one pastor and the failure of another.

94.   If you were a member of the national or regional governing
body of your Church and one of your pastors was completely un-
productive, what would you do?

     Every administrator needs exact knowledge of the way in
which the churches under his responsibility are growing. All the
data mentioned earlier help him to have a realistic picture. By
improving the methods of obtaining and interpreting these facts
it will be possible to determine more exactly the receptivity of
people, the most effective ways of reaching them and the best
allocation of workers to carry out plans and projects.

/   results,
     fruits
//   men

95. What suggestions could you give now to your denominational leaders to help them reach the goals mentioned above?

The New Testament Example

The principles governing church growth which have been presented in this study are seen clearly in the New Testament Church. It is important for the student to be convinced that these principles originate in the wisdom of God and not of men. Therefore it is worthwhile to digress a little to study some teachings in Acts. During its first expansion, or until about 48 A.D., the Church grew among the Jews of Palestine.

96. Acts 1:8 is one of the keys for our study. It indicates that the power that drove the Church came from the see /// _____.

97. It also points to four divisions or centers of missionary labor. They are:

_____, _____, _____

and _____ . see &

98. The Church had to evangelize first the _____ . see &&

99. Paul preached first to the _____ . see / (Acts 13:46)

100. On the Day of Pentecost the Holy Spirit descended on the disciples in the city of

_____ . (Acts 2:14) see //

/ Jews
// Jerusalem
/// Holy Spirit
& Jerusalem, Judea, Samaria, the ends of the earth
&& Jews

101. Peter's first sermon was directed to _____ . see $
(Acts 2:14)

The Jewish people were very closely knit. They had a strong conviction that they were the people of God, a firm belief in the Scriptures (of the Old Testament), knowledge of Jesus of Nazareth, a common language - aramaic - and an intense desire to win their freedom from the Roman occupation. The Holy Spirit used these factors to create a large number of Christian congregations throughout all Palestine.

102. The Jews who became Christians still kept the _____ of Moses.   see //

103. They thought that they did not cease to be Jews by becoming

_____ .   see &&

104. They even considered Christianity to be another sect within

_____ .   see $$$

105. The persecution of the Christians began with the martyrdom of Steven. He did not want Christianity to be limited to those who worshipped in the
   (Acts 7:48f.)   _____ in Jerusalem.   see &

106. The Jews did not mix with gentiles. They didn't want to concede that the gospel was for

_____ .   see ///

107. Peter's visit to the house of Cornelius was so important because it demonstrated that one could be a Christian and receive the Holy Spirit without becoming a

_____ . see &&&

108. Many Jews became Christians in the beginning when this did not require them to have contact with the

_____ . see /

109. In this way the Church expanded among the Jews while they were

_____ .   see $$

/ gentiles
// law
/// everyone OR SIMILAR WORDS
& Temple
&& Christians
&&& Jew
$ Jews
$$ receptive
$$$ Judaism

110. Later when it was recognized that Christianity was a religion for all peoples,
    see ///   _____ Jews joined the Church.

    During the second expansion - from 48 A.D. until the death
of the apostle Paul - the Church grew vigorously in the communities formed around the synagogues of the Diaspora. In this
population other factors operated. For example, the God-fearers
were converted in great numbers. These gentiles were attracted
by the morality and the monotheism of the Jewish religion, but
repelled by circumcision and other aspects of the Jewish law.
When they learned that they could be saved by faith in Christ
without assuming the burden of the law and when they saw that in
Christ men become new creatures that manifest the fruits of the
Spirit, they became fervent members of the Church. Joyfully
they proclaimed the gospel among their relatives who were not
Christians. It was the same Church as in the first period that
was growing, but the second expansion is distinguished from the
first in that the elements which promoted the faith were combined
in different proportions. The source of this study of the
Church is the New Testament, mainly Acts.

111. Many gentiles entered the Church when they discovered that
they could do so without becoming

                              _____ first. see &&&

112. We see, therefore, that it was impossible to attract at the
same time large numbers of
        see &   _____ and of _____ .

113. When it expanded throughout the Roman Empire the Church became a community composed largely of

                              _____ . see //

114. Nevertheless, the apostles began their missionary work in
each city among the Jews and God-fearers that met in the
                    see $
                                            _____ .

115. The nucleus of many of the churches was made up of gentiles
that were attracted to Judaism but did not want to become prose-
lites. These pious men were known as

                              _____ . see /

116. The proclamation of Christian liberty in relation to the
Jewish law was the reason for the entrance into the Church of
many

  _____ __ _____ .   see &&

/ God-fearers
// gentiles
/// few
& Jews, gentiles
&& gentiles
&&& Jews
$ synagogues

117. However, this same proclamation was a great obstacle for many

_____. see //

118. In the wisdom of God the Church grew greatly among the Jews before

_____. see /

As a summary of this chapter and of all that has been studied up to this point let us consider briefly some reasons why churches grow. A list of eight reasons follows. Later we will consider them one by one.

1. The gospel is preached to a receptive element of the people.
2. Some Christian leader finds a plan of action that serves to multiply congregations.
3. Some pastors, laymen or missionaries dedicate their lives to establishing churches.
4. Some church leaders refuse to be limited to activities which do not produce new congregations.
5. Church leaders are filled with the Holy Spirit.
6. Social and religious factors favorable to growth coincide.
7. The Church provides good post-baptismal instruction for its members and their children.
8. Indigenous principles are employed among a prepared people.

119. The first reason is illustrated by the example of the first expansion of the Church in Palestine. While the Christians kept the law, the gospel was preached first to the see && _____.

120. When the universality of the message of Christ was recognized the gospel was presented also to the _____. see &

121. In every case the gospel was preached to a _____ sector of the people.   see ///

/ Christian liberty was proclaimed OR SIMILAR WORDS
// Jews
/// responsive
& gentiles
&& Jews

122. The second reason for growth is that some leader finds a plan that serves to multiply congregations. In the second lesson we examined the case of the Peruvian Evangelical Church. Taking advantage of contacts made by means of a newspaper, John Ritchie

_____ . see &&&

123. Before leaving a town he named leaders to direct _____ .
see $$

124. Many of the groups became _____ . see /

125. Ritchie found a plan to _____ .
see %

126. The first reason for growth is that _____

_____ . see &&

127. The second reason is that _____

_____ . see //

128. Thirdly some leaders dedicate their lives to founding churches. They decide that the principal need of man is
see $
_____ .

129. And they think that God's agent to propagate the Christian faith is the
_____ . see %%

130. Therefore they give themselves to the work of _____ .
see ///

131. The fourth reason is the negative side of the third. Some church leaders refuse to limit themselves to activities which do not produce churches. In addition to evangelism there are

_____ that the Church can do. see &

132. These things are good, but in comparison with evangelism they are

_____ . see $$$

/// churches
someone finds a plan to
multiply churches OR SIMILAR WORDS
/// evangelism
& many things OR SIMILAR WORDS
&& the gospel is preached to a responsive people OR SIMILAR WORDS
&&& visited towns OR SIMILAR WORDS
$ salvation OR SIMILAR WORDS
$$ the group
$$$ secondary
% multiply churches OR SIMILAR WORDS
%% church

133. Therefore the Church grows when men refuse to be limited to

_____ . see /

134. In some areas of the world the Church grows because Christians are dedicated to

_____ . see &&&

135. Keeping their emphasis on the spiritual need of man they are not distracted by activities that
          see $ _____ .

136. Write below the four reasons mentioned so far why some sectors of the Church grow.

_____

_____

_____

_____

See the list on page 6-21

137. All these men are guided and empowered by God. But in some cases God works in a special way and men are filled with the

_____ . see ///

138. The Church of the Disciples of Christ in Puerto Rico grew because it had experienced a

_____ . see &&

139. The fifth reason why the Church grows is that the Holy Spirit fills

_____ . see &

140. The sixth reason refers to a less direct way in which God works. It has to do with evangelistic efforts made at the same time that social factors have prepared the people for the gospel. We find an example in the Korean Church. In 1919 Christians led a movement to free their country from Japanese domination. For this reason Christianity won much popular support. At the same time the Methodists began a great evangelistic effort. The Church grew because of the combination of religious and

factors.   see //   _____

/ secondary things OR SIMILAR WORDS
// social
/// Holy Spirit
& church leaders
&& revival
&&& evangelism
$ church planting do not produce churches OR SIMILAR WORDS

141. The important thing is that this evangelistic effort was made when

_____ . see /

142. The Church grew for a combination of _____ and

_____ factors.   see &&

143. The fifth reason is obviously the work of God and the sixth apparently of men. Write below the six reasons for growth already considered.

•——•

•——•

•——•

•——•

•——•

•——•

See the list on page 6-21

144. The seventh reason is that the churches instructed well their new members and their families. Generally the instruction of new converts is in preparation for the act of
                    see //   _____.

145. But if instruction terminates there believers remain children in their

_____ life.   see &&&

146. Church members must also be taught after _____ . see $

147. The quality of members depends in great degree on the amount of

_____ that they receive.   see &

148. Some churches grow more than others because they give their members

_____ .   see ///

/ social factors were favor- able OR SIMILAR WORDS

// baptism

/// more instruction

& teaching, instruction

&& social, religious

&&& spiritual

$ baptism

149. The last reason why some churches grow more is that they give attention to indigenous principles. That is, they use methods and forms that are

see / _____ to their region.

150. At the end of the second lesson we learned that one of the measures of the Church is

_____ . see ///

151. A church has greater possibilities of extension if its faith is expressed according to

see // _____ .

---

152. Write below the eight reasons why churches grow.

_____

_____

_____

_____

_____

_____

_____

_____

See the list on page 6-21

Now another list is presented, not to be learned by memory, but to be read and studied. This list contains negative factors which correspond to some of the points on the first list. They are reasons that explain the lack of growth in certain churches.

1. Leaders do not learn to avoid the errors of the past.
2. Churches confronted with little growth do not seek the help of experts to remedy the situation.
3. No one studies the results of their efforts and there is no realization of how little remains from their work.
4. Churches and missions are dedicated to obsolete policies that don't produce churches.

/ natural
// indigenous principles OR SIMILAR WORDS
/// Indigeneity

5. Churches follow a policy that produces slow growth and they are satisfied when they could do more.
6. Churches continue in preparatory work for the gospel, winning many friends, but few converts.
7. Christians work among difficult elements of the population instead of concentrating on peoples responsive to the gospel.
8. Baptismal standards are so high that many are discouraged from becoming evangelicals.
9. Evangelism is limited to sectors where the Church has institutions or residences for pastors or missionaries.
10. A ministry is established with salaries and preparation so high that it separates pastors from their people and doesn't permit churches to sustain them.
11. The gospel is not expressed in the social patterns of the people. Therefore conversion to the gospel signifies a change of culture.

The most important aspect of this study is not learning some theories about church growth, but rather the application of knowledge to the situation of each student. Taking into consideration the reasons mentioned above and your analysis of the church that you attend, indicate at least five factors that have hindered the progress of the church in its evangelistic expansion. Write also some recommendations to correct the situation.

7
EVANGELISM,
PERFECTING OR REVIVAL

In Lesson IV some causes of the darkness that hides the
facts of church growth were presented. In Lesson VI some reasons for little growth in some churches were named. Lesson VII
treats another obstacle for the extension of the Church. It is
the confusion that exists in regard to the meaning of evangelism,
perfecting and revival. It is necessary therefore to study the
meaning of each term. It will also be helpful to examine the
motives behind conversion. Finally we will name some conditions
necessary for revival and the relationship between revival and
church growth.

"Make Disciples"

Someone has said that in evangelism there are two dangers:
that of changing the message and that of not changing the form
in which the message is presented or expressed. The cultural
differences that exist in Latin America have already been mentioned. The Christian faith is not a new culture but a truth
that can be expressed in any culture. All preachers should realize that explanations or illustrations have to be based on the
experience of the audience. The same message will not serve
a community of fishermen, a group of university students and
the beginners in Sunday School. The form of the message must
be adapted to the culture and preparation of the persons that
are to receive it.

1.   In evangelism it is necessary to change constantly the way in which the message is

_____ .   see /

2.   The forms of expression have to be those that conform to the

_____ of the audience.   see ///

3.   The experience of the listeners should determine _____

_____ .   see &

4.   Write a list of all the factors which an evangelist should take into consideration when preparing his messages for a certain group.

see //

       While the forms and methods of presenting the gospel change, the message never changes. It continues as the good news of salvation. Christ died for our sins. God so loved the world that He gave His only Son. Salvation is a gift of God that is received by faith. By grace are we saved, not by works. But at the same time that we affirm the truth and necessity of this message we must ask: Is this message complete? Have we given so much emphasis to the grace of God that some people interpret the invitation to accept Christ as an offer of salvation without cost and without obligation?

5.   We are saved by the _____ of God.   see &&&

6.   This salvation is received by _____ .   see $

7.   What can man do to gain his salvation?_____ .
                                              see &&

8.   The message that ends with salvation is an _____
message.   see $$

/   presented OR SIMILAR WORDS

//   age, sex, education, culture, environment, economy OR SIMILAR WORDS

///   experience, culture OR SIMILAR WORDS

&   the form in which the message is presented OR SIMILAR WORDS

&&   nothing

&&&   grace

$ faith

$$ incomplete OR SIMILAR WORDS

9. Such a message _____ nothing of the believer. see ///

10. In the Great Commission Jesus said: Go and make _____.
(Mat. 28:19)   see &&&

11. What does it means to be a disciple? (It may be necessary to consult a dictionary)

                                                    see //

12. What does a disciple do? _____ see &

13. The principal task of the Church is to produce:

_____a) Converts.

_____b) Disciples.

_____c) Saints.   see $

      In the book "Y Será Predicado Este Evangelio (And This Gospel Will Be Preached,) Juan Carlos Ortiz distinguishes between the gospel of "offers" and the gospel of the "kingdom." Without necessarily accepting everything in the book, we must admit that the Argentine preacher has discovered a weak point in the preaching and practice of the churches. Mr. Ortiz is not the only contemporary writer that has been concerned with the nominalism and passivism of many believers. When everything is offered without demanding anything, the complaint that many members are useless is well founded. Many believers have never recognized the implications of the gospel and their Christian obligations. They are converts, but not disciples. The Church and its ministers have failed. They have preached an incomplete message that has produced incomplete Christians. The task of disciples is to make other disciples.

14. Sometimes the gospel is presented only as the way of obtaining salvation, peace, prosperity, healing, happiness, etc. It has been a series of

                         _____. see &&

15. Jesus preached the gospel of the _____. see /
                                        (Mark 1:14)

/ kingdom
// one who follows and learns from another OR SIMILAR WORDS
/// demands, requires OR SIMILAR WORDS
& learns
&& promises
&&& offers
&&&& disciples
$ b

16. This gospel should be preached also by the _____.
      (Luke 8:1; Matthew 24:14)   see $

17. The preaching of an easy gospel leads many believers to
think that they don't have to

_____. see &&

18. What proportion of the members of the student's church do
not participate actively in evangelism or other programs of the
church?

19. Who is to blame for their inactivity?_____
                                  see ///

20. What do inactive Christians need? _____
                              see //

21. Disciples should produce other _____. see &

     The student will remember the definition of the Church's mis-
sion presented in this study: Preach the gospel of Jesus Christ
and persuade men to become His disciples and responsible members
of His Church. The emphasis on church growth does not propose to
produce multitudes of nominal Christians. We must accept all the
implications of being Christians. There is not necessarily a
conflict between the quantity and the quality of Christians. Our
Lord wants great numbers of true disciples. He wants them to be
responsible members of His Church.

22. The goal of evangelism is that men become _____
of Christ.   see /

23. A part of this discipleship is taking an active part in the

_____.   see &&&

24. Emphasis on numbers does not signify indifference to their

_____.   see $$

25. The concept of the "gospel of the kingdom" belongs to bibli-
cal theology. But even a brief examination of the evidence in-
dicates that the mission of the Church, according to the
Great Commission is

_____.   see $$$

/   disciples
// instruction OR SIMILAR WORDS
/// pastors and other leaders
&   disciples
&& do anything OR SIMILAR WORDS
&&& Church
$ disciples OR SIMILAR WORDS
$$ quality
$$$ make disciples

26. A verse well known to many is the answer of Paul to the Phillipian jailer. He said, in Acts 16:31: Believe in the

_____. see &

27. A study of the preaching and teaching of the early disciples as revealed in the book of Acts tells us that the most commonly used title of Jesus was

_____. see &&

28. One of the earliest confessions of faith of the Church is found in Romans 10:9, 10. In order to be saved one must believe that Jesus is the

_____. see &&

29. Accepting that Jesus is the Lord seated on the throne is part of the gospel of the

_____. see //

There is still another consideration to be contemplated with regard to the message of the Church for the present. The present tendency in many areas is toward a more secular and less religious world. Materialism in its various forms has captured the interest and energies of many peoples. The Christian frequently encounters a person that senses no need of salvation. His interests and aspirations are limited to this earthly existence. However many people are seeking some purpose in this life. They want something that deserves their loyalty and dedication. We know that the answer is Christ. Christ is the Lord of the universe and of the life of His disciples. The lordship of Christ is the other part of the Christian message to which we must give more emphasis.

30. The tendency in our contemporary world is to give (more/less)

_____ importance to the Church and its message.
          see /

31. Even many church members demonstrate by their lives that their main concern is with

_____ things.   see &&&

/   less
//   kingdom
/// Lord
&   Lord Jesus and your will be saved ...
&&   Lord
&&& material

32. If someone lives only for this world he doesn't recognize his need of

_____. see /

33. Many persons seek something that will give them purpose in this

_____. see &&&

34. We know that we should live for _____. see //

35. Christ is the one who gives _____ to our existence.

see $

36. More importance should be given to the _____ of Christ in our preaching. see &&

37. Christ must be proclaimed as _____. see ///

38. This message has meaning and importance not only for the religious world, but also for the

_____ world. see &

39. If Christ is Lord, our position is that of _____.

see $$

40. The duty of a servant is _____. see %

41. In order to serve intelligently the servant must _____.

see %%%

42. The responsibility of teaching the believers the way in which they should live is that of

see $$$ _____

43. It is interesting to note that the requirements of bishops and deacons in the letters of Paul to Timothy and Titus include many social elements. They refer more to daily life than to doctrine. If church leaders are to teach God's people how to live, they themselves must serve as

_____. see %%

/ salvation
// Christ, God
/// Lord
& secular
&& lordship
&&& life
$ purpose, meaning
$$ servants OR SIMILAR WORDS
$$$ church leaders
% serve, obey
%% examples OR SIMILAR WORDS
%%% learn OR SIMILAR WORDS

44. How many sermons on the lordship of Christ did you hear last year?

45. What does the lordship of Christ mean to you?

46. Taking into consideration the requirements for church leaders that Paul mentions in I Timothy 3, II Timothy 2 and Titus, make a list of qualities which you lack as a spiritual leader.

Teaching them to Observe all ...

Now let us consider discipleship from another point of view. One obstacle to church growth has been the confusion between making disciples and perfecting them. Think again about the Great Commission (Mat. 28:19, 20). The task of the Church is (1) Go, (2) make disciples, (3) baptizing them, (4) teaching them. We have established that the gospel of the kingdom demands that we make disciples and not just converts. Nevertheless, scriptural evidence seems to indicate that as soon as a person accepts Christ as Lord and Savior he should be baptized. He can identify himself as a Christian even though he has not yet learned "all that I have commanded you."

47. According to the Great Commission there are various stages in the church's responsibility toward those whom it seeks to win. In the first place, it must present a clear message that Christians are

_____ of Christ.   see /

/ disciples

48. If they commit themselves to Christ on this basis they can give public testimony of their faith by means of
                              see ///   _____.

49. After baptism instruction is needed. The church must

_____ .   see &

50. The major part of the instruction comes _____
baptism.   see $$

51. This means that there will be some members of the church that have had relatively

_____ . see //

52. The last stage is that of _____ the saints. see

53. Although Christians are not perfect, they are where they can

_____ .   see &&&

54. The three steps or stages in the formation of Christians according to the Great Commission are

                              _____,
_____ and _____ .   see / _____

      The stages in the growth of a Church and its members are as clear as those in the development of a child. The Church that is surrounded by ten thousand people receptive to the gospel has a God given duty to make disciples. It should not stop winning many to perfect a few. Christian perfection that exalts educational achievements, increases economic capacities, focuses on social justice and, consequently, decreases its concern for winning others to eternal life, betrays the gospel.

55. We must affirm again that the basic need of man is _____.
                              see &&

56. The believer joins the church, not as a mature Christian, but as a spiritual

                  _____ .   see $$$

/   make disciples,
     baptize them,
     teach them
//   little instruction
     OR SIMILAR WORDS
/// baptism
&   teach them all
     things OR SIMILAR
     WORDS
&&   spiritual,
     salvation
&&& receive
     instruction OR
     SIMILAR WORDS
$ perfecting
$$ after
$$$ child

57. Children also are _____ of the family. see /

58. In the same way, immature Christians should form an integral part of the
_____. see &&&

59. The Church can not shut its doors in order to dedicate itself to perfecting its members while there are many others who have never had the opportunity of
see // _____.

60. Although education, economic factors and social justice are important, they are
_____ things. see $

For theological as well as practical reasons, the improvement of the Church and its members is necessary. God demands it and the Church decays without this emphasis. This is precisely the emphasis of the first part of this lesson. It is sad to see a person with an adult body but the mind of a child. The presence in our churches of Christians that have never developed spiritually should concern us also.

61. Children should not remain children all their lives. They must
_____. see &&

62. A child develops intellectually in the home and in the _____.
see ///

63. A "spiritual infant", that is a new believer, should grow by means of the instruction that he receives in the
_____
and in the _____. see &

64. At the same time we insist that multitudes must be "added to the Lord" before they can be perfected. Only those who identify in some way with the Church receive its
see $$ _____.

/   members, part
//   salvation OR SIMILAR WORDS
/// school
&   home, church
&&   grow, develop
&&& church
$ secondary
$$ instruction, teaching

65. A church can discipline only its _____. see //

66. A pastor has greater influence over

_____a) A believer who has been in the church for a long time.

_____b) A new believer.

_____c) A non-believer.   see $

67. Explain your choice of the answer to the preceding question.

68. The Church does not exist for itself. It's purpose is to glorify

_____ .   see &&&

69. It should not become a social club. Its doors should be open to

_____ those who wish to enter. see /

       Church members have been saved to save others. They always have a double responsibility: that of winning souls for Christ and that of growing in His grace. It is necessary for them to do these two things constantly and simultaneously. Each church must decide if its principal ministry is to evangelize the unconverted that attend its services or if its services should be primarily for the edification of its members.

70. If all the sermons are evangelistic, the members receive little

_____ .   see &&

71. If a pastor alone does the work of evangelism, the church will win

_____ .   see ///

72. The Church should _____ its members for evangelism.
                                                 see &

/   all
//   members
///   few OR SIMILAR WORDS
&   prepare OR SIMILAR WORDS
&&   instruction, edification
&&&   God
$ b

73. Christians are responsible for those outside the Church too. What is this responsibility?

_____ . _____ see &&

74. Christians should think also of their own lives as disciples. Every Christian needs to

        see //   _____ spiritually.

75. In view of the double responsibility of evangelism and perfecting the saints the church should do

        see &   _____ .

76. But it must always remember that the initial process that the individual needs is

        _____ . see ///

77. In an area open to the gospel the Church should open its doors to

_____a) All those who want to become Christians.

_____b) Those that the pastor can instruct well.

_____c) Those that have already been well instructed. see /

78. Why did you select your answer in question 77?

The confusion with respect to the importance of making disciples and of perfecting them produces concepts contrary to church growth. The essential thing for the Church and its members is their relationship with Christ. This relationship does not disappear just because there is a deficiency in carrying out some duty. For example, the Church existed and expanded greatly in the midst of slavery. This was a curse that brought much misery to large sectors of humanity. Nevertheless the Church prospered in the midst of a culture that permitted the practice of slavery. There is even evidence that the revival which took place in the United States around the year 1860 had as great effect in the South where slavery was practiced as in the North where it was prohibited. But we must recognize also that slavery was abolished

* grow OR SIMILAR WORDS
/ evangelism
// both things OR SIMILAR WORDS
/// make them into disciples OR SIMILAR WORDS
&
&&

in England as the result, although indirect, of the revival produced by the preaching of John Wesley and others. It was when
the Church had grown and acquired political power that it was
able to eliminate slavery.

79. A Christian is a person that

_____a) Hates slavery.

_____b) Demonstrates exemplary behavior.

_____c) Has faith in Christ.   see ///

80. If the Church notes some defect among its members it should

_____a) Cease to call itself a Church.

_____b) Overlook the defect.

_____c) Try to correct the defect.   see //

81. In order to eliminate an evil what is needed is

_____a) A revival.

_____b) The instruction of church members.

_____c) The Church to stop meddling in social matters. see /

82. In relation to social conditions, the Church

_____a) Is indifferent to them.

_____b) Can exist in any kind of conditions.

_____c) Tries to preserve the status quo.   see &

83. The Church that is in the best position to change the culture
is one that has

_____ members.   see &&

/ b
// c
/// b
& b
&& many OR SIMILAR WORDS

Where men turn to Christ, are baptized in His name, accept
the Bible as their rule of faith and practice and manifest the
fruit of the Holy Spirit, there is born a new branch of the
Church. The power of Jesus is within reach of its members.
They live on a higher moral level. The fact that they may not
conform completely to our ideas or even to our interpretation
of the Bible does not prevent their being a true Church and
growing as a Church.

84. The only indispensable requirement for becoming a Christian
is
_____ . see ///

85. But this faith is in Jesus as Savior and _____ . see &&

86. The practices of Churches in distinct cultures will be

_____ . see //

87. But all Churches must submit to the authority of the _____ .
see &

88. Nevertheless, there may be differences in the _____
of the Bible. see &&&

89. A Church, even though it does not conform to our concepts,
may enjoy the
_____ of God. see /

Someone has said, "Baptized pagans do not constitute a
Church." That is certain. Nevertheless perfecting is possible
only in populations which have been discipled, that is, where
persons consider themselves to be disciples of Christ. Many
congregations are made up of baptized persons whose lives do not
fully reach the biblical norms. But we do not thrust such persons from the church unless they continue in serious sins without
repentance. Generally we try, by means of instruction and exhortation, to bring them to a higher level of spiritual maturity.

/ blessing OR
// SIMILAR WORDS
/// distinct,
& different
&& faith in Christ
&&& Bible
Lord
interpretation

90. An individual should be received as a Christian when he

_____a) Attends the church the first time.

_____b) Drops all his vices.

_____c) Makes a profession of faith.   see /

91. With regard to smoking, the Bible

_____a) Prohibits the practice.

_____b) Encourages the practice.

_____c) Says nothing about it.   see //

92. This silence on the part of the Bible means that

_____a) The church should say nothing about smoking.

_____b) The church decides according to its interpretation of biblical principles.

_____c) The church can speak infallibly about smoking.
                                              see &

93. In order to be a Christian one must reach

_____a) A certain social level.

_____b) A certain educational level.

_____c) A certain cultural level.

_____d) None of these levels.   see ///

94. Explain your answer to question No. 93.

The least perfected Church is better than the pagan people from which its members came. If their faith is sincere and if they receive adequate instruction congregations always improve. We can trust that the Holy Spirit will work through the Bible to demonstrate the implications of the Christian faith in every aspect of life. Sometimes less perfected congregations grow more. This is partly due to the fact that the Christianity which they profess is something simple that the common man can achieve. It is also due to the contact that these Christians have with parents and friends who have not yet been converted. Although they lack extensive knowledge of the Bible and don't always show the fruit of the Holy Spirit, they produce more evangelistic fruit than better prepared Christians. And their evangelistic fruit is genuine even though imperfect.

95. If some members of the congregation have certain bad habits it is better

_____a) To exclude them from the congregation.

_____b) To instruct them with patience.

_____c) To tolerate their habits.   see /

96. The Christian must recognize that those who practice bad habits

_____a) Never will rise to his own level.

_____b) Can be transformed by God in time.

_____c) Are not real Christians yet.

_____d) Should not be allowed in the church.   see //

97. New converts produce more evangelistic fruit because they have

_____ . see &

98. The person who can best communicate the gospel to those in the world is the

_____ . see ///

/ b
// b
/// new convert OR
SIMILAR WORDS
more contact with
the world OR
SIMILAR WORDS
& the world OR
SIMILAR WORDS

99. For the perfecting of new Christians we must trust

_____ .   see /

100. We must remember that the objective of the Church is to make men into true

_____ of Christ.   see &&&

101. Precisely because of his greater opportunities and contacts we should urge the new believer to

_____ . see &&

102. He should not wait to witness until he is _____.
                                    see //

103. If the process of perfecting means cultural change the older Christian will have
        see &   _____ contact with the world.

Many people say that the church can't expand until it goes deeper. It is equally true to say that it can't go deeper until it expands. Small congregations that can not sustain a pastor nor participate in educational programs do not have the spiritual guidance that they need.

104. The Church must expand and go deeper. That is, it must concern itself with the

_____ and the _____

of its members.   see ///

105. Small churches lack the resources necessary to obtain the spiritual direction of a

_____ .   see $

Congregations that receive financial aid from a mission run the risk that some of the new members will come to the church for unworthy motives. They hope to receive some benefit from the institutions or programs run by the Church or mission. If the mission maintains clinics, schools or pays the salaries of pastors, many people think about these material benefits that come from outside instead of relying on their own efforts. Spiritual maturity is difficult for those who depend materially on others.

/ God
// perfect, mature
/// quantity, quality
& less
&& witness OR SIMILAR WORDS
&&& disciples
$ pastor

Instead of talking about the holiness of the little flock it should be recognized that the congregation that does not grow is spiritually sick. Growth is one of the signs of health.

106. For its own spiritual welfare every congregation needs to work for

_____ independence. see //

107. One of the criteria of the quality of the Church is the percentage of

_____ : see //

108. Now we arrive at a very important matter. Many people think that there is some conflict between quality and quantity. In a certain sense there could be such a conflict if the resources and time are limited severely. We should advance in both directions at the same time. But if you were a leader in a congregation that had to choose between opening a new evangelistic effort in another town or building a school for the children of evangelicals, which would you choose? Why?

Motives for Conversion

When the gospel is preached many of those who hear it decide to become Christians for unworthy motives. This is particularly true when the preacher is a relatively well off missionary. Some will confess Christ because they love material benefits, not because they love Christ. Without a genuine experience such "converts" seek all the missionary can give them. When they can obtain no more from him they cease to identify themselves as Christians. We should all beware of such "converts."

/ material, financial
// growth

109. When Christians offer certain material benefits it is to be
expected that the motives of some of those who appear will be

_____. see &&&

110. Here, therefore, we have another reason for preaching the
gospel of the kingdom instead of a gospel of
                                        see $ _____.

111. Generally these "converts" remain _____ time in
the church. see //

     On the other hand the preacher should avoid the other ex-
treme of putting off with his suspicions those that grope toward
salvation. Our Lord accepted men that wanted to share His glory
when He drove out the Romans. But in His presence these men
were transformed into disciples. If it is within reach of our
resources we should try to satisfy social and spiritual needs
at the same time.

112. Even the apostles in the beginning followed Christ for

_____ motives. see &&

113. They did not understand that His reign was not of _____.
                                             see /

114. We can offer to those who come to the church for whatever
reason
          _____. see ///

115. If we suspect that some have come to the church for unworthy motives we can

_____a) Wait until God purifies their motives.

_____b) Overlook their motives.

_____c) Ask them about their motives.   see &

116. Defend your answer to question No. 115

SIMILAR WORDS
/   this world
//   little
/// salvation
&   a
&&   unworthy OR
&&& material,
        unworthy
$ offers

117. Some people are unable to express spiritual motives because they know very

_____ about the gospel. see //

118. Should we insist that decisions be based entirely on spiritual motives? Explain your answer.

In a study made in India, Waskom Pickett (Christian Mass Movements in India, 1933) calls our attention to the problem of motivation to accept the gospel. Many people have become Christians for reasons which were good although not spiritual. Perhaps it would be more exact to say that these persons identified themselves as Christians. But, according to Pickett, this phenomenon should not disturb us very much. The outstanding discovery of the study is the relationship between the motives for adopting the Christian faith and their progress in it. 3,947 individuals were interviewed to determine their motives for becoming Christians and also their spiritual progress. Pickett distinguishes between four types of motivation:

1. Spiritual motives - seeking salvation, finding peace, knowing God, etc.
2. Secular motives - seeking a good education for children, bettering one's social position, seeking the help of the missionaries.
3. Social motives - joining relatives and friends who were Christians.
4. Natal motives - following the faith of their parents.

In the space after each phrase that follows (119-126) write: spiritual, natal, secular or social according to the type of motivation that is expressed in the phrase.

119. I was seeking peace._____ see /

/ spiritual
// little

120. Some of my friends were already Christians._____

see ///

121. The Church distributed free clothing._____see &

122. I was born into a Christian home _____ see &&

123. I realized that Christ died for my sins._____

see //

124. My girl friend was an evangelical. _____see $

125. The evangelicals had the best high school. _____

see &&&

126. I was disillusioned with the religion of my parents. _____

see /

127. What factors operated in your own life to bring you to the church the first time? Christian friends? Church activities?

128. What should our attitude be toward a person that attends church in order to receive some material benefit?

/   spiritual
//   spiritual
///   social
&   secular
&&   natal
&&&   secular
$ social

In Pickett's study, spiritual progress was measured by knowledge of the Lord's Prayer, the Apostles' Creed and the Ten Commandments. It was also noted if a person kept the Lord's Day, if he had become a member of a church, if he attended regularly and if he made financial contributions to the church. With regard to his conduct it was observed whether the believers had abandoned all forms of idolatry, whether they participated in pagan festivals and if they used alcoholic beverages. They were graded higher also if they had no fear of evil spirits and if they had married a Christian. Pickett indicates that those who had entered the church for spiritual motives demonstrated a little more progress, but really the difference between those who became Christians for spiritual, social or secular reasons was small. The quality of instruction received after baptism was more important than the motive for conversion.

Pickett demonstrated in his study that of those who became Christians for spiritual reasons 75% attended church regularly. Of those who became Christians for non-spiritual reasons 70% attended church regularly. We are unable to determine the motives of the Christians in our community, but the student is able to compare their progress in the faith with that of the Christians in India who entered the church for non-spiritual reasons. According to the categories indicated state the approximate percentage of those who have made professions of faith in your local church. Include all those who have made definite commitment to Christ, not just church members.

	In India	In your church
Regular attendance (Sundays)	70%	_____
Free of idolatry	93	_____
Contributions to the church	91	_____

One of the conclusions of Pickett's investigation was that the quality of instruction received after baptism was more important than the motive for conversion. What instructional program has your church for all those who attend?

Does someone supervise the quality of instruction? _____

Does someone coordinate the program to guarantee that there is periodic and systematic instruction on all the different aspects of the Christian life?

_____

Write down some suggestions to better the educational program of your church.

We doubt the sincerity of many professions of faith, particularly in evangelistic campaigns or other special efforts. Some leaders are not willing to receive as Christians these converts who know so little about Christ. But in spite of their ignorance, these persons, for some reason, want to follow Christ. If their motives are spiritual, so much the better. But whatever the circumstances we must minister to them. The care that they receive in the church and outside of it determines their Christian progress more than the motives that caused them to turn to the evangelical faith.

129. The majority of those who enter the church after an evangelistic campaign know

_____ about Christian doctrine.   see /

little

/

130. What they need, therefore, is _____.see ///

131. In spite of their lack of knowledge, their decision could be

_____. see &

132. These persons should be considered as _____.

see/

133. For this reason they are ready to receive _____.

see //

134. Christians need instruction whatever the _____
for conversion. see &&

135. For the recent convert a dangerous situation exists in many of our churches. The church receives them with reservations and considers them among "the friends who visit us." Meanwhile, the world, their families and their friends keep insisting that they return to them. What can the church do so that the new believer will feel that he is a part of it.

/ Christians OR SIMILAR WORDS
// instruction, teaching
/// instruction
& sincere OR SIMILAR WORDS
&& motive, reason

Revival and Church Growth

Revival is closely related to church growth, but many times this relation is not understood. Under certain conditions revival produces growth. In other circumstances the relationship between the two movements is so distant that apparently they are mutually exclusive. The two must be carefully considered if we are to understand the function of each and the redemptive purpose of God.

136. Revival is studied here because it can produce _____.
see &

137. Revival produces growth only under certain _____.
see ///

The word "revival" has different interpretations. For some revival is an emotional orgy produced by professional promoters of revival. When the excesses wear off the congregations are in the same conditions as before. For others, revival implies a great ingathering of members. For this reason, when there are many conversions they call this phenomenon a revival. For the majority of Christians revival signifies principally the purification and renewal of the Church.

138. Some people criticize revivals for certain _____ excesses that sometimes accompany them. see &&

139. Others confuse revival with _____ campaigns.
see &&&

140. For these people revival would be the cause of _____.
see //

141. But the majority of Christians understand that a revival does not touch the unconverted but rather the
see /   _____.

Dr. J. Edwin Orr defines revival as a movement of the Holy Spirit in the Church of Christ which produces the restoration of New Testament Christianity. Although revival depends on the sovereignty of God, there are certain conditions which generally prepare the way for this visitation of the Spirit. The student

/   Christians
// growth
/// conditions, circumstances
&   growth
&& emotional
&&& evangelistic

is recommended to read The Light of the Nations by J. Edwin Orr.
This book contains explanations and illustrations of this theme
in details which can not be included here.

142. In revival the Church returns to the spiritual conditions
of the

_____ century. see &

143. Revival is the result of the work of the Holy Spirit in
the

_____. see $

144. It depends on the sovereign will of _____.see ///

145. Nevertheless, there is greater probability of revival when
certain

_____ exist. see &&

       One of the essential conditions is prayer. In many cases
prayer has produced revival. It is a gift of God. Men can not
produce it. But God answers the sincere and persistent prayers
of His children.

146. Christians believe that God answers _____. see //

147. If our request does not coincide with His divine will,
God may answer in a

_____way. see $$

148. We believe that one of the things that God wants for His
Church is

_____. see &&&

149. Therefore we should pray with _____.see /

150. The first condition for revival is_____.see $$$

       Another necessary condition is the study of the Bible.
Revivals in Europe, the United States and Korea came after many
years of Bible study in homes and churches.

/   faith OR
         SIMILAR WORDS
//   prayer
///   God
&   first
&&   conditions
&&&   revival
$ Church
$$ negative
         OR SIMILAR
         WORDS
$$$ prayer

151. Knowledge of God and His purposes comes through studying the
_____. see $$$

152. Revival has been defined as a return to the spiritual conditions of
_____. see &

153. Up to a certain point the New Testament Church serves us as
_____. see $

154. It is through the study of the Bible that we acquire knowledge of
_____. see ///

155. The second condition for revival is _____.
see &&

Confession of sin is sometimes another condition for revival. Although it is accompanied by strong emotions, revival is not just an emotional excess. In the restoration of New Testament Christianity humility, contrition and consecration result in the confession of sins and in restitution. This confession and restitution sometimes constitute the key to revival and sometimes are the result of it.

156. What hinders our communion with God is _____.
see //

157. In order to experience the forgiveness of sin it is necessary to
_____. see $$

158. The principle governs our relationships not only with God but also with
_____. see &&&

159. If our sin is public knowledge of the congregation, perhaps confession should be made
_____. see /

/   in public
//   sin
///   God, the Church OR SIMILAR WORDS
&   The New Testament Church OR SIMILAR WORDS
&&   Bible study
&&&   men, brethren OR SIMILAR WORDS
$ example, model
$$ confess it
$$$ Bible

160. In such confession of sin there may be tears and other demonstrations of

_____. see &&&

161. A more convincing proof of repentance than tears is when the person that confesses his sin also makes
see &   _____.

162. The value of the confession of sin depends more on what is

_____ than on what is said.   see ///

163. The third condition for revival is _____.
see /

164. God is freer to act when there exist _____.
see &&

165. Write below three conditions which are necessary for revival.

see //

166. Even if revival does not come, these three conditions

_____ the church.   see $

     The greatest blessing of a revival is that it releases tremendous power to do God's will. When the Holy Spirit comes, He does miracles in the lives of the believers. The example of transformed lives attracts even more than the verbal testimony of Christians. That which is of greatest interest for this study is the conviction that revival impels men to proclaim the gospel. As a result of the indwelling Holy Spirit's activity they go everywhere proclaiming the Word of God.

/   confession of sin
// prayer, Bible study, confession of sin
/// done
&   restitution
&& certain conditions
&&& emotion, contrition OR SIMILAR WORDS
$ bless, help OR SIMILAR WORDS

167. The promise of Acts 1:8 is that "you shall receive _____ when the

_____ has come upon you." see $$

168. God grants this power to Christians so that they will do

_____. see $

169. God's will for the Church is that it _____.

see &

170. Unconverted men are not impressed as much by our words as they are by our

_____. see &&

171. Nevertheless, a Christian can not remain silent. He must

_____. see ///

    Revival can occur only where there is already life. It affects believers, and only indirectly unbelievers. It is impossible to have revival throughout the whole city of Managua because only the few Christians there can experience it. It could be that revival would shake the whole city. But in this case God world work through Christians instead of sending the Holy Spirit directly to the unconverted. Revival doesn't generally happen on the mission field where the Church is just starting to grow. That which is known as a "people movement" is clearly distinguished from revival.

172. Revival directly affects those who are _____.

see //

173. Nevertheless, by means of believers who experience revival God can touch

_____. see &&&

174. The entrance of many persons into the church (is/is not)

_____revival. see /

    Revivals in missionary communities or in Church or mission institutions do not always produce church growth. Usually the effects are of short duration and on a local scale. Besides,

/   is not
//   believers, Christians
///   witness OR SIMILAR WORD
&   grow, make disciples OR SIMILAR WORD
&&   lives, deeds actions
&&&   the people
$ His will OR SIMILAR WORD
$$ power, Holy Spirit

revival in itself does not produce growth. It only contributes
under certain conditions. Let us examine an example from India.
In 1936 the Holy Spirit granted a genuine revival to the Free
Methodist Church in Yeotmal, India. The congregation was
anxious to tell others about what God had done. In order to
do this the Christians decided to meet on the steps of the
City Hall every afternoon to testify of God's wonders. These
Christians were of the lower social class and the government
officials were of the higher class. Many listened and read
the tracts that were given out. Some wanted to know more about
the Savior that the Christians proclaimed. But not one accepted
Christ and no one was added to the Church. The social distance
was too great. After a few months the meetings were discon-
tinued without having produced any evangelistic fruit of the
revival.

175. Sometimes revivals do not produce growth because those
affected by the revival are a

_____ group. see &

176. The presence of the Holy Spirit in revival gives _____
to witness. see //

177. But even sincere witness does not always produce _____.
                                         see ///

178. In the case in India, the obstacle was the difference in

_____. see /

179. Although a revival does not produce evangelistic success,
should we conclude that it had no value for the Church? Why
or why not?

          The Church did not extend itself in Yeotmal as a result of
the revival there. But two men who had been in the revival
left the city and began to establish new congregations in a new
area among persons of their own social class. God was pleased
to bless these individual efforts more than the misdirected

/   social class
// power
/// fruit, results
&   small OR SIMILAR WORDS

efforts of the churches which were socially isolated from the people they tried to reach. Revival results in growth only when the spiritual power liberated is directly intelligently in accord with the circumstances in which the Church is found.

180. The two men were successful partly because they worked among the same

_____. see /

181. Their efforts were well _____. see &

The dynamic of revival is so great and the possibilities for church growth so tremendous, that all who are interested in the advance of the Church are also interested in revival. The same God gives growth and revival. He doesn't want the revival to be limited to a few small churches. God has given His people power, which they have not always used, to reap the harvest that He has prepared. There are three requirements that will ensure that revival results in growth.

1. Revival in the Church can produce a great harvest if the Christians are in intimate contact with the unconverted population and if the spiritual power is converted into testimony to win these people for Christ.
2. Revival produces growth when the Church is already growing and its leaders pursue this objective.
3. Revival results in growth when it is combined with knowledge of how the Church grows.

182. The case in Yeotmal demonstrates that evangelistic efforts can be frustrated in Christians who do not have contact with those whom

_____. see //

183. The problem is not always that of social differences. We have seen that those who have been Christians for some time have less

_____ with the world. see///

/ social class
// they seek to win OR SIMILAR WORDS
/// contact, relationship OR SIMILAR WORDS
& directed OR SIMILAR WORDS

184. If the Church emphasizes the intellectual and economic achievements of its members, it is creating a division between them and those who are most
see & _____ to the gospel.

185. The first requirement for directing revival power into growth is that the Church have
see% _____ .

186. The Church which has greater likelihood of growing in the future is that which
_____ now. see &&&

187. Greater growth results when this is the goal of the
_____ of the Church. see $

188. Revival will not result in the expansion of the Church if this expansion is not
see // _____ to the Christians.

189. Growth will be accelerated by revival if the church leaders believe that growth is an important aspect of the
_____ . see $$ _____

190. The second condition for revival to result in growth is that
_____ . see /

191. Wisdom must be mixed with zeal. Church leaders need to know the
_____ for growth. see &&

192. They must study the _____ about why and how the Church grows. see $$$

193. Human knowledge must be added to _____ power.
see ///

/ the leaders believe that growth is important OR SIMILAR WORDS
// important, OR SIMILAR WORDS
/// divine
& receptive OR SIMILAR WORDS
&& reasons, causes conditions
&&& is growing
$ leaders OR SIMILAR WORDS
$$ mission of the church OR SIMILAR WORDS
$$$ facts OR SIMILAR WORDS
% contact with the unconverted OR SIMILAR WORDS

194. Revival should result in greater growth in the Church if
the three requirements or conditions are met. Write them
below in your own words.

see the list on page 7-30

Many Christians want and pray for revival. Do you believe
that a church that waits for revival in order to be able to
evangelize is more ready for revival than a church that is already making an effort to grow? Explain your opinion on this
matter.

8

COMPARATIVE STUDIES
OF GROWTH

In the preceeding chapters we have seen some examples of rapid and slower growth. We have considered different ways in which the Church grows and we have learned to measure and interpret its growth. One of the techniques used in this study is that of the graph of growth. By means of the graph it is possible to study the progress of a denomination or of a congregation in the various stages of its development. Church growth is a complex process. Because there are so many factors to be considered it is difficult to make comparisons between churches or mission fields. Nevertheless, in Lesson VIII we will indicate the conditions in which comparisons are valid and what they can teach us.

This lesson is shorter than earlier ones. In the class which ends the week's work the mid-semester exam will be given. Since the examination is based on all that has been studied up to this point the student will have to review earlier lessons, with special attention to the review questions in the various sections.

The Comparison of Two Churches

The comparison of churches which work under similar conditions can be of great value. The basic method used is the same for studying a single church. We must obtain exact data and construct a graph which represents the churches' history. On the basis of this comparison we can seek the reasons that have caused differences in rates of growth. But it is important to note that only churches in similar circumstances can be compared. It is impossible to make a valid comparison between a church in Montevideo and one in Maracaibo. We must compare two churches in the same city.

1. The evangelistic success of a church depends partly on the

_____ in which it works. see /

2. A church located in the city of Lima must be compared with
another church in

_____. see ///

3. Churches must be compared that work in the midst of _____
conditions. see //

4. The best way to observe the progress of a church is by
means of a

_____. see &

5. The progress of each church will be represented on the
graph by a

_____. see &&&

6. If the conditions in which two churches work are the same
we can know that the differences that are seen in their growth
patterns are caused by

_____. see &&

        The case presented below is based on two Churches that
really exist.   Nevertheless, it is convenient to call the two
denominations Church A and Church B. Churches A and B entered
the same city in 1935 and have continued the evangelistic work
since that time. The results are seen in the columns of numbers that follow. One of the purposes of this lesson is to review what has been studied about the construction and use of
graphs.

Church A		Church B
0	1935	0
900	1940	300
2000	1945	500
1500	1950	900
1500	1955	1500
1500	1960	1000
2700	1965	900
3900	1970	1200

/ conditions, circumstances
// similar
/// Lima
& graph
&& other factors OR SIMILAR WORDS
&&& line

7. The comparison of these two Churches is valid because they are in

_____. see /

8. When constructing the graph space must be left for _____ years. (1970 minus 1935). see &&

9. Years are indicated along the _____ axis. see ///

10. In the vertical line are indicated the number of _____.
see &

11. In this case the number of members goes from ___ to ___.
see $

The Growth of Churches A and B from 1935 to 1970

12. Church A is represented by the _____ line. see //

13. It experienced good growth from the beginning of its work until

_____. see &&&

/   the same city
//   solid
/// horizontal
&   members
&&   35
&&& 1945
$ 0,3900

14. In 1945 it began to _____. see //

15. It remained at the same level from _____until_____,
that is, for a period of

_____ years. see &&

16. Church B is represented by the _____ line. see$$

17. This Church grew constantly until _____. see ///

18. Nevertheless, its growth was _____ rapid than that of
Church A.   see &&&

19. The membership totals of the two Churches were equal in ___.
see $

20. After that year Church B declined for a period of _____
years. see /

21. With the exception of the period between 1955 and 1960 one
or the other of the Churches was

_____. see %

In the comparison of these two Churches we will eliminate
two factors that should be considered in any comparative study.
One is the possibility of using wrong or incomplete figures.
We must accept that the figures are correct. The other
factor that we can not take into consideration here is the trans-
fer of members from one Church to the other. We will suppose
that all the members of these two Churches were converted and
baptized in their respective Churches.

22. In this study we will not accuse the pastors of "sheep
stealing." We will not take into consideration growth through

_____. see &

23. Graphs are based on _____. see $$$

24. In this study it is assumed that the figures are _____.
see%

/ 10
// descend, decline
/// 1955
& transfer
&& 1950, 1960, ten
&&& less
$ 1955
$$ dotted
$$$ data, figures
% growing
%% exact, correct

There are four general observations which can be made with regard to the comparison of these two Churches. In the first place, the two lines in the graph prove that the people of the city were responsive to the gospel during almost all the period studied. With a single exception one or the other of the Churches grew during the thirty-five years. It was possible to win men and women for Christ during all this time.

25. With the exception noted, during the thirty-five years one or the other of the lines

_____. see ///

26. This tells us that one or the other of the Churches was

_____. see &&

27. We can conclude that during this period it was possible to

_____. see /

28. The first observation is that from 1935 to 1970 the city was

_____. see $

29. The second observation is obvious. Sometimes the Churches grew. Under certain circumstances, employing certain policies or methods both Churches grew well. When Christians used appropriate methods they saw good results of their work. Good growth was a

_____ for the Churches. see &&&

30. If one Church was growing and the other did not in the same city and under the same conditions, it is probable that the difference was due to the use of different

see &   _____.

31. The second observation is that the Church grew normally when it

_____. see //

In the third place, the people were not very responsive to the gospel. Sometimes the work was hindered by the wrong methods or by other factors. When emphasis was given to institutions instead of to church planting, or to perfecting

/ make disciples OR SIMILAR WORDS
// used appropriate methods OR SIMILAR WORDS
/// climbed, rose
& policies, methods
&& growing
&&& possibility
$ responsive

the saints instead of winning new disciples, growth was slowed.

32. Sometimes conditions exist which permit the Church to grow in spite of its mistakes. This was not the case here. When the Churches used the wrong methods they

see $ _____.

33. Perhaps one of the errors committed was that of giving more emphasis to the care of church members than to the salvation of people

_____. see ///

34. It is possible that there was confusion between the importance of perfecting and making

_____.see &&

35. Whatever the cause of obstruction the descents on the graph indicate that the people were not overly

_____. see /

     In the fourth place, we must concede that neither of the Churches did everything that it could have to win this city for Christ. It was possible to have achieved a constant increase in membership during the whole period using adequate policies and methods. With the proper emphasis placed on the growth of the Church during these years there could have been a much larger harvest of disciples.

36. Neither of the Churches grew constantly during _____.

see //

37. But growth would have been possible through the use of

_____. see &

38. Therefore it can be seen that the Churches did not take advantage of

_____. see &&&

/ responsive

// the whole period

/// outside the churches OR SIMILAR WORDS

& appropriate methods OR SIMILAR WORDS

&& disciples

&&& all the opportunities for growth OR SIMILAR WORDS

$ did not grow OR SIMILAR WORDS

Comparative studies reveal two types of very useful information. In the first place they indicate the responsiveness of a given population. Some index of responsiveness is very important for church planters. It indicates where resources can be used to ensure best results.

39. The case of Churches A and B reveals that the population was more or less responsive to the gospel during
                        see &&&   _____.

40. Periods of stagnation indicate that the population was not very
_____. see ///

41. If the people are open to the gospel there is an opportunity for
_____ growth. see &

42. Comparative studies are valuable because they indicate the
_____ of the people. see /

The second type of information that is obtained through comparative studies is related to the methods that God uses to extend His Church. We don't have to depend on theories. We can observe the results of various groups that work in the same city. Although we may not be in agreement with the theology of a certain group, we can learn from its methods. This does not mean a change of doctrine on our part, but rather a change in policy. Generally the differences in the rates of growth of different groups are due to differences of methods and not doctrinal distinctions. We must confess that the reason why we don't adopt a certain practice that has been blessed in the work of other groups is because our tradition hinders it, not our doctrinal position.

43. Probably the difference in evangelistic success in two Churches that work under the same conditions is due to the use of different
_____see &&

44. The best way to evaluate a given method is to observe the
_____. see //

/ responsiveness OR SIMILAR WORDS
// results OR SIMILAR WORDS
/// responsive, open to the gospel
& greater
&& methods
&&& the whole period.

45. Comparative studies give us the opportunity to observe the merits of

_____. see &&

46. The success of some sects in numerical growth demonstrates that the extension of a group does not require that it teach correct

_____. see //

47. We are not interested in their doctrines, but in their

_____. see ///

48. Many of their practices could be adopted without changing our

_____ position.   see &

---

49. Write below the two types of information which comparative studies afford us.

---

see /

Let us consider another example of the comparative study of two Churches. We will call them Church X and Church Y. They have largely worked among the same class of people. The two Churches have their headquarters in the same city. This time the figures and the framework of the graph are provided, but the student must locate the points, trace the lines and interpret the graph.

Church X		Church Y
20	1938	0
50	1949	200
50	1952	200
50	1957	582
574	1960	372
1000	1966	890
1603	1968	977

/ the responsiveness of the people,
the best methods to reach the people OR SIMILAR WORDS
// theology, doctrine
/// methods
& doctrinal, theological
&& various methods

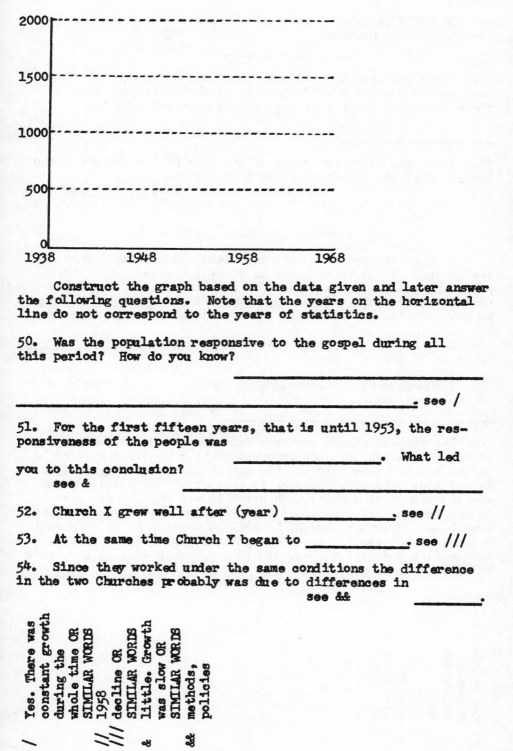

Construct the graph based on the data given and later answer the following questions. Note that the years on the horizontal line do not correspond to the years of statistics.

50. Was the population responsive to the gospel during all this period? How do you know?

_____

_____. see /

51. For the first fifteen years, that is until 1953, the responsiveness of the people was

_____. What led

you to this conclusion?
see &
_____

52. Church X grew well after (year) _____. see //

53. At the same time Church Y began to _____. see ///

54. Since they worked under the same conditions the difference in the two Churches probably was due to differences in
see &&   _____.

/ Yes. There was constant growth during the whole time OR SIMILAR WORDS

// 1958

/// decline OR SIMILAR WORDS

& little. Growth was slow OR SIMILAR WORDS

&& methods, policies

55. It would be helpful to compare the methods of the two
Churches in the year

_____. see ///

56. Since the two Churches grew more rapidly after 1960
than during the ten previous years, we should compare for
these two periods not only the methods used but also the

_____ that existed during those periods. see //

57. After the first few years of the life of the Churches, the
two had the same number of members in the year
(where the lines cross)_____.see &

How Is My Church Doing?

We have arrived at a very important and practical part of
the lesson. It is interesting to study the cases from other
years and other places. But it is more important for the student to analyze his own congregation. How is your church doing?
We now have the tool to measure more objectively its progress.

58. This tool is the comparative study of _____
by means of graphs. see /

59. A church must be compared with another or with others in

_____. see &&

The student should now have data concerning the membership
of his church. The minimum information that he could have would
be the actual membership and the number of members a year ago.
He can also determine the year in which the church was founded
and the number of members with which it was organized. Even
though he may only have these three figures with respect to his
church and one other church, it will be worthwhile to construct
a graph to compare the two congregations. Of course the more
information the student has, the more valuable will be the study
which he makes.

/ two or more churches
// conditions
/// 1958
/// 1959
& similar conditions
&& OR SIMILAR WORDS

On the rest of this page the student can indicate the information from the churches and make the calculations necessary to construct the graph on the page of squared paper which follows. Choose the values for the axes well in order to present most adequately the information in the graph.

60. Is the city in which the student lives very open to the gospel?
_____ Explain your answer.

61. Are there other churches in the same city or region which grow more rapidly?
_____

62. Do they work among the same social class? _____

63. Are there other differences in the conditions in which the churches work that should be mentioned?

64. What evangelistic methods does the student's church use?

65. Are there methods used by other congregations that have not been tried in the student's church? What are they?

66. Why haven't these methods been tried?

Up to this point the principle emphasis has been given to the number of Christians. We must always remember that the quality of their Christian life is also important. Numbers are important, but they are not everything. The student is advised to review the criteria of the Church which were mentioned at the end of the second chapter. An illustration follows.

A Church can begin in a new city or area with a large scale campaign and later open a rented meeting place in which to preserve and increase the fruits of the campaign. Another Church that begins with home Bible studies, without a large investment of funds will perhaps not be able to show the same number of converts and baptisms after a year. We must consider, however, the lasting results after five, ten or more years. And we must consider the character of the church formed. Some Churches have rejected certain forms of evangelism because they believe that they do not contribute to the formation of the kind of churches which they want to establish.

We must not judge others. We all have the same Judge. We must also remember the very human tendency to justify what has been done in the past and to resist changes. Taking into consideration all this, what more can the student's church do to demonstrate its faithfulness to God and to fulfill His mission for the Church?

9
SOCIAL FACTORS IN CHURCH GROWTH

In this chapter emphasis will be given to the social factors which determine in part the responsiveness of peoples to
the gospel. As has already been said, it must be understood
that everything depends on God. However there are many good
books which concentrate on the spiritual necessities of the
Church. God operates in human society by means of human in-
struments in addition to working directly in men's hearts.
In Lesson IX we will examine the social structures and sociological findings which will guide us in our evangelistic work.
It will be necessary to identify some of the social barriers
to the gospel and try to eliminate them on the basis of biblical
teaching.

Social Structures

Church growth takes place within the societies in which
men live. Therefore, it is necessary to understand their
structure in order to grasp how the Church grows. Men do not
exist as isolated individuals, but rather as members of some
society. The laws of social change are very significant in
determining the direction, speed and size of movements toward
Christianity.

1. Since the Church is a social organism, religious change is
a type of

_____ change. see /

/ social

2. Man can not be understood apart from his relationships with

_____. see //

3. We must understand the way in which society is organized, that is its

_____. see &

4. Sociologists have formulated certain laws which describe the diverse ways in which societies
see /// _____.

Man is a product of his environment. For example, he doesn't chose the language which he speaks. This is determined for him by his parents and by those with whom he plays as a child. In the same way society exercises a strong influence in everything that a person says, thinks and does. The more that we study the society, the more we will understand man as a member of society. It is necessary to analyze social structures in order to understand better how the Church may extend itself within these structures.

5. Man is formed by the circumstances in which he lives. This means that

_____a) Everything that a man is and does is predetermined.

_____b) Early home life exercises a profound influence on the personality.

_____c) Man can choose freely what he wants to be.   see /

6. The study of the characteristics of a society is valuable in order to

_____a) Understand how the men in that society think.

_____b) Change the inherited factors of the individual.

_____c) Understand the characteristics of all societies. see &&

/ b
// others, society,
   OR SIMILAR WORDS
/// changes
& structure
&& a

7.   As a result of the influence of society over its members

_____a) Men think more or less in the same way.

_____b) Men are unable to change their way of thinking.

_____c) Men think exactly alike.   see /

8.   The culture in which a person lives has an important role
in the formation of

_____a) His eternal destiny.

_____b) His intelligence.

_____c) The system of values which he observes.   see //

    The social structure has various component parts. One
is the concept that the members of a certain society have of
themselves. This concept reflects the society's values.
In Latin America the social structure of the ranch owners
is completely distinct from that of the laborers who work
on the ranches. And the society in which the urban factory
worker lives is clearly distinguished from the other two.

9.   Write below, on the basis of your own experience and study,
the values which you think are of greatest importance for the
culture or sub-culture to which you belong.

    Each society has a power structure or aristocracy. Even
the urchins who roam the city streets have such a social structure. Some members of a given sub-culture have more prestige
than others. Some are leaders. When someone who is on the
fringe of the group makes a suggestion nobody pays any attention to him. But if one of those who form the opinions and
norms of the group makes the same suggestion, all the members
consider the possibility of accepting it to stay with the leaders

of the group. When one of these individuals who is important in his own little circle is converted, the faith has a good chance of being extended among relatives, neighbors and friends.

9.   Societies which have a definite structure are

_____a) All societies.

_____b) Aristocratic societies.

_____c) Powerful societies.   see /

10.   Within a given society

_____a) Some members have more influence than others.

_____b) The urchins have the greatest influence.

_____c) All the members are equals.   see //

11.   The leaders of a group or society

_____a) Are always formally elected.

_____b) Always bear titles

_____c) Are always recognized by the group.   see &&

12.   It is better to win for Christ first

_____a) Any member of the group.

_____b) One who is on the fringe of the group.

_____c) One whose ideas the group will accept. see ///

13. If a leader suggests many ideas that the group does not want to accept

_____a) He increases his prestige in the group.

_____b) He ceases to be a leader of the group.

_____c) His position within the group does not change. see &

Churches are small societies with a more or less formal organization. The same social realities exist within the congregation as in other societies.

14. Within the evangelical church

_____a) All members have equal influence.

_____b) All members are leaders.

_____c) Some members are leaders   see /

15. It is important to recognize who the church leaders are.

_____a) Those with greater influence are always elected to office.

_____b) One who holds no office may be a real leader.

_____c) Only God knows who are the real leaders.   see ///

16. For the maximum extension of the gospel Christians should

_____a) Be separate from all human organizations.

_____b) Remain silent with respect to material things.

_____c) Try to be leaders in the community.   see //

17. What are the characteristics of a leader? What similarities and differences are there between leaders within and outside the church?

18. What are the kinds of community activities in which a Christian can be a leader? Parent-teacher association? Athletic club?
Committee for community action? Make a list of the activities
in which a Christian should participate and those in which he
should not participate.

19. What are the advantages and disadvantages of participating
in these community affairs?

20. Christians are members of various social groups that vary
in size and formal organization from the family to the political unit in which he lives. They have greater influence over
other members of the more intimate groups. They can best communicate the gospel to persons such as

see / _____.

   Even land ownership can affect chruch growth. For example,
in Puerto Rico the fertile lowlands belong to rich land owners.
The peasants that work on the farms have no rights. They live
on the owner's property and can be evicted from their huts at
his wish. But in the mountains of the interior those who
grow coffee own their lands. These independent people can
become evangelicals and have meetings in their homes if they
wish. The farm workers can lose their homes and their jobs
by becoming evangelicals.

/ relatives,
friends,
OR SIMILAR
WORDS

21. A man that works for a fanatical Catholic, if he should become an evangelical, runs the risk of losing his
                              see &/   _____.

22. In the same way someone who lives on property belonging to
the Catholic Church can be evicted if he identifies himself as
an
    _____. see //

23. People are freer to become Christians if they _____
their houses. see &&&

24. The fact of being a home owner can _____ the
decision to become an evangelical. see /

25. Therefore, we may note that economic conditions may influence in
    _____ decisions. see &&

26. Those who most easily can decide for Christ are people who
are

____a) Independent.

____b) Rich.

____c) Poor.   see ///

27. With regard to their place of residence

____a) Those who live in the mountains are always more respons-
ive to the gospel.

____b) Those on the coast are always more responsive to the
gospel.

____c) Place of residence in itself does not determine recep-
tivity.   see $

The mere fact that a person is the owner of a piece of land
does not predispose him to become an evangelical. It was hoped
that the Otavalos, a group of Quechus in Ecuador, because they
were relatively well off and independent would respond more
readily to the gospel. But few have been converted in more than
thirty years of work among them. Land ownership, like many other
conditions, helps, but does not guarantee conversion.

/ Facilitate
OR SIMI-
LAR WORDS
// evangeli-
cal, pro-
testant
///a
& work,
position
&& relgious
&&&own
$ c

28. The example of the Quechuas demonstrates that the economy is not the most

religion. see // _____ factor in determining men's

29. Evangelistic plans should not depend on a single _____.

                                                see &

        It is important to know also if the members of a sub-culture are very conscious of belonging to a distinct people. We have the example of the Jews with their "racial" pride. Their existence as a people after so many centuries of sufferings and pressures to be absorbed into other peoples and cultures is a miracle.

30. The providence and mercy of God are demonstrated in the preservation of the

                _____. see /

31. The existence of the Hebrews as a nation throughout centuries is due to the fact that

_____a) They are conscious of being the people of God.

_____b) They have suffered so much.

_____c) They are a superior race.   see ///

32. In which regions of your country is there greater growth? Cite some reasons for the differences in growth, including such factors as social structure, economy, etc.

/ Jews
/// Important
a
& factor OR
SIMILAR WORDS

The same desire to be identified as a special people set
apart from the rest is found in many Indian tribes. Tribes which
consider themselves to be distinct from the other inhabitants
of a country and want to maintain their tribal identity and unity
resist the gospel. The reason is that many times the gospel has
been presented in such a way as to demand a cultural change.
For the Indians, therefore, the act of becoming a Christian
means joining another people and betraying one's own people.
These persons reject Christ for social rather than religious
reasons. It is not that they love their sins, but that they
love their brothers. The greatest value for them is the preservation of the unity of the group. Tribal identity is measured by its capacity to discipline the members of the community.

33. Extreme group loyalty is seen in Latin America among some

_____ groups. see ///

34. They believe that they are separate from other _____.
                                            see &

35. The most important thing for these peoples is the preservation of their

_____. see /

36. It is important to show them that Christianity is not something foreign to their

_____. see //

37. Christianity must be expressed as a natural aspect of their

_____. see &&

38. If the Indians think of Christianity as something belonging to Spanish speaking whites, they will
                        see $ _____ it.

39. Paul said that he became weak to the weak in order to win

the _____ (I Cor. 9:22). see &&&

40. If someone wants to win Indians he must identify himself
with
        _____. see $$

/   identity,
     unity, group
//   people,
     culture
/// Indian,
     tribal
&   peoples
&&   culture
&&& weak
$ reject OR
     SIMILAR
     WORDS
$$ Indians

41. In order to win the Aymaras it is necessary to preach to them in

_____. see ///

42. If they are preached to in Spanish, Christianity will be identified by them with

_____. see &&

43. In many cases Indians consider whites as their oppressors and enemies. For this reason tribal members consider the Indian who accepts the enemy's religion as a

see $ _____.

44. Therefore, Christianity is seen as an evil influence because it constitutes a threat to the

see //   _____ of the group.

45. If an Indian accepts another people's religion it is probable that the community will

_____him. see &

46. A society that maintains very close relationships between its own members

_____a) Accepts everything that comes from outside.

_____b) Accepts that which doesn't seem to threaten the unity of the group.

_____c) Rejects everything that comes from outside.   see /

47. To an unconverted Indian it seems to be most important to be a

_____a) Christian.

_____b) Member of his community

_____c) Sinner.   see &&&

/ b
// unity OR SIMILAR WORDS
/// Aymara
& expel OR SIMILAR WORDS
&& Spanish speaking people OR SIMILAR WORDS
&&& b
$ traitor

48. For someone who identifies himself completely with his tribe, the strongest disciplinary measure would be to

_____a) Ostracize him from the group.

_____b) Fine him.

_____c) Not permit him to leave the group.   see //

49. If an Indian accepts Christ and is expelled from his community it is (likely/unlikely)

_____that others from the same tribe will make the same decision.   see /

50. Under such circumstances it is better for men not to identify themselves as Christians individually but rather in

_____. see ///

51. If everyone becomes a Christian at the same time there is no danger of destroying the

_____ of the group. see &&

When conversion to Christianity is considered more a racial than a religious decision, church growth is very slow. The Church must find a way of making it easier for members of very exclusive groups to accept Christ without betraying their families. One answer to this problem is the promotion of "people movements", a type of evangelism that will be explained in lesson XIII. The goal is for the whole tribe to be converted at once. People accept the Christian faith in great numbers only when they find a way to do so without leaving their relationships.

52. Christianity extends more rapidly when it is not presented as a cause of division between the person and his

see &   _____.

53. Conversion to Christianity is considered a selfish decision if the individual makes it without considering the opinion and the welfare of his

_____. see &&&

/ unlikely
// a
/// groups
& relatives OR SIMILAR WORDS
&& unity
&&& group, people

54. If the head of a family is converted to Christ, should he be baptized and join a church even if it means that his whole family will suffer for his decision? Should he wait to make a public confession of faith until his family is ready to make it with him or at least is sympathetic with his decision? Explain your answer.

55. What tribes or culturally separate groups are there in your country? Has the Church had much evangelistic success among them? What methods have been used with best results?

The biggest obstacles to conversion sometimes are social rather than theological. It was thought that the conversion of the Moslems was impossible, but the opposite has been proven in Indonesia. Whole Moslem communities decided to accept Christ when the social barriers were removed. In some communities the mosque was converted into an evangelical church. An individual may be afraid to become a Christian and face the opposition of the rest of the community, but if everyone decides together such conflict within the group does not arise.

56. Many Moslems knew very little of Islamic doctrine. Therefore they did not present many arguments of a _____ nature against the change of religion. see &&

57. Social obstacles to conversion were removed when the decision to accept the Christian faith was made in
see ///   _____:

58. The principle obstacles for the Indonesians were not theological but
_____. see //

59. It was possible for Christian evangelists to remove these obstacles without compromising the
_____. see &

There are millions of persons who live in two worlds: 1) that of primary relationships, with those who speak the same language; and 2) that of trade and work with those who speak another language. One example of this duality is the case of the Quechuas of Ecuador. Perhaps 60% of them speak Spanish, but the language of the home and of other activities and relations central to their life is Quechua. The government urges the use of Spanish because it is the language of national unity. But for the Indians Quechua is the language of their hearts. If the Church seeks to win their hearts for Christ, it must communicate the gospel to them in Quechua. The experience of many years of frustrating work has demonstrated that not many Indians are won through Spanish speaking churches.

60. For the Quechuas, Spanish is used with (family/outsiders)
_____. see /

61. In worshiping God the Indians would use _____.
see &&&

62. If the gospel is communicated only in Spanish, they will believe that Christianity is a religion of
see $ _____.

/ outsiders
// social groups
& doctrine OR SIMILAR WORDS
&& theological OR SIMILAR WORDS
&&& Quechua
$ Spanish speaking people OR SIMILAR WORDS

It was thought that the solution to this problem was to employ bilengual persons, that is, persons who speak both languages and would be able to preach in Quechua. But a Christian worker, trained in a Spanish speaking Bible Institute, does not easily identify with the Quechuas. He is on the edge of the group. If he has cut his hair and put on a coat instead of a poncho he is no longer one of them.

63. The person who can best win the members of a group is not someone who is on the fringes of the group but rather one who is in the center, that is, one who is a

_____ of the

group. see /

64. The education of a Christian worker can _____ him from his former people. see &&

65. The communication of the gospel to a certain group is always easier for someone who is completely

_____ with

the group. see //

66. Considering the two examples, that of Indonesia and that of the Quechuas of Ecuador, some general observations can be made that are applicable to situations similar to those mentioned. These two examples prove that

_____ a) Mohammedans are converted more readily than Quechuas.

_____ b) Communities are converted more readily than individuals.

_____ c) The reasons for conversion are always theological.
see ///

67. In order to win the Quechuas it is necessary to preach to them

_____ a) In Quechua, the language of the heart.

_____ b) In Spanish, the language of the dominant culture.

_____ c) In either of the two languages. see &

/ leader
// identified OR SIMILAR WORDS
/// b
& a
&& separate OR SIMILAR WORDS

68. Our first responsibility as Christians is to

_____a) Cooperate with the government.

_____b) Win the greatest number of persons for Christ.

_____c) Maintain tribal unity.   see /

69. As a review of this section, write in your own words why it is better not to try to win Quechuas by means of Spanish speaking churches.

Another important aspect of the social conditions is the place of residence of the people. Generally, there is more or less uniformity within a neighborhood or sector. In other words, most inhabitants are of the same social class. A difficult problem for the Church is the location of congregations, because it is inevitable that people identify the churches with the social class of the sector. Nor can the problem be solved by erecting a building in the city center. Sometimes the centers of the city deteriorate leaving the church surrounded by bars and pawnshops. The believers have moved out to other areas and do not want to attend the central church at night. The building does not possess the same mobility of its members to move to a more suitable location. This is the much discussed inner city problem.

70. The division of the people into social classes is something recognized by

_____a) Church members.

_____b) The unconverted.

_____c) Everyone.   see //

71. Generally, one's neighbors are

_____a) Of the same social class.

_____b) Of a different social class.

_____c) A mixture that can not be classified.   see &

72. If the church is located in a middle class sector, Protestantism will be identified as a religion of the
                              see ///   _____.

73. A church composed of members of the lower class attracts those of the
                    _____ class. see /

74. Because of the people's mobility in moving from one place to another, the social level of a sector can
                              see &&   _____.

Anticipating an element of the discussion of the urban church, it is fitting to mention briefly one of the solutions to the problem of church location. This is to follow the New Testament model of establishing churches in homes. In this way some difficulties are avoided. One advantage is that there is no need to buy or rent a building. The evangelistic work is not limited to areas where there are buildings set aside for church services. Another advantage is that social class conflict is avoided. A Christian can invite to his home those who would come for purely social reasons. At the same time, but in different homes there can be middle class and lower class meetings without having to consider class prejudices and the possible problem of bringing together persons who would not normally mix socially. This point will be treated later in more detail.

75. The problem of church location is found mainly in (rural/urban)
            _____ areas. see //

76. The New Testament tells us of churches that met in

_____. see &&&

/   lower
//   urban
/// middle class
&   a
&&   change
&&& homes

77. All Christians live in some type of _____. see /

78. If believers meet there, the house becomes a _____.
    see $$$

79. The home church can be organized wherever _____
    live. see &&

80. This seems to be the solution for churches which do not
    have the funds necessary to

    _____ a building. see %

81. A middle class Christian would normally invite to his home
    people of the

    _____ class. see $

82. A day laborer would invite those of the _____ class.
    see &

83. An unconverted person who would respond to the invitation of
    his Christian neighbor would be among those of the

    _____ social class. see ///

84. Therefore, the unconverted man would be convinced that the
    gospel was for

    _____. see $$

85. In this way we avoid the inconvenience of mixing un-
    converted friends with persons of another

    _____ whom they might not accept. see &&&

    There is another advantage of home churches. The isolation
of the church from the rest of the community is avoided. Every
Christian home is open to the sector of the society in which
it is found. Every place of Christian worship attracts neighbors and relatives to close contact with fervent Christians.

86. If the Christian homes are scattered throughout the whole
city, each home will attract

    _____ persons. see //

/   home
//   different, distinct
///   same
&   lower
&&   Christians, believers
&&&   social class
$ middle
$$ people like himself OR SIMILAR WORDS
$$$ church
%   buy, rent, OR SIMILAR WORDS

87. Each place of Christian worship serves the people in its

_____. see ///

88. The distance that any person has to walk to the closest church would be

_____. see &&&

The system of forming churches in homes also overcomes the problem of the lack of leadership. Because of the necessity and the opportunities presented, in every home church at least one leader will appear. It could well be that this leader would not be able to direct a large congregation. But the gifts that God has given to His Church are wonderful. Under the guidance of the Holy Spirit the leaders arise that the Church needs. There is no need for a paid pastor of every congregation. Unconverted persons are more impressed when they hear the gospel from a friend or neighbor. They know he is speaking from conviction, not because he is paid to do so.

89. Since services in homes must be directed by some member of the group, in every group there will arise at least one

see & _____.

90. These groups depend on the guidance and the gifts given by the

_____. see //

91. In this situation it is not necessary to pay the salary of a

_____. see $

92. The gospel is communicated better by someone who is (more/less)

_____ like his listeners. see $$

93. A professional pastor can not share all the experiences of the members of his church because he does not _____

with them in the factory or store. see &&

94. There is less suspicion of the motives of someone who does not receive

_____for preaching. see /

/ salary, money
// Holy Spirit
/// neighborhood, sector
& leader, director
&& work
&&& little, short
$ pastor, worker
$$ more

95. The formation of churches in homes is one way of producing more

_____. see &

96. Perhaps these leaders would not be able to direct large groups. But all they have to do is direct

see &&& _____.

The suggestion of the organization of home churches will not work as well in all situations. Nevertheless, we should consider this possibility since we find this form of evangelism in the New Testament.

97. A church can be organized where

_____a) A home is opened for the preaching of the gospel.

_____b) There is a special building for church services.

_____c) There is lack of interest in the gospel.   see /

98. Normally those who attend such meetings are

_____a) Friends of the owner of the house.

_____b) People who don't know the owner of the house.

_____c) Enemies of the owner of the house.   see &&

99. Each home church attracts

_____a) The same persons.

_____b) Neighbors and relatives of the home owner.

_____c) Only convinced Christians.   see ///

100. The number of home churches is limited by

_____a) The interest of the people.

_____b) Funds available for rent.

_____c) Pastors who can serve the churches.   see //

/ a
// a
/// b
& leaders
&& a
&&& home churches OR SIMILAR WORDS

101. The leaders of such groups depend on

_____a) Their preparation in a Bible institute.

_____b) The guidance of the Holy Spirit.

_____c) Foreign funds.   see /

102. In relationship to pastors, home churches

_____a) Eliminate the necessity of full time pastors.

_____b) Depend on the continual presence of a pastor.

_____c) Are aided by the supervision of a pastor. see ///

The Jamaican Example

Now let us consider an example of how the social structure
influences in church growth. In 1820 the population of Jamaica
was made up of three elements: a) the English and Scottish
plantation owners who were members of the Anglican and Presbyterian churches; b) the mulatto population in the villages, some
educated, some free, that belonged to a social class a little
elevated; c) the Negro slaves that formed the largest part of
the population.

Up to this time the Anglicans and Presbyterians did not
want to evangelize the slaves for fear of creating discontent.
However, Baptists and Methodists arrived from England and began a large scale movement toward Christianity among the slaves.
The Baptist churches multiplied among the Negroes and the Methodist churches among the mulattos. The Baptists found it difficult to extend their churches among the mulattos because these
lighter skinned people did not want to mix with the Baptist Negroes. They did not want their children to marry into the lower
social class. Each denomination prospered in its particular
sub-culture. These Christians preferred to worship God with
others like themselves.

103. In Jamaica the whites were Christians and the Negroes practiced the religions of their African ancestors. The religion which won converts was that of the

_____a) The lower social class.

_____b) The predominant culture.

_____c) The majority of the population.   see /

104. The denominations followed the social lines of the_____.
                                        see &&

105. Conversion to Christianity did not destroy _____
prejudices.   see ///

106. People prefer to attend a church whose members are of

_____. see //

107. The land owners did not evangelize the Negroes because they did not want to admit into their churches the
                        see &
                                _____.

108. Racial discrimination existed not only between Negroes and whites, but also between Negroes and

                        _____. see &&&

    The Disciples of Christ sent missionaries to Jamaica in 1868 and established churches principally among the Negroes. Around 1915 a very capable pastor served a church made up mainly of domestic workers. This pastor organized a youth movement which enjoyed great success. Young people of the middle and lower classes of that sector of the city attended the meetings. The pastor tried to win these young people for Christ and for his church. Many of them did accept Christ but only those of the lower class joined his church. The parents of the middle class young people insisted on their children's becoming members of the Presbyterian and Methodist churches. The influence of social structure on church growth is very important.

/   b
//   their own people
     OR SIMILAR WORDS
/// racial, social
&   slaves, lower class
&&   races, classes
&&& mulattos

109. Sometimes the membership of a congregation or denomination changes. At least one Presbyterian church ceased to be a church for whites and was converted into a mulatto church of the

_____ class. see //

110. But the Disciples of Christ worked among the _____ of the lower class. see &&&

111. Generally each successive generation is (more/less) _____ concerned about social distinctions than its parents. see /

112. The middle class parents permitted their children to _____ the church of the Disciples of Christ. see &&

113. It seems that the discrimination was not so much between denominations as between

_____. see $

114. Although the church of the Disciples of Christ did not grow much due to the social factors involved, the pastor, with an ecumenical spirit, could rejoice because there had been growth also in

_____. see ///

115. People join churches which are of _____.
                                      see &

Social Obstacles to Evangelism

Men prefer to become Christians without crossing the barriers of race, language or class. It is easier to understand this truth in regard to the linguistic barrier. If the Quiche Indians had to attend services in Spanish or if they could be baptized only if they could read the Scriptures in Spanish, very few would be converted.

116. Large numbers of the Mam Indians of Guatemala are converted only in churches directed by

_____. see $$

/   less
///   middle
/// other churches OR SIMILAR WORDS
&   the same class OR SIMILAR WORDS
&&   attend
&&&   Negroes
$ classes, races
$$ themselves, Mam Indians OR SIMILAR WORDS

117. The most obvious barrier that exists for the communication of the gospel is that of

_____. see /

    But we must consider other obstacles and characteristics that divide mankind. When there are differences of skin color, economic conditions, personal cleanliness or education, people understand the gospel better when it is presented by those of their own group. They prefer to attend churches where the members talk and act as they do.

118. It is easier to accept the gospel when it is presented by persons who are

_____. see //

    Sometimes the differences seem insignificant to those who proclaim the message, but very important for those who listen to it. Even though they may be of the same general social class in other aspects, the young man from the country and another who has been brought up in the city think in different ways. The student should apply these principles to his own experience.

119. Have you ever attended a church service in another language?

120. If you have, were you greatly blessed or edified? Why?

121. Would you regularly attend such a service? _____

122. Would you have arrived at an intelligent and vital faith in such a meeting? Explain your answer.

123. To what social class do the members of your congregation belong?

/ language
/ similar OR SIMILAR WORDS

124. How many professional people are members of your church? __

125. In your city are there congregations made up largely of middle class families and others which are lower class?_____

126. If there are middle class churches, are they of certain denominations?
_____ which? _____

127. Can you tell from what state, department or province the members of your church have come?
_____

128. Would it be easy for a missionary to make this distinction? Why?

129. Do people like to be correctly identified as to their origen, and occupation? Why?

In the nineteenth century the high plateaus of Mexico were divided up into many large ranches which had been formed from lands granted by the king of Spain in representation of the pope himself. On the ranches small villages sprang up. The population was nominally Catholic and composed of the exploited masses and the higher classes. The land owners lived in the towns and were allies of the Roman Catholic Church.

During the revolutions of the early years of the twentieth century, and in particular that of 1927, when the central government divided up the lands to hand them over to the peasants the people were divided into two camps: the agraristas who were willing to fight for the distribution of land, and the cristeros who were convinced that taking the lands away from the big land owners meant robbing them. God would punish the people for this sin since the land had been given to the rich by the pope.

The peasants of the two parties looked the same. They all spoke Spanish, considered themselves to be Roman Catholics, shared the same culture, cultivated the same lands and dressed in the same way. Nevertheless, for the spread of the gospel, there was an important difference. The agraristas were more open to the gospel. They thought of the Roman Church as an ally of their oppressors. For the first time it was possible for them

really to listen to the gospel and consider it. But the evangelical missionaries and pastors were not aware of this openness and they did not make any special effort to plant churches
in the villages of the agraristas. If they had begun a movement
which would have provided a biblical basis for agrarian reform
it is possible that they could have enjoyed great evangelistic
success in this region.

130. With regard to the relationship between the church and the
people

_____a) All were Catholics.

_____b) Only the rich were Catholics.

_____c) Only the poor were Catholics.   see /

131. In this conflict between the rich and the poor the Church

_____a) Favored the poor.

_____b) Favored the rich.

_____c) Preserved its neutrality in the matter. see &

132. The agraristas differed from the cristeros in that

_____a) They were not Catholics.

_____b) They belonged to another culture.

_____c) They were ready to oppose the Roman Catholic Church.
                                              see ///

133. Because of their attitude, the agraristas

_____a) Accepted the gospel.

_____b) Were more open to the gospel.

_____c) Wanted to leave the Catholic Church. see //

134. The agraristas saw the Roman Church as

_____a) Their protector against oppression.

_____b) An instrument of oppression.

_____c) A neutral force.   see /

135. The Evangelical Church can

_____a) Aid and guide just movements.

_____b) Avoid all conflicts.

_____c) Try to maintain peace and order even in an unjust
        system.   see //

136. The central teaching of this example is that

_____a) The Church should foment revolution.

_____b) Economic factors affect the receptivity of peoples.

_____c) Racial factors affect the receptivity of peoples. see ///

        Another difference that people from outside do not notice
is that of blood or godfather relationships. It is interesting
to note that in many towns the evangelicals belong to two or
three families. From other families, which are perhaps rivals,
not one has been converted. We must learn to exploit these
conditions that contribute to the receptivity of certain families
or sectors of the population.

137. Indicate the order (1 to 4) in which the Church should take
the following steps to evangelize a town. Afterwards indicate
the reasons for proceeding in the manner indicated.

_____Determine the lines of relationships.

_____Evangelize the families which have no evangelical members.

_____Evangelize the families which have no evangelical members.

_____Try to join or reconcile the families.

Church planters that let men become Christians without crossing social barriers have more success. The offense of the cross
is a biblical obstacle to Christian faith and can not be removed.
Accepting the truth that one is a sinner, whose salvation depends
not on what he himself can do, but rather in accepting what Christ
has already done on the cross, offends one's ego. Repenting of
one's sins and abandoning them is another barrier. Confessing
Christ openly before others is a third obstacle. Surrendering
oneself completely to the lordship of Christ is a difficult decision. For those of us who accept the authority of the Scriptures
these barriers can not be taken away. But the Church must fight
against the tendency to impose other obstacles. In most cases
that which hinders men in their decision for Christ is one or more
non-biblical obstacles.

138. The obstacles which we can not remove in the proclamation of
the gospel are those which are

_____. see /

139. If the biblical obstacles are preserved, the evangelist
should seek ways of making the acceptance of the gospel (easier/
more difficult)

_____. see //

140. The greatest obstacles to the faith have often been imposed
by

_____. see ///

The Biblical Evidence

There is nothing in the Bible that requires that to become
a Christian one must cross barriers of language, race or class.
To demand this is to place emphasis on human requirements rather
than on biblical principles. The Scriptures affirm that in Christ
there is "neither Jew nor Greek, there is neither slave nor free,
there is neither male nor female" (Gal. 3:28). But this teaching
applies only to those who are already in Christ. This unity is a
fruit of the Holy Spirit. We must recognize that sometimes the
fruit delays in maturing unless we can believe that the members
of the Early Church, which preached only to Jews and maintained
its social distance from the gentiles, were not really Christians.
We must also consider the last phrase - there is neither male nor
female. Certainly Paul doesn't mean that the Christian should
live as though there were no differences between the sexes. Nor

/ biblical
// easier
/// men OR SIMILAR WORDS

does the first phrase mean that as Christians we should declare
that the differences of class and race do not exist.

14. The apostle Paul in his letter to the Galatians teaches that
in Christ there is neither

_____ nor Greek

slave nor _____

_____ nor female.   see //

142. This unity exists only in _____. see &&

143. Nevertheless, we recognize that there still exist _____
                                        see ///

144. Men should not be accepted as identical, but as _____.
                                        see &

     Nineteen centuries ago the Church discovered that the Jews
could more readily become Christians if they did not have to cross
social barriers. The Jewish society was tightly knit together.
It insisted that Jews marry Jews. It had nothing to do with Samaritans who were considered as mestizos, descendents of marriages
between Jews and gentiles.

145. Jews had fellowship only with _____. see /

146. They did not allow in their synagogues as full members the

_____. see &&&

     This solidarity provided a path for the expansion of the
Jewish Church. While the Jews could become Christians without
ceasing to be Jews, the Church grew greatly among them. When
the Church was extended to the communities around the synagogues
throughout the Mediterranean world, the first disciples were Jews
who awaited the Messiah. These Jews, becoming Christians within
the synagogue community, did so without crossing barriers of
race or class.

/   other Jews
//   Jew, free, male
/// differences
&   equals
&&   Christ
&&& gentiels, non-Jews

Nevertheless, when the gentiles were converted to Christianity, this meant for the Jews that the Church became the means of ceremonial contamination. Joining the Church meant joining a society that included gentiles. Admitting the gentiles into the Church created a barrier for the Jews. If being a Christian meant eating pork with the gentiles, they no longer were interested in becoming Christians.

147. Demanding that one become a Christian among those of another culture

_____a) Differs from the biblical teaching.

_____b) Is in agreement with the teaching of the Apostles.

_____c) Follows the pattern of the New Testament Church.   see //

148. It is to be hoped that men will lose their social prejudices

_____a) Before listening to the gospel.

_____b) When they listen to the gospel.

_____c) When they are converted to Christ.

_____d) When they reach spiritual maturity.   see /

149. The first Christians maintained social relations only with

_____a) The gentiles.

_____b) The Jews.

_____c) The Samaritans.   see &

150. Among some elements of the Early Church the practice was continued without condemnation by the Apostles, of

_____a) Slavery.

_____b) Immorality.

_____c) Idolatry.   see ///

151. The first Jewish converts considered themselves to be

_____a) Equal to the gentiles.

_____b) Jews zealous of the Law.

_____c) Members of a universal people.   see /

152. The principal mission of the Church is to

_____a) Change the social structure.

_____b) Destroy prejudices.

_____c) Win men for Christ.   see ///

153. When the universality of Christianity was recognized

_____a) Many Jews joined the Church.

_____b) Many Jews left the Church.

_____c) Few Jews joined the Church.   see //

154. When the gospel is presented to non-Christians is it necessary to explain all the social implications of being a Christian? Explain your position and give biblical evidence for it.

Examples from History

In the conversion of Europe the same social phenomenon was
seen. When accepting the Christian faith meant identifying with
political enemies who were Christians, the linguistic and racial
barriers hindered for years the conversion of many peoples. But
when some military or political change provided a way to be converted without crossing these barriers, multitudes entered the
Church. These movements have been much criticized for having
admitted the "world" into the churches. But if it had not been
for these mass movements there would not have arisen later the
gathered churches of our tradition. In the beginning of the
christianization of Europe, social obstacles maintained entire
countries outside the Christian faith and salvation for centuries.
When at last a way of becoming Christians within the same social
unit was presented, whole countries declared their allegiance to
Christ.

155. The European people were evangelized more easily by

_____a) Their political allies.

_____b) Their political enemies.

_____c) Persons of another race.   see //

156. The receptivity of a people changes when there is a
change in its.

_____a) Language.

_____b) Political position.

_____c) Race.   see ///

157. The entrance of multitudes in the Church happened after
the conversion of the emperor Constantine. This great expansion

_____a) Completely contaminated the Church.

_____b) Admitted only nominal Christians.

_____c) Admitted many who became sincere Christians. see /

We have already mentioned the case of the Church that grew so
rapidly among the Italian immigrants to Brazil. For the first
twenty years these churches extended only among those who spoke
Italian. In order to become evangelicals in other churches the
Italians would have had to cross linguistic and class barriers
and separate themselves from their own community. For the same
reasons that those of Italian descent entered these churches,
non-Italians did not.

The mere capability or opportunity to become a Christian
without crossing social barriers has never converted anybody.
In the United States, for example, almost everyone has the
possibility of joining a church of his own sub-culture, but
many do not do so. There are other equally important factors
for church growth. The gospel must be proclaimed and Christian
love demonstrated. Christians must try to presuade their friends
and relatives that it is good to be a follower of the Lord of Life

158. Brazil and the United States are examples of nations composed
of persons of many countries, cultures and languages. Many other
countries also have colonies which are more or less separate from
the life of the rest of the people. The denomination founded by
the Italian immigrant in Brazil was successful only among the
Italians because.

_____a) The Church conformed to the Italian culture.

_____b) The Italians constituted a distinct economic class.

_____c) Only the Italians were open to the gospel.   see //

159. The act of removing social barriers

_____a) Guarantees conversion to Christianity.

_____b) Facilitates conversion to Christianity.

_____c) Hinders conversion to Christianity.   see /

160. The following factors contribute to conversion (choose two)

_____a) The preaching of the gospel in the language of the people.

_____b) Early presentation of rules for Christian conduct.

_____c) Demonstration of the gospel in the lives of Christians.

_____d) Instruction in how to adapt to another culture.   see ///

b a a,c
////

Now it is the student's turn to make some investigations concerning the reality within the church and community of which he is a member. Since not all students will live in the same circumstances it will be necessary to adapt the following project to the student's situation.

The student should obtain a map of his city or region and indicate the various sectors on it. He should identify the social class of the various sectors of the city and locate the evangelical churches. What kind of persons surround the churches? Do the churches attract mainly persons from their own neighborhood? In what types of areas are the churches growing more rapidly? What examples are furnished locally of the principles indicated in this lesson?

10

THE RECEPTIVITY OF PEOPLES

Lesson IX dealt with social factors that affect the receptivity of peoples to the gospel. In Lesson XI we will consider some social implications of the gospel that the Church can not ignore if it hopes to win the sympathy of the people and carry out its obligations in the world. In the present lesson we are going to study other factors, some social, others political, that have permitted rapid growth. On the basis of this knowledge we must take advantage of every opportunity. We ought to give special attention to the lower class which constitutes the largest sector of the population in the Latin American countries. After choosing the sector of the people that we want to evangelize we can compare various suggestions for the urban church in Lesson XII and for the rural church in Chapter XIII.

Variable Receptivity

Our Lord speaks of fields in which the seed has just been sown and of others already white for the harvest. Sometimes persons, hearing the gospel, do not respond. The field is no closer to being harvested than before receiving the seed. Sometimes, however, men who hear the Word hurry to obey it. They receive it with joy, accept Christ, and are added to the Church.

1. When persons hear the gospel, _____ respond.

see /

/ some

2.   Not every field is white and ready for the _____.

        see ///

3.   Our Lord has sent His laborers specifically to the _____
fields.   see &

        Our Lord referred to the variable capability of individuals
and societies to listen to and obey the gospel. The changing
receptivity is a prominent aspect of human society. It is
found in all sectors, urban and rural, advanced and primitive,
educated and illiterate. It affects profoundly every aspect of
the Church's mission and must be studied in depth if we are to
understand how churches grow. Let us examine, therefore, the
fact of receptivity, its causes and its application to the advance of the Church.

4.   The capacity of a society to receive the gospel_____.

        see /

5.   This variation in receptivity is found in _____
societies.   see &&&

6.   Recognizing this variability is of _____ importance
for the Church.   see $

7.   The Church should reap when the level of receptivity is____

        see &&

8.   In some cases perhaps it would be possible to produce receptivity if we knew

        _____. see //

        The responsiveness of individuals increases and decreases.
No one is equally ready at all times to follow the "Way." A
young person brought up in a Christian home more readily accepts
Christ at the age of 12 than at 20. Even the sceptic is more
responsive after an illness or other crisis in his life than before. During a war many sceptics learn to fear God.

9.   Variable receptivity is a phenomenon that can be noted not
only in societies but also in

        _____. see $$

/   changes, varies
//   the causes OR
     SIMILAR WORDS
/// harvest
&   whitened, ready
     greater OR
     SIMILAR WORDS
&&   all
&&& much, great
$ individuals,
$$ persons

10.   One is more disposed to receive instruction when he is (old/ young)

_____. see ///

11.   A young person is more open to the gospel (before/after)

_____ he finishes high school.   see &

12.   Someone is more likely to respond to the gospel when his health is

_____.   see /

13.   Do you believe that the Sunday School and the Youth Society are important for the life of the church?   Why?

Peoples and societies also vary in their responsiveness. Whole sectors of mankind resist the gospel for some time, and then suddenly open up to the good news.   This is the case in many parts of Latin America where we see opportunities as never before.   In populations that resist the gospel congregations can barely survive.   Meanwhile, among receptive peoples, many congregations can be established which will not only grow, but will in turn establish other churches.

14.   Many peoples of Latin America are now _____ open to the gospel than before.   see //

15.   The emphasis of this study is not in how churches can survive, but how they can

_____.   see &&

16.   With equal preparation will two areas open to the gospel at the same time?
_____ Why or why not?

/ poor OR SIMILAR WORDS
/// more
& young
&& before
grow, increase

17. If a field is open to the gospel at one time, does this mean that it always will be? Explain your answer.

Examples of Responsive Peoples

Irregularity of growth has been a characteristic of the Church from the beginning. The common people, say the Gospels, received the Savior's message more readily than the Pharisees or Saducees. For the first three decades of the Christian era the Jews responded more than the gentiles. When Judea had already been Christian for one hundred years, Philistia on one side and Arabia on the other were still pagan.

18. A phenomenon that has been observed throughout the history of the Church is that not in all sectors has it grown _____.
see //

19. Even among the Jews the Christian faith found greater favor among those of the
_____ class. see /

20. At first Christianity was considered a religion of the____.
see ///

21. The gospel was not well received in Arabia because the Arabs in that time also were
_____ of the Jews. see &

22. For that reason it is not surprising that the Church grew
_____ in Arabia. see &&&

23. Among the other enemies of the Jews, from the time of David, were the
_____. see &&

/ lower
// in the same way, equally
Jews
/// enemies
& Philistines
&& little,
&&& slowly

When Christianity spread throughout Europe, it was not always true that the closest countries were the first to accept the gospel. Ireland was converted, then England and later Germany. It was impossible to win the Germans at the same time as the Irish because the germanic tribes resisted the gospel.

24. The case of the evangelization of northern Europe shows us that some times the (cultural/geographic) distance between peoples is more important.
_____. see /

The Southern Baptists maintained missionary forces in Thailand and Hong Kong between 1950 and 1960. In 1960 they had 42 missionaries in Thailand and 38 in Hong Kong. But there were big differences in results. After ten years of work in Thailand the membership of the churches was 355 and in Hong Kong 14,000.

25. On the basis of the lessons already studied and your other reading concerning the conditions in Hong Kong and Thailand, state some reasons why the Church in Hong Kong grew more.

26. If you were the person responsible for allocation of missionary personnel for the Southern Baptists in the Orient, what would you have done after 1960?

One of the most noteworthy cases of openness to the gospel in recent years has been that of the Tiv in Central Nigeria. This tribe numbers more than one million. In 1960 the Church had 7,352 members. But in the villages of the Tiv hundreds

/ cultural

of religious instruction classes were established. These classes were really small church schools. In these centers Christian workers, many of them with little preparation and minimal salaries, taught the Bible, reading and arithmetic and led services on Sundays. In 1963 Sunday attendance was 105,242 - testimony of great receptivity.

27. In 1963 the Church included.

_____a) 3% of the total population.

_____b)10% of the total population.

_____c)50% of the total population.   see ///

28. Many of those who attended the religious instruction classes were children and others who attended to receive the secular teaching. However, this is still a case of

_____

receptivity. see /

29. In comparison with the number of persons reached, the funds expended were

_____. see &

30. Those who directed the centers of instruction required_____ preparation.   see //

31. The Church demonstrated that it was not concerned only with spiritual needs, but also with

_____needs. see &&&

32. The success of the program depended on the establishing of

_____ religion instruction centers. see &&

There are innumerable causes of responsiveness or its lack. Some are so common that they should be mentioned. New towns or neighborhoods are more responsive than older established areas. Colonies and the poor sectors of many Latin American cities are open to the gospel for a few years. But when a Roman Catholic church is built and the people have erected permanent homes and sent their children to school they become deaf to the gospel. It is not accidental that the tremendous growth of the Pentecostals in Brazil has been among migrants who have left their homes in the north to settle in the large cities in the southern part of the country.

/ great OR SIMILAR WORDS

// little
/// b low OR SIMILAR WORDS

& many
&&& social, economic OR SIMILAR WORDS

33. A change of residence, for just a week or permanently, makes
it easier to change religion. Those who move from the country to
the city are

_____a) Indifferent to the conditions in which they live.

_____b) Those who are satisfied with the way they live.

_____c) Those who want to change the way they live.   see ///

34. The evangelization of a new neighborhood is easier because

_____a) It does not have a Roman Catholic Church.

_____b) It has not identified with some social class.

_____c) It always has good roads.   see &&

35. The most responsive people to the gospel in Brazil are

_____a) Those who live in the north.

_____b) Those that moved to the southern cities.

_____c) Those born in the south.   see //

36. It is easier to change religions if one has already changed

_____ .   see &

37. The pentecostals have been very successful in southern
Brazil because they have worked among
                          see /   _____ .

38. The same opportunities in Brazil and other places can be
used by
              _____ .   see &&&

　　　　Travel and the wider perspective which it affords sometimes
produce receptivity. Mexican workers, during 1940 to 1962, in-
vaded the United States in great numbers to work on farms. Sometimes New Testaments were given to them and the workers took them
back to their homes in Mexico. Later evangelical missionaries in
Mexico found that these farm workers were rather open to the gospel. Some congregations were established among them. Unfortunate-

/ migrants
/// b
// c
& resi-
dence OR
SIMILAR
WORDS
&& a
&&& all,
others

ly evangelicals did not realize the importance of 300,000 Mexicans on the farms of evangelicals in the United States and the spiritual harvest was not what it could have been.

39. With regard to the farm workers

_____a) Some were more responsive because of their experience in the United States.

_____b) Many were converted in the United States.

_____c) They returned to Mexico the same as they had left. see //

40. The blame for not taking advantage of the evangelistic opportunities in the United States would be mainly that of

_____a) The farm workers.

_____b) Evangelicals in Mexico.

_____c) Evangelicals in the United States.   see &

Nationalism can exercise a strong influence for or against the Church. In Korea, after nine years (1910-1918) of slow growth in most of the provinces, there came five years of great receptivity (1919-1924). The circumstances were the following: After the First World War and the proclamation by President Wilson of the self determination of small nations, Korean patriots began in 1919 a non-violent resistance movement against the Japanese. They sought to force Japan to concede autonomy to Korea. Almost half of those who signed the Declaration of Independence were evangelical ministers. The Church became a center of resistance of the Korean people against the Japanese oppression. Evangelism that took advantage of the Church's policy produced considerable growth in some provinces. Nationalism helped the Church.

41. In Korea Christianity was identified with the spirit of

_____. see ///

42. Probably _____ Japanese were won for Christianity in Korea.   see /

43. Explain your answer to question 42.

/ few
// a
/// nation-
    alism
& 0

44. During the early years of this century some Central American countries were occupied by the U. S. Marine Corps. In this case Protestantism was (aided/hindered)
see &&& _____ by nationalism.

45. In Korea Christianity was aided by _____. see ///

46. Rapid growth resulted because

_____a) The Church stopped evangelizing to enter into politics.

_____b) The Church refused to recognize the rebel ministers.

_____c) The Church harvested when conditions were good. see //

    In Mexico in 1857, during the revolution of Juarez, a fairly large group of priests left the Roman Catholic Church. Without support or allies some married and became laymen; others asked forgiveness and returned to the Church; others were converted to the evangelical faith. If the evangelical missionaries had taken advantage of this revolution to give it a biblical basis it is possible that they would have started a large scale movement. But in those days the missionaries were convinced that Latin America was closed to the gospel and they did not understand that nationalism can make a people more receptive.

47. In Mexico in the time of Juarez the people

_____a) Were converted to Protestantism in large numbers.

_____b) Were more open to the gospel.

_____c) Considered that Protestantism was their enemy. see /

48. The priests left the Roman Catholic Church mainly for reasons which were

_____a) Doctrinal.

_____b) Economic.

_____c) Political.   see &&

49. The evangelicals did not take advantage of the situation because of lack of
_____. see &

/ b
// c
/// nationalism
& understanding, vision OR SIMILAR WORDS
&& c
&&& hindered

50. Around seventy years ago several million Filipinos left the Roman Catholic Church to form a National Church. If such a movement occurred in Latin America, what should be the relationship of the Evangelical Church to such a Church?

Taking Advantage of Receptivity

We study receptivity not as an exercise in anthropology but for its application to the complex process of church growth. We want to be good stewards of the opportunities that God has given us for the extension of the Church. We are still not ready to feed all the data into a computer which will give us an answer in regard to the receptivity of a certain people. However, within a few years science may provide us with even more information to help the Church in its mission. Meanwhile we can all observe conditions around us. It is very important to note if groups of persons are joining the Church. Is there a Church working among a certain people or a similar population with much success? If receptivity is demonstrated in one sector of the society it is reasonable to believe that other similar sectors will be open to the gospel.

51. We study the receptivity of peoples to apply this knowledge to

_____. see /

52. The best way to determine if a people is responsive to the gospel is

_____. see ///

53. In order to carry out God's mission we may use human

_____. see //

/   church growth OR SIMILAR WORDS

// wisdom, knowledge, science to note if the church is growing OR SIMILAR WORDS

/// to note if the church is growing OR SIMILAR WORDS

54.   If in one sector of a country an industrial city has provided a great harvest for the gospel, probably another city in the same region

_____ . see ///

Although the best measure of receptivity is the rate of growth of the Church in a given sector, sometimes it is impossible to wait to measure the results. We must apply the theory. The study of anthropology and sociology teaches us something of the conditions that produce social changes, including religious changes. The Church's experience is that migrants to a country or to a city, and societies which have been oppressed and deprived hear and respond to the gospel more readily than those which are content with their social conditions.

55.   The surest indication that a people is open to the gospel is

_____ .   see /

56.   Nevertheless, the social sciences tell us some conditions that tend to produce

_____ in individuals. see $

57.   Generally the gospel finds fertile ground among colonists and other recent

_____ to a country.   see &&&

58.   This responsiveness is illustrated by the formation of

_____ (type) churches among Italians and other groups in Argentina.   see //

59.   Also those that move from one sector of the country to another are readier to listen to the gospel. There is greater possibility of a change of religion after a change of
see &
                                                        _____ .

60.   We have noted the successful evangelism among those who left the rural areas in northern Brazil to seek work in the

_____ .   see $$

61.   The Aymaras in Peru that became Adventists were more disposed to do so because they had been oppressed by
see &&
                                                   _____ .

/   the rate of growth OR SIMILAR WORDS
//   ethnic
/// will be receptive OR SIMILAR WORDS
&   residence
&&   the Roman Church
&&& arrivals, migrants
$ changes
$$ cities

62. In the midst of oppression and privation men need a religion that gives them

_____.   see $

63. When men come from the country and see the riches in the city they are

_____ satisfied.   see &&&

64. Is there greater contrast between the life of the rich and the poor in the cities or in the country?

_____ see &

65. In the future the Church should expect great ingatherings in (rural/urban)

_____ sectors.   see /

66. The Church should take advantage of the receptivity produced among the people because of the dissatisfaction with the

_____

in which they live.   see $$

     The society and its institutions exercise certain controls over their members. The government dictates laws which its citizens must obey. There are other controls which are less obvious but just as strong in our lives. These social controls hinder receptivity to Christianity because they oppose change. Receptivity is increased when the controls are loosened. A large proportion of the two billion non-Christians in the world live under rigid controls. When these controls dissolve men remain free to consider the merits of Christianity.

67. No man is completely free. All live under certain _____.
                                                       see ///⌐

68. Social controls _____ change.   see &&

69. When an individual escapes certain controls he is _____ open to the gospel.   see //

     Controls are of various types. The most intimate is that of the family. Persons do not exist as independent entities to make decisions without concern for others. They exist in society. Their thoughts and emotions are conditioned and determined to a certain degree by family controls. What will they say? is a very serious consideration in many societies where everyone depends on the family for almost every aspect of life.

/ urban
/// more
/// controls
& cities
&& oppose
OR SIMI-
LAR
WORDS less
hope
OR SIMI-
LAR
WORDS
&&& condi-
$ tions,
$$ circumstances

70. As an example of the control that parents exercise over their children, the student should indicate the restrictions that they try to place on choosing a wife. That is, what types of girls would be unsuitable? Think about all the factors - religious, social, economic, personal, etc.

71. The social institution or entity which has greatest influence or control over the individual is the
                        see //   _____ .

72. Men are not independent. They have to think how their decisions will affect
            _____ .   see ///

The controls of the town, tribe or companions are also important. Therefore there is greater liberty to consider the evangelical faith in the cities of Latin America than in the country. City dwellers are free from the pressures of family, neighbors and the priest. In the city there is greater anonymity and freedom to do what one wants without being concerned about what others will say.

73. Individuals are concerned (more/less) _____ about the opinions of people whom they don't know.   see /

74. It is possible to be surrounded by strangers in the _____ .
                                            see &&

75. Therefore it is (easier/more difficult)_____ to become an evangelical in the city.   see &

76. Each group controls its members, for good or for evil. Name the entities or social institutions which exercise some control over your conduct or thinking.

/ less
// family
/// others
& easier
&& city

10-14

77. Does the Evangelical Church control its members? In what aspects of their lives?

78. How can the Evangelical Church discipline its members in order to maintain control over them?

79. What biblical basis is there for the Church's control over the life of its members?

80. Are there some areas in which your church should exercise more control over its members so that they would conform more to biblical standards? Are there areas in which the church should give its members more liberty for greater contact with those who are in the world?

If we take advantage of whitened fields, what should we do about fields in which we can harvest little now? Should we abandon them? By no means. We must sow with the hope that at the right time the Lord of the harvest will change hearts there.

81. Does the fact that we have seen few results in an area necessarily mean that it is not ready for harvest? Why or why not?

82. Do scanty results in a sector mean that God's servants there have not been faithful? Explain your answer.

83. It is always possible that receptivity will change because of

_____ factors.   see /

We should occupy unresponsive fields with a minimal missionary force. Someone must be there to note any change in receptivity. But it is better to free the greatest number of workers from unfruitful fields to concentrate in areas of great possibility. We must maintain a witness to the gospel without flooding difficult areas with so many workers and institutions that we increase the resistance. As good military strategists we must maintain the defense on all fronts while we feel out the enemy to know where to concentrate our forces for a decisive victory. Above all there must be sufficient flexibility to reinforce responsive areas.

84. Our forces should be concentrated in areas of _____ possibility.   see //

/ social OR SIMILAR WORDS

// greater

85. Difficult fields should be occupied by (no one/few/many)

_____.   see //

86. While we occupy all the territory we look for _____

_____.   see &&

87. The presence of many workers and institutions in an unresponsive field sometimes results in

_____ the
opposition to the gospel.   see &

88. Flexibility is needed for the relocation of _____.
                                    see &&&

It is sometimes easier to exploit receptivity than to discover it. Each people is a distinct case. There is no general
formula that will work under any circumstances. Each population
needs its own formula. The essence of the gospel, the authorita-
tive Bible and the unchangeable Christ remain the same. But the
way to express Christian truths and the combinations of institutions, literature, radio, campaigns and visitation vary in each
situation. Under certain circumstances all the things mentioned
above can produce results. In other conditions only the precise
combination of these elements will give the church growth desired.
We must remember that nothing grows except local congregations
and that the Church does not grow in a geographical area as
much as in certain sectors of the population.

89. Each field needs its own _____ of evangelistic methods.   see /

90. There is need to change the _____ of the message.
                                    see $

91. A combination of literature and campaigns will give good
results in

_____ conditions.   see ///

92. An evangelistic formula is valid only for _____.
                                    see $$

/   combination
// few
/// certain, some
    increasing OR
    SIMILAR WORDS
&   areas of greatest
    opportunity OR
    SIMILAR WORDS
&& workers, forces
&&& expression
$ certain conditions
$$ OR SIMILAR WORDS

93. The Church grows through membership increases in the _____.

see &&&

94. For maximum growth in a sector of the population it is necessary to choose the best

see &&

_____.

Of the more than 250,000,000 inhabitants of Latin America today, many are open to the gospel and we can win them only if we use the correct methods. It could be that if they hear the gospel from a neighbor they will listen, but for a foreigner or even a pastor from elsewhere they will seem as deaf as ever. If those who accept Christ are really converted the people will listen to the good news of salvation that has the power to transform lives. Consecrated disciples of Christ can have an influence that nominal Christians will not. If Christians are as sad as others and if they fight among themselves, thousands will remain indifferent to the gospel.

95. The success of the Church in Latin America will depend on the

_____ that it uses.   see ///

96. However no method will produce results for all who use it, but only if it is used by

see &

_____.

97. The number of persons reached for Christ will be determined in part by the

_____ of Christians within the

Church.   see //

It is impossible to fix principles outside the situation. Sometimes it is necessary to experiment with some methods and choose that which has worked out best over a period of time. The essential task is to determine receptivity and, when the ready fields are identified, to adjust methods, institutions and personnel until responsive peoples accept Christ and in turn invite their friends and relatives to enjoy the same eternal life.

98. When making evangelistic plans we should

_____a) Seek the solution in some book.

_____b) Seek a different solution for every situation.

_____c) Seek the formula which will always work.   see /

/ b
// quality OR SIMILAR WORDS methods
/// certain persons OR SIMILAR WORDS
& combination of methods OR SIMILAR WORDS
&& congregations, churches

99. In order to adapt to individual conditions we must

_____a) Change the message proclaimed.

_____b) Change the way of proclaiming the message.

_____c) Do the same as in other places.   see &&

100. In a non-responsive area the methods used for evangelism
are

_____a) Very important.

_____b) Of little importance.

_____c) Of no value.   see ///

101. Sometimes while making plans to take advantage of receptivity we must begin with the negative side. List factors which
can hinder receptivity to the gospel.

          There are certain general principles that can guide us in
the search for people responsive to the gospel. It has already
been mentioned that generally new neighborhoods contain persons
in the process of changing many aspects of their lives. These
persons can consider also a change in religion. Another general
principle is that the masses are more open to the gospel than
are the higher classes.

102. A person that changes his place of residence is _____
open than before to the gospel.   see //

103. We find this type of person in _____ neighborhoods.
                                                     see /

104. Those who suffer material needs sense _____ need
of salvation.   see &

/   new, transient
// more a
/// more b
&
&&

105. Therefore the gospel will be better received among those of the
_____ class.   see //

---

106. Two sectors of the population that generally are more responsive are:

.   .

.   .

---

see &&

The Masses

We live in an era in which everyone is very conscious of
the masses and their demands for justice and participation in
the prosperity and opportunities possible in our societies.
In the twentieth century the masses have gained influence in
many countries. Communism has shown the power of the masses and
the Church also has become aware of the need to correct injustices. We can not accept the marxist system, not because it is
not right in trying to better the conditions of the masses, but
because it ignores the basic problem - the sinfulness of man
and his need of spiritual transformation.

107. The basic need of man is _____. see /

108. When a person is saved

_____a) All his material problems are solved.

_____b) Material problems lose their importance.

_____c) He still has material problems.   see &

109. The error of communism is that

_____a) It is not concerned about human conditions.

_____b) It does not recognize the sin of the masses.

_____c) It doesn't recognize the sin of capitalists. see ///

/ salvation
/// lower
/// b
& c
&& new neighbor-
hoods,
the masses
OR SIMILAR
WORDS

110. In the twentieth century the masses

_____a) Are in worse conditions than before.

_____b) Are in much better conditions than before.

_____c) Want to change their condition.   see /

111. What percentage of your city or community is of the

lower class?_____% middle class?_____% upper class?_____%

112. What percentage of the members of your church are of the

lower class?_____% middle class?_____% upper class?_____%

113. What is the greatest need of the poor? What is their hope
for the future? Work? New houses? Education? Explain your answer

   The Bible gives special attention to the common man. It
begins with the declaration that all men are sons of Adam and
therefore brothers and equals. It ends with the affirmation
that all men "great and small" will appear before the great white
throne of judgment. Riches, education, social position and
power will count for nothing in God's judgment. The only criterion is: Is your name written in the book of life? Have you
confessed Christ before the world and abandoned all sin; have
you been faithful unto death?

There are at least six biblical arguments for the equality of men and the special concern of God for the humble. Two of these arguments are mentioned in the preceeding paragraph and the rest are presented in the paragraphs that follow. The arguments are:

All men were created equal.
All men will be judged equally.
The choosing of the Israelite slaves in Egypt.
The prophetic preaching on behalf of the poor.
Jesus' incarnation in humility.
The humble majority in the Early Church.

114. All men have descended from _____.   see ///

115. With regard to their origen, all men are _____.
                                               see &

116. In the final judgment they will be judged _____. see &&&

117. In that great judgment the basis for judging men will be

_____ .   see /

118. What place will material riches have in that judgment?

_____   see $

119. All men were created _____ .   see $$$

120. In the Day of the Lord they will be equally _____.
                                                 see //

121. Our belief in the equality of men rests on the authority of the

_____ .   see &&

122. Two arguments for the equality of all men are:

●——●

●——●
                                        see $$

/   faith in Christ
      OR SIMILAR WORDS
//   judged
///   Adam
&   equal
&&   Bible
&&&   equally, all
$ none
$$ created equal,
      they will be
      judged equally
      OR SIMILAR WORDS
$$$ equal

When God chose a people and made a covenant with them, He did not choose the erudite nor princes nor aristocrats nor students, but slaves in Egypt (Exodus 3:7,8; 19:5,6).

123. An outstanding event in the history of the Jews was when God

_____. see ///

124. In Egypt the Jews lived as _____. see &

125. Nevertheless God _____ them to be a holy nation. see $$

Later when the Jews were settled in Canaan and wanted a king, God was not pleased that they wanted a society with an aristocratic structure. He warned them ahead of time how the aristocrats have always oppressed the poor and humble. The forms have changed from century to century and from country to country, but the oppression still exists (I Samuel 8:11-18). When the aristocratic order was already developed and these prophecies were fulfilled God sent His prophets to plead the cause of the poor and to demand justice for the common man (Isaiah 10:1-20). We could cite other exhortations in Micah, Nathan, Jeremiah and Amos. God is a God of justice who does not permit the oppression of the masses.

126. God knew that the rich always _____ the poor.
see /

127. He wanted to avoid this division of the people that He had

_____. see &&&

128. Therefore it did not please God when, to conform to other peoples, the Israelites demanded a

_____. see //

129. Under God's covenant with Israel all men have certain ____.
see &&

130. Injustices were denounced by the _____ sent by God.
see $

/ oppressed OR SIMILAR WORDS
// king
/// delivered them from Egypt OR SIMILAR WORDS
& slaves
&& rights OR SIMILAR WORDS
&&& chosen, elected
$ prophets
$$ chose

131. These servants of God demanded _____ for the humble.   see &&

132. One evidence of God's concern for the poor is found in the preaching of the

_____ .   see //

133. In the history of the beginning of Israel and its later development we see two evidences that God loves the poor. These two proofs are:

•——•

•——•

see &

     The New Testament tells us that, when the Word became flesh and dwelt among men, Jesus was born of a country maid in Nazareth and brought up in a carpenter's home. The Son of God learned the carpenter's trade and carried the heavy boards on His shoulders. Like humble people everywhere he ate bread in the sweat of His face. And when our Lord announced in Nazareth this purpose of His coming he said: "The Spirit of the Lord is upon me, because he has anointed me to preach good news to the poor. He has sent me to proclaim release to the captives and recovering of sight to the blind, to set at liberty those who are oppressed, to proclaim the acceptable year of the Lord." (Luke 4:18).

134. Joseph and Mary were of the _____ class. see &&&

135. Jesus learned the trade of a _____ . see /

136. Our Lord preached the good news particularly to the _____.
                                                              see $

137. To the oppressed he offered _____ . see ///

138. The divine concern for the poor is seen in the example of

_____ .   see $$

/ carpenter
// prophets
/// liberty
& the choosing of slaves, the preaching of the prophets for justice OR SIMILAR WORDS
&& justice
&&& lower, humble
$ poor
$$ Jesus

139. God took the form of a _____ man.   see &&

Of the twelve apostles, eleven were Galileans - peasants who talked with an accent. The elders, scribes and the high priest looked down on them as "uneducated, common men." The book of Acts tells us that Christianity spread among the masses in Jerusalem and Judea. The humble people gladly listened to the apostles. The Jewish governors did not take more drastic measures because they feared the people (Acts 5:26). The Early Church was made up of humble persons and even many of the leaders were of the same class. Compared with the large number of Christians from the masses there were very few from the upper classes.

140. Eleven of the apostles were from the province of _____.
                                                       see $$

141. At least four of them earned a living on the Sea of Galilee as
_____.   see ///

142. In comparison with the scribes and others, the apostles did not have much
_____.   see &

143. It is easier to share the gospel with someone of the same
_____.   see //

144. Therefore it should not surprise us that the gospel spread among
_____ people.   see $$$

145. The majority of the first disciples were of the _____ class.
                                                       see &&&

146. Jesus identified with the poor in His _____. see /

147. The last evidence for God's concern for the poor is that in the Early Church most of the disciples were
                            see $ _____.

/ incarnation
// class
/// fishermen
& education, preparation
&& humble OR SIMILAR WORDS
&&& lower
$ humble people OR SIMILAR WORDS
$$ Galilee
$$$ humble

When the Church grew in the communities which surrounded the synagogues throughout the Roman Empire, a large number of less priv-privileged people entered it. The only description is in I Corinthians 1:26-29. Certainly there were men of means and culture in the Church. Only well-to-do men had houses large enough for the meetings and generally Jews are not paupers. Nevertheless, on reading the biblical evidence it seems that the Early Church was quite similar to many congregations in Latin America among humble people.

148. We have already noted that in Christ there is no difference between

_____ and free.   see $$$

149. This equality is mentioned because there were many _____ in the Church.   see //

150. The Church grew throughout the Roman Empire among _____ men.   see &&

151. But this Church of the poor did not exclude the _____.
                                        see $

152. The equality of men before God is taught from the beginning through our common descent from

_____.   see ///

153. On the last day also men will be _____.
                                    see &

154. In the Old Testament the history of the rise and decline of the Hebrew nation illustrates the same principle. In order to form the nation God chose
          see $$ _____.

155. When the people wandered away from God and His commandments the prophets
    see &&&   _____.

156. In His incarnation Jesus identified with the _____.
                                    see /

/   humble OR SIMILAR WORDS
//   slaves
/// Adam
&   judged equally OR SIMILAR WORDS
&&   humble OR SIMILAR WORDS
&&& denounced the oppression of the poor OR SIMILAR WORDS
$ rich
$$ slaves
$$$ slave

157. The Early Church was made up in great measure of _____.

see //

158. Write below the six biblical evidences of God's special concern for the poor.

See the list on page 10-21.

These passages do not say that God loves the poor and not the rich. With God there is no partiality. While the Old Testament prophets preached against the rich who sold the poor for a pair of shoes, His judgment fell not only on the rich but also on the poor that abandoned God to serve idols. Wealthy women were among the disciples of our Lord and Nicodemus and Zaqueas were far from being poor. Nevertheless, the humble people are precious to God. His revelation demands that we consider the masses.

159. According to the Bible the poor man is

_____a) Better than the rich man.

_____b) Equal to the rich man.

_____c) Inferior to the rich man.   see ///

160. God judges men according to their

_____a) Culture.

_____b) Economic position.

_____c) Spiritual conditions.   see /

/ c
// poor, humble
/// b

161. The prophets denounced the rich for

_____a) Having more than others.

_____b) Their ways of getting rich.

_____c) Not offering sacrifices to God.   see /

162. God condemns sin in the rich and in the poor. The mere
fact of being poor does not sanctify a person. What are some
of the sins more common among the poor than among the rich?
Why are they more common?

Priority Between the Classes and the Masses

In Latin America much of the missionary effort has been
directed toward the middle class. Beautiful schools have been
built with high standards to attract middle class children.
Attractive churches have been erected in good neighborhoods
in order to reach a "good" class of people. But in spite of
all these efforts the great majority of those converted to
the evangelical faith have come from the lower class. Often
attempts have been made to mold these lower class converts
into middle class churches. Many examples can be found of
churches located in middle class neighborhoods that do not
really serve the people who live nearby. Instead the lower
class members come from other parts of the city to attend the
services.

163. In the beginning some schools were founded to help _____
children.   see ///

164. But the standards and tuition were raised until now many
evangelical schools (and clinics) are within the reach only of
those of the
          _____ .   see //

/ b
/// middle class
/// poor

165. As in the days of the apostles most Latin American evangelicals are of the

_____ .   see &&

166. Nevertheless the culture expressed in their churches is that of the

_____ .   see ///

167. The larger churches in the student's city are located in

_____ class neighborhoods.

Sometimes education and the transforming power of Christ help men to leave their vices and live better. These church members or their children climb to middle class status. But even in this way they win few persons of the middle class for their Lord and His churches.

168. Christians tend to _____ in the social and economic scale.   see &

169. The class which is most responsive to the gospel is the ____.
                                                              see $

170. Even when they become middle class themselves Christians find that they can win

_____ of this class.   see //

171. Meanwhile their education and economic status has separated them from the

_____ .   see &&&

172. Therefore they have _____ opportunity to share the gospel with those who are most open to it.   see /

One of the key questions for the policy of the Church is this: Should we try to win the classes first with the hope that more capable and prepared persons won will be able to win the masses later? Many missionaries and pastors who have had this idea have dedicated themselves to work among university students. It seems to be a good plan since from the middle class will come the leaders of the future. (Although today many secondary school students are from the masses.)

/ less, little
// few
/// middle class
& climb, rise
&& lower class
&&& lower class
$ lower

173. The Church must set evangelistic priorities between the

_____ and the _____ . see &&&

174. Much attention has been given to student work because one
way to climb to the middle class is through
see &&
_____.

175. Examples can be cited of how the lower classes accept the
faith of the upper classes. The slaves in the United States
became Christians because their masters were. In the case of
Jamaica we see that the
_____ accepted the faith of
the
_____ . see ///

However, in general this strategy has not produced good
results. Those in the upper levels of society are satisfied and
do not want to risk their social position by leaving the religion of their parents. Evidence from India, Brazil, and Chile
indicates that greater numbers of middle class persons have been
converted when hundreds of thousands from the masses were already converts. In other words, the efforts to win less priv-
ileged persons in Brazil and Chile have won more middle class
converts than have efforts directed toward that class in other
countries. The situation is complex and there are other factors
to be considered. However, the historian Arnold Toynbee has
demonstrated that often the religion of the masses has been
accepted by the classes.

176. A middle class Latin is anxious to preserve the social
position he has attained. He would loose prestige by becoming
an
_____ . see &

177. Although his Roman Catholic faith is nominal it is difficult for him to leave his traditional religion because of the

_____ controls. see /

178. It is easier to become an evangelical when _____,
although they may be mainly from another social class, have
accepted the evangelical faith. see //

/ social
/// many, others
//// Negros, whites
& evangelical,
Christian
&& education
&&& masses,
classes

179. But if we want to win a large number of Christians now it will be best to work among the
  see /   _____.

180. It is possible tp win more from the middle class if the evangelistic efforts are directed principally toward the
                                          see &&   _____.

181. A social class may accept the religion of another class which is

_____a) Inferior.

_____b) Superior.

_____c) Inferior or superior.   see //

     Our policy with regard to the classes and the masses should be based on two presuppositions: 1) that the masses are opening more and more and will continue to listen to the gospel because the influences on their lives make them more dissatisfied with their present condition; 2) the masses, in certain countries and sectors of countries, vary in receptivity according to the way in which economic and social factors operate on them. In some places they are closed to the gospel, in others very open. On the other hand the upper classes will generally be closed to the gospel although their attitude also can change.

182. In view of the prosperity which has been denied them, the masses will be
see &&&   _____ content with their social situation.

183. In their search for a solution to this situation they will be
     _____ open to the gospel.   see ///

184. This receptivity depends on _____ factors. see &

185. Therefore receptivity _____ from one place to another.
                                          see $

     Since the gospel should be preached to every creature, no one denies the need to present it to everyone whether he is responsive or not. But those elements of the population which are

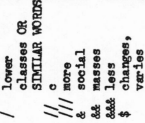

lower
classes OR
SIMILAR WORDS

c
more
social
masses
less
changes,
varies

/
///
&
&&
&&&
$

responding to the gospel have a higher priority. When we must choose between harvesting whitened fields and sowing in others, the first option is God's command.

186. The gospel must be preached to _____. see //

187. The Church should take advantage first of opportunities to

_____. see &

188. Harvesting does not mean only winning souls, but making

_____. see /

189. (Harvesting/sowing) a sector requires greater effort.

_____see $

190. Winning the winnable while they are winnable seems to be a sound policy. This is the strategic significance of our Lord's words "beginning in Jerusalem." While it was possible to win the Palestinian Jews the Holy Spirit directed the Church to concentrate its efforts there. When a sector of the population, whether of the masses or the classes, opens to the gospel this sector must hear the gospel, be baptized and added to the Church immediately. Without resting to consolidate, Christians should seek to win others whom God has prepared. If a sector becomes indifferent or hostile, evangelistic emphasis should be transferred to other sectors where men are ready to listen and obey.

191. We must gain the _____ while they are _____.
see ///

192. At present this means giving priority to the _____.
see &&&

/ disciples
// everyone, all
/// winnable, receptive OR SIMILAR WORDS
& harvest
&& sowing
&&& lower class, masses
$ harvesting

193. In your city or area which elements of the population are most responsive to the gospel? Why are they?

11

THE CHURCH AND SOCIAL PROBLEMS

The Church must always fight to maintain its universality and its identity. The universality requires that it be accessible to anyone who approaches God by faith in His Son Jesus Christ. The identity refers to the preservation of the distinctive qualities of Christianity without being absorbed in the world. Those who promote church growth are concerned with its extension and also want to insure that the members of the Church are genuine Christians.

The Latin American Church faces great opportunities and dangers. Certain factors, some of them religious, permit the entrance of great multitudes in the Evangelical Church today. However we know that numbers aren't everything because the Roman Catholic Church still claims some ninety per cent of the population. There is no lack of nominal Christians. This continent needs disciples of Christ and responsible members of His Church. Such disciples and members will interpret biblical principles for the political and social conditions in which they live. True Christianity has the answers for the problems found in the Latin American countries. However, these answers are not easy nor are they always obvious. The Church needs to study the biblical evidence and God's dealing with the world now to be able to interpret and explain the relationship between the Christian faith and the social problems which cry out for attention in our world.

The Opiate of the Masses?

Karl Marx accused religion of being the opiate of the masses. He meant that religion is like a tranquilizer that is given to the people so that they will be content with the conditions in which they find themselves. Others have said that all

religions are inventions of men to control other men. We can
see the truth of this accusation in Hinduism which has established certain social distinctions or castes as part of its
teaching. Nevertheless, we are not so interested here in the
errors of other religions as we are in the problem of how the
Church can answer these accusations.

One way would be to denounce them as the unfounded statements of insane men. However, if we are honest, we must confess
that there is a certain element of truth in their statements.
There could be just complaints against the Church and its expression of Christianity. It is possible to present here only
an introduction to this topic to show its importance for the
quality of Christians we seek. It is really a matter to be
taken up in Christian Ethics.

1. Marx accused religion of

_____a) Agitating for social change.

_____b) Approving social change.

_____c) Resisting social change.   see /

2. According to Marx the Church taught its members to be

_____a) Dissatisfied with the conditions in which they live.

_____b) Ignorant of the conditions in which they live.

_____c) Satisfied with the conditions in which they live. see ///

3. Therefore he believed that the Church supported

_____a) The rights of the poor.

_____b) The equality of all men.

_____c) The privileges of the rich.   see &

4. According to Marx the Church had become an instrument of the

_____a) Aristocracy.

_____b) Communists.

_____c) Proletariat.   see //

5.   In order to see if it has departed from Christian principles we must examine critically the teachings of

_____a) Communism.

_____b) The Church.

_____c) Another religion.   see ///

Some sectors of the Church have avoided all discussion of the social implications of the gospel. In the minds of many the "social gospel" was a part of liberalism which divided the Church at the beginning of the twentieth century. In contrast with the "liberals" the "fundamentalists" emphasized the supernaturalness of Christ. They stressed the fact that no one can save himself nor establish the milenium in this world. They were correct doctrinally, but this position carried to its extreme separated conservative theologians from some activities which are expressions of Christian compassion and conscience.

6.   At the beginning of this century there arose a division between fundamentalists or conservatives and
                              see &   _____.

7.   Social action was left for the _____ . see /

8.   The fundamentalists emphasized what God has done in Christ and forgot what
                        _____ can do.   see &&&

9.   Therefore the fundamentalists avoided _____(type) activities.   see //

10.   The conservatives didn't want to be accused of preaching a

_____ gospel.   see &&

Faced with the needs of Latin America many conservatives participated in programs which could be called "good works," since it was necessary to serve the evangelical community and the community in general. However, they didn't want to have anything to do with social action for fear of being contaminated by politics. In some places Christians were forbidden to belong to political parties.

/   liberals
    social
/// b
&   liberals
&& social
&&& man

11-4

11. In Latin America clinics and schools were established by the

_____ also.   see &&

12. Nevertheless, Christians were taught that they should not participate in

_____ activities. see ///

13. Therefore the political parties were deprived of the

_____ influence.   see $

During its early years the evangelical movement in Latin America was dominated by missionaries from North America and Europe, who, because they were foreigners, did not have the right to criticize the political and social conditions of the countries in which they lived. On the other hand, nationals not only have the right, they have the responsibility for doing so. Nevertheless, it was never made clear that the missionaries' silence was because they were foreigners and not because they were evangelicals. Many nationals thought that they must imitate the missionaries in everything, including avoidance of politics and social action projects.

14. The right to criticize the conditions which exist in any nation is that of the

_____ of that nation.   see &

15. Foreigners that criticize the government can be _____ from the country.   see /

16. Missionaries are silent about political matters because they are

_____.   see &&&

17. In social and political matters the initiative must be taken by

_____.   see //

Another factor which contributed to the lack of participation by the Church in social matters was the message which it proclaimed and the methods used by many Christians to transmit it. The message was apocalyptic; that is, it put more emphasis on the life to come than on life in this present world.

/ expelled
// nationals
/// political
& citizens
&& conservative
fundamental-
ists
&&& foreigners
$ evangelical,
Christian

The method employed was to evangelize the individual, snatching him from his place in society. Separated from normal social relations and with his hope fixed in heaven the Christian was not interested in what happened around him. His philosophy was that the world passes and therefore we should not be concerned with transitory things. There are still many Christians who are not aware that this is a distortion of the gospel. God seeks to redeem the whole man. Material things are not insignificant in the sight of God.

18. In evangelism emphasis was placed on decisions by _____.
    see /

19. It was necessary, therefore, to remove the Christian from the

_____ . see $$$

20. Thus were broken _____ relations. see $$

21. The characteristic emphasis in preaching was on the _____ age. see //

22. In this way the concept was formed that there was no need for concern about

_____ which exist now. see &&&

23. But the purpose of God was to redeem not only the soul but

_____ . see &&

24. The whole world was created by _____ . see ///

25. Although sin has corrupted much, in the sight of God the material things of this world are (good/bad)
    see &
                                    _____ .

26. The Christian should be interested not only in the transformation of the individual but also in that of the
                                    see $
                                                _____ .

    There is still another element which has been misinterpreted in the message of the Church. The gospel is the good news of peace. It offers peace within for the Christian even though he is in the midst of troubles. He should be at peace with all men. He must turn the other cheek. He should love his enemies.

/ individuals
// future, coming
/// God
& good
&& the whole man OR SIMILAR WORDS
&&& conditions OR SIMILAR WORDS
$ society
$$ social
$$$ world, society

11-6

Without denying all this, it is necessary to recognize also
that as Christians we must love our friends and brothers so
much that we are willing to defend their rights. We must distinguish between personal and social ethics. The police offi-
cer resorts to violence, not for selfish purposes but to defend
the rights of other citizens. Such means will always be necessary in this imperfect world. The Christian is also a citizen
and there are occasions when he must act on behalf of the people and for the sake of justice.

27. The man who accepts Christ as Savior and Lord always has

_____a) Peace with the enemies of his nation.

_____b) Peace with his neighbor.

_____c) Peace in his heart.

_____d) Peace in every area of his life.   see /

28. If the Christian sees a thief commit a theft he should

_____a) Beat up the thief.

_____b) Inform the police.

_____c) Forget it.   see ///

29. Explain your answer to question 28.

30. The Christian should not be careless of his civic rights and
responsibilities as a
                    _____.   see //

31. This world will never be perfect because of the _____
that has entered into every aspect of it.   see &

/ c
// citizen
/// b
& sin OR SIMILAR WORDS

32. A nation can not be governed by the same rules which guide
an

_____ .   see /

33. Sometimes it is impossible to follow the ideals of the
Christian life because the world has been corrupted by

see &   _____ .

Since the Church has been silent with regard to social injustice, other voices have been raised in protest. Consequently, for
many, the current heroes are Che Guevara and Camilo Torres. Even
though we can't approve all of their actions and words, we must
admire their dedication and some of their ideals. Someone has
to protest against the dehumanizing forces in society.

34. In regard to Che Guevara, the Church can approve

_____a) All his actions.

_____b) All his declarations.

_____c) All his dedication.   see ///

35. When the Church observes social injustice it should

_____a) Say nothing.

_____b) Say that it doesn't matter.

_____c) Work for change.   see //

Someone has said that communism is a Christian heresy; that
only within Christianity, with its biblical teachings of the
dignity of the individual and a just society, could such a movement have arisen. Nevertheless, communism distorts the Christian
message when it excludes God from its consideration of man. It
is obvious that the Christian can not accept unreservedly a
system that rejects the biblical teachings of Christianity. Communism is a materialistic system, but so is capitalism. The
Church can survive under any political and economic system but
it can not approve in its entirety any of them.

individual
/ c
/// c
& sin.

11-8

36. Communism is based in part on _____ teachings.
see //

37. Nevertheless, it rejects many of the central doctrines of

_____. see /

38. Communism, like capitalism, forgets the spiritual realm to concentrate on the

_____. see &

39. No economic system yet devised conforms completely to

_____ standards. see ///

Communism prospers in certain areas not only because of instigation from outside but also because certain conditions exist which are favorable to its dissemination. In the past the proletariat was resigned to its miserable conditions. Poor people thought that there was no chance to change their circumstances. But now the masses are aware of the fact that they don't have to live in poverty. Educated men tell them that they have the right to share the fruits of the soil and of their labors. There are seeds of revolution in all the Latin American countries although in varying degrees. Some people are saying that those who hold power, land and privileges will never let them go willingly. They must be seized by force. In some cases the Church must remain neutral, recognizing that honest convictions may place its members on both sides of the conflict. Even so, the Church must interpret constantly the implications of the gospel for the current situation.

An unfortunate aspect of this Latin American dilemma is that many people see no alternative to communism. In their anxiety for social change they despair of change through normal channels and adopt violence to obtain it. Some see the Church as an ally of the oppressors because it does not offer a significant and wide scale plan to satisfy the problems of the masses. As in the case of the "cristeros" and "agraristas" in Mexico, the Church has not provided a biblical base for the recovery of lands lost through conquest and exploitation.

/, Christianity
// Christian, biblical
/// Christian, biblical
& material

40. Many oppressed people feel that the only persons who offer escape from their conditions are the
see / _____.

41. The masses are now (more/less) _____ restless than twenty years ago.   see $

42. Many peoples have risen up to claim their _____.
see &

43. Some people teach that the masses will get what they have coming to them only through the use of
_____. see //

44. Every Christian should follow

_____a) The official position of his Church.

_____b) The example of others.

_____c) His Christian convictions.   see &&

45. Often it seems as though the Church is on the side of the

_____. see ///

46. In all its activities the Church must be governed by the

_____.   see &&&

47. What is the platform of communism in your country? What does it demand? Are these demands just?

communists
violence
rich
rights
o
Bible
more

/ /// & && &&& $

The Church should not instigate revolution among the masses in order to exploit the insecurity and restlessness that results. It should rather help the oppressed to achieve their political, social and economic aspirations through peaceful means. The task of the Church is to reconcile men with their God and their neighbors. Nevertheless, the Church can not avoid completely the conflict between social classes. According to the circumstances it must decide what is God's will to be followed in each situation.

Not only are we in the age of the common man, the future belongs to him. What God requires of His Church depends on the new forms which society is taking, not on the conditions of an age gone by. No one knows what the future will bring. The important thing is that the Church not be a reactionary force that ignores the aspirations and rights of the people and thus alligns itself against the people whom it could win.

48. In times of crisis there are many social, economic and emotional factors which drive people. Therefore the Church should:

_____a) Take advantage of conditions to evangelize.

_____b) Wait until the crises pass before evangelizing.

_____c) Promote conditions favorable to evangelism.   see //

49. The primary responsibility of the Church toward man is to treat his problems which are in nature

_____a) Emotional.

_____b) Spiritual.

_____c) Social.   see /

50. The Church should be a _____ force.

_____a) Reactionary.

_____b) Conciliatory.

_____c) Revolutionary.   see ///

51. The Church must shape its program according to the conditions in the

_____ .   see &

52. The Church can not follow selfish purposes. It must in every case seek what is

_____ .   see //

The Biblical Basis for Social Justice

Sometimes God leads His people, as He did in the days of the Early Church, to suffer patiently social injustices such as slavery (Eph. 6:5-8). There are other passages, such as Romans 13, which teach us the need to submit to established authorities. Study these passages and later answer the following questions.

53. These passages indicate that

_____a) All authorities are just.

_____b) All authority comes from God.

_____c) All government is in rebellion against God.   see &&

54. Civil authorities and the laws which they administer

_____a) Guarantee order in the society.

_____b) Guarantee justice for all.

_____c) Guarantee the elimination of all social conflict.
                                                     see /

55. The Bible teaches that authorities

_____a) Are worthy of respect.

_____b) Can not be changed.

_____c) Always follow biblical standards.   see ///

/ just, right, correct

// a society OR SIMILAR WORDS

/// a

& society OR SIMILAR WORDS

&& b

Although Christians should live in peace with their neighbors and although God desires order in the society, there are occasions when God orders His people, as He did with Moses, to defy and rebel against their oppressors trusting in the help of God. Study Exo. 3:7-10.

56. God wanted to redeem His people because they lived

_____a) In unjust conditions.

_____b) Under religious persecution.

_____c) Without laws to govern them.   see /

57. The basic purpose of the Exodus was to

_____a) Punish the Egyptians.

_____b) Provide an example for the nations.

_____c) Free the Israelites.   see ///

58. Finally, to liberate His people, God used (Exo. 12:29).

_____a) Persuasion.

_____b) Violence.

_____c) Elections.   see &

When He established the Hebrew nation God provided certain rights in His covenant with His people. They should not give up their inherited land nor serve others for an indefinite period. At least in certain ways, all men were equal before God. When Israel asked for a king God warned His people through Samuel (I Sam. 8:11-18). But the people were unwilling to obey and they set up an aristocracy in Israel.

59. According to God's covenant with Israel His people should be

_____a) Land owners.

_____b) Equally rich.

_____c) Servants of Moses.   see //

60. The covenant guaranteed to every Israelite

_____a) Certain civil rights.

_____b) The opportunity to be elected king.

_____c) Peace and prosperity.   see /

61. God didn't want an aristocracy in Israel because

_____a) Some men would have to be subservient to others.

_____b) This form of government is less efficient.

_____c) No other nation had a king.   see ///

       The prophecy of Samuel with regard to the abuses to which the
people would be subject under a king was fulfilled in the time of
Solomon. In order to construct magnificent palaces and keep all
his women in splendor he contracted tremendous debts. He levied
more and more taxes and required forced labor of the Israelites
to provide the materials for various building projects. The revolution exploded in the time of Solomon's son. Read the story
in I Kings 12:1-24.

62. Solomon's mistake was

_____a) Not being wise enough.

_____b) Not being the legitimate king.

_____c) Not respecting the rights of the people. see &

63. In Solomon's time the people were divided between

_____a) The religious and the irreligious.

_____b) The rich and the poor.

_____c) The wise and the fools.   see //

64. The ten tribes of Israel broke off from the united kingdom because the king

_____a) Didn't allow them religious liberty.

_____b) Didn't want to govern them.

_____c) Didn't respect their rights.   see /

65. In addition to the examples cited of how God had mercy on oppressed people, the Bible offers clear teachings against social injustice. Study the following pasages: Isa. 3:11-15; 10:1-4; Mc. 2:1-3:12. What are the evils that God condemns?

66. What form do these evils take in Latin America today?

67. Does God teach in these verses that the masses should rise up in arms against their oppressors?
                                    _____ see //

/ no

·/ //

68. Noting that these profecies were written some 700 years before Christ, we see that God's judgment was carried out by means
of

_____. see $

69. Downtrodden peoples should always seek to be guided by _____.
see /

Racism

Let us consider another matter that presently occupies many
people in various parts of the world. In the United States the
Church has finally awakened to the need to do something to eliminate this form of social injustice. In some circles the fight
is on against segregation with the object of tearing down the
social barriers which have been mentioned. For example, it is
no longer acceptable to have one church for whites who speak
Spanish and another for Indians who speak Quechua. They are all
brothers in Christ and the proof that they are Christians is that
distinctions have been eliminated and they are all one in Him.

70. In many areas there is social discrimination based on certain inherited traits, that is, according to

_____. see &&&

71. This discrimination is one form of _____.
see &

72. Nevertheless, for some the attendance of persons of another
race at a church may present

_____ to their

acceptance of the gospel.   see //

73. It is possible to win the Indians only in churches which are
identified with

_____. see &&

74. These differences disappear only in _____.
see ///

/ God
// social barriers
/// Christ
& social injustice
&& Indians OR
   SIMILAR WORDS
&&& race
$ other nations or
   SIMILAR WORDS

We are not arguing for the preservation of social segregation. However, we must recognize that it exists and that possibly it won't disappear in this generation. It seems necessary to accept as a provisional stage churches which make certain social discriminations. One of the chief purposes of the Church is to win the lost. We must permit all men to become Christians without crossing social barriers and later teach them that among brothers in Christ such barriers should not exist. But for now we must choose between winning people in conformity to the existing social conditions or trying to change the system at the risk of obtaining minimal fruits of evangelism. Those who make up the various races and classes must be converted into disciples of Christ before they can be one.

75. With regard to social discrimination the Church must

_____a) Ignore it.

_____b) Preserve it.

_____c) Recognize it.   see /

76. The chief mission of the Church is to

_____a) Eliminate social discrimination.

_____b) Instruct its members about social realities.

_____c) Win the lost.   see ///

77. The formation of congregations according to cultural or other differences is

_____a) A necessary condition at present.

_____b) The Christian ideal.

_____c) The permanent form of the Church.   see &

78. The individual should get rid of his prejudices

_____a) Before becoming a Christian.

_____b) When he accepts Christ.

_____c) As he reaches Christian maturity.   see //

A few years ago many Puerto Ricans, some of them evangelicals, migrated to Bridgeport, Connecticut in search of jobs. The church people there said to themselves, "It would be a tragedy to set up Puerto Rican churches. Let's open our churches to these brethren, welcome them and consider ourselves fortunate and en- riched by their presence." The Puerto Ricans attended a few times, but later decided that they felt more at home in their own Spa- nish speaking churches. Even more important was the fact that their unconverted parents and friends attended these meetings, but they didn't like the more formal services of the traditional New England churches. Therefore the Puerto Rican evangelicals established congregations in rented quarters and the Church grew. They avoided premature integration. The integration of two groups, if they are not ready, often reduces the growth of the minority group or of both groups.

79. The example of the Puerto Ricans in Connecticut allows us to make a few general observations which are historically proven. The Puerto Rican evangelicals preferred to attend a church where

_____a) They could mingle with English speaking people.

_____b) They could be with others of their own culture.

_____c) They could participate in both cultures.   see /

80. The Puerto Ricans willing to attend a church of another culture were

_____a) The evangelicals.

_____b) The unconverted.

_____c) None of them.   see ///

81. The decision to integrate two cultural or racial groups in a single congregation must be made by

_____a) The majority group.

_____b) The minority group.

_____c) Either one of the groups.

_____d) Agreement between the two groups.   see //

a
b
c
///

82. Really the invitation of the Bridgeport church members meant

_____a) Accepting the Puerto Rican culture in their churches.

_____b) Mixing the two cultures in all the church activities.

_____c) Forcing the recent arrivals to conform to the culture already established in the churches.   see //

83. When two classes or cultures are mixed in a single congregation

_____a) The dominant class runs the church.

_____b) The minority runs the church.

_____c) The two groups have equal influence in the church.   see &

When there is great class or racial consciousness and Christian churches begin to multiply among the people, the right policy is to evangelize each group to its limits. Insisting on integration even when the church doesn't grow is inviting defeat and is contrary to God's will. Christian brotherhood is the result of the work of the Holy Spirit in the lives of believers and not a requirement for baptism and even less for salvation.

84. In a population composed of two races it is better to evangelize

_____a) Both races jointly.

_____b) Each race separately.

_____c) Neither of the races until they unite.   see ///

85. An indispensable purpose of the Church is to

_____a) Obtain political influence.

_____b) Achieve social integration.

_____c) Produce growth.   see /

86. Christian brotherhood is the result of

_____a) Teaching in the public schools.

_____b) Government regulations.

_____c) Being transformed by God.   see //

There can be an exception to this principle. In the large cities a church can be successful simply because it boasts of welcoming everyone and having a fellowship where all are accepted without discrimination. Because of urbanization and social change some class and regional distinctions disappear. If a church has this universal image and prospers and grows, we should be thankful to God. But the majority of such churches never prosper. If we have to chose between spiritual change and social change, we must always seek the first, that is, the salvation of men.

87. The Church of the future will be characterized by

_____a) Greater social integration.

_____b) Less social integration.

_____c) The same conditions which exist now.   see /

88. God prefers a church in which

_____a) Everyone is accepted as an equal and the church grows.

_____b) Everyone is accepted as an equal, but the church doesn't grow.

_____c) There are social distinctions, but the church grows.
                                        see ///

What Can the Church Do?

The Church of Jesus Christ can not ignore social problems and their causes. It must speak and act. One of its responsibilities is the conversion of millions of Latin Americans. Men transformed by God can transform the world. But they will not do it unless they are convinced that this transformation is part of God's plan for the world. Faith in Christ does not automatically resolve all problems. It is necessary to examine again what it means to be a Christian. The Church can not be silent in the face of social injustice. It can not be indifferent to human need. When the Evangelical Church shows Christ's love for men they will be attracted to it. The quantity and the quality of Christians are inseparable.

89. One great contribution that the Church can make toward the transformation of society is the
                see /   _____ of many persons.

90. But faced with conditions which reflect values and practices contrary to her convictions the Church has the
                                    _____

of condemning them.   see &&&

91. After conversion men need to be _____ by the Church.   see ///

92. This teaching should include a study of the _____ obligations of the Christian.   see &&

93. The Christian's social relations should reflect Christian

_____ .   see $

94. The Church that is concerned with the needs of men _____ more members.   see //

95. There should be a simultaneous increase in the _____ and the
             _____ of Christians.   see &

      The Church should provide a theological basis for an equalitarian society. Men live and die for what they believe is the will of God, for what they accept as revealed truth. Christianity offers the only basis which will allow the emerging masses to reach a position of power and justice in the world. The only religion in which the common man can take his fair place in society is Christianity. Marxism arose in a Christian society, impelled by the hopes which the Christian faith had inspired in the common man even though the Church had failed to transform social values in the application of the revelation it had received.

/ conversion OR SIMILAR WORDS

// will win OR SIMILAR WORDS

/// taught, instructed

& quantity, quality

&& social, political

&&& obligation, responsibility

$ love OR SIMILAR WORDS

The Christian foundation for a just social order is quite superior to that of atheistic ideologies that argue for justice, believing that there is nothing beyond this life. The proletariat needs a Christian undergirding in the present era. The revolution to establish the rights of men will be defeated time after time because the men who wield the power are sinners, without faith in a just and all powerful God who has provided the way through which all man may reach personal justice and righteousness.

96. A solid basis for a just society is provided only by _____.
see &&&

97. In the future the humble masses will possess _____ power.
see /

98. Therefore it is essential that they have an orientation which is
_____.   see $

99. Not only for the life to come, but also for the present Christianity offers
_____ to the common man.   see //

100. Any social or political theory is inadequate if it leaves out
_____.   see &&

101. Atheistic theories see the sins of the bourgeosie, but don't recognize those of
_____.   see ///

102. There can be no just society until redeemed men find personal
_____.   see &

103. State in your own words why a just social order can be based only on Christianity.

/   more
//   hope
/// themselves,
     all men OR
     SIMILAR WORDS
&   justice OR
     SIMILAR WORDS
&&   God
&&& Christianity,
     the Bible OR
     SIMILAR WORDS
$ Christian,
     biblical

104. How would you characterize such a society? In other words, what does Christianity offer to the masses?

105. In Latin America there is need for agrarian reform, tax reform, the elimination of corruption in government, and provision of better educational and medical facilities. Complete religious liberty has not yet been achieved nor have all their rights been awarded to the Indians and other minority groups. Read today's newspaper. From your reading and your experience state some of the evils which the Church should combat.

106. The Church can teach the humble to endure patiently any injustice since this life will soon be past. It can also teach that Christians should work to better their condition and to change the structure of society. Another possibility is to teach men that they are being mistreated and that they should demand now their just rights and benefits. If you were the pastor of a lower class church, what would you advise your people and why?

The Church should not only criticize, but also act in a positive way. In the local situation it should labor to better conditions and eliminate social evils. It should teach its members to live and work in an exemplary way in the community. The Christian should work so that he can give his tithes and offerings to God and also supply the needs of his family. Another motive of his labors is to have something to give to the needy. There are obligations for the employer (James 5:1-6) and for the employee (Eph 6:5-9). The servant of God must teach these Christian truths by means of his life and through his exposition of God's Word.

106. If we have experienced new life in Christ, we should be able to teach others how to

_____ . see /

107. In his work the Christian should set an _____.

see //

/ live
// example

108. The Christian should work to be able to give an offering to

_____ . see &

109. He should also labor to supply the needs of his _____ .

see &&&

110. In addition, his work will allow him something to give to the

_____ . see //

111. Christian charity is distinct because it is not done in an impersonal way but in a spirit of

_____ . see &&

112. For all of life we must submit to the teachings that are found in the

_____ . see ///

113. Every church should seek first to ameliorate conditions in its own

_____ . see /

    The Church must make plans to grow. It needs also to plan for the good of its nation. It should inculcate in its members, and particularly in its young people, a spirit of service and sacrifice. In the future the Church will contain a growing number of young people and adults with greater preparation and capabilities. These Christians should not think only of what they can earn in various professions. They shouldn't select a job just because it pays more. Christians should seek opportunities to serve God and their fellow men. There will be opportunities to serve and be of influence that the Christian should seize. Some Christian young people should prepare for careers in journalism, radio, teaching, medicine and other technical fields which will help to resolve the problems of an increasingly complex society. Although urbanization is an irreversible phenomenon, the Church and its members should think also of those in rural areas who need help in rising above deficient and degrading circumstances.

114. Christians should think not only of their own welfare, but also of that of their

_____ . see $

/ community, OR SIMILAR WORDS
// needy, poor
/// Bible
& God
&& love
&&& family
$ neighbor OR SIMILAR WORDS

115. Instead of a selfish spirit the Christian should demonstrate a spirit of

_____ .   see /

116. Economic considerations should not come first in determining a career. A Christian should think more of how a certain position will enable him to

_____ .   see //

117. Mention some careers in which a Christian can more readily serve others.

118. What can the student's church do to better local conditions? What is the responsibility of the church and what that of the individual members?

/   service, sacrifice
//   serve

12

THE URBAN CHURCH

In the preceeding chapters we have presented some growth principles and the social factors that contribute to growth if these
are exploited. In Chapter XII we will examine in greater detail
one sector of society, the city. In Chapter XIII "People Movements"
the same attention will be given to the rural sector. Many of
those who study this book live in cities. Therefore we are
touching upon something of which they have direct experience.
They can react and discuss with greater knowledge and conviction
the ideas presented. This chapter does not pretend to solve
every problem. The student should remember also that his experience is not normative for everyone else. He should approach
open-mindedly the ideas suggested and seek a way of adapting and
trying new methods in the search for greater growth. It will
first be convenient to study the causes of urbanization and its
advantages and disadvantages for the Church. We will also present six keys to cities.

Urbanization

Christianity was born in the City of David and developed in
the major cities of the Roman Empire. The expansion of Christianity is associated with the centers of Roman power in the old
world - Antioch, Ephesus, Corinth, Alexandria, Carthage and Rome.
Saint Paul, evangelizing a population prepared for the gospel,
traveled from one urban center to another. Eight of his letters
bear the names of the cities to which they were directed. The
cities had great significance for the Early Church and they
should have the same importance for us.

12-2

1. Christ was born in the City of David which was also called

_____ (Luke 2:4).   see /

2. The Savior died outside the city of _____ . see &&

3. Paul gave special attention to the administrative centers
of the
_____ Empire.   see ///

4. After a few centuries the headquarters of the Catholic Church
was established in
_____ .   see $

5. From the beginning Christianity has prospered in some _____.
see &

6. Read rapidly Chapters 13 to 18 of Acts and write the names
of the cities mentioned there.

       The importance of cities for church growth increases when
we see that an ever larger proportion of the world's population
lives in them. The movement to the cities has begun and possibly
within a few decades 75 per cent or three out of every four
persons will be born, live and die in urban areas. Urbanization
has been so rapid in Latin America that today the majority of
Latin Americans live in cities. For many years Sao Paulo was the
fastest growing large city in the world. In some countries the
capital has a high percentage of the total population. In nations in the early stages of economic development the movement
of people to the cities is startling.

7. The proportion of the population that lives in urban sectors
is
_____ .   see //

8. Today in Latin America the majority of the population is
(rural/urban).
_____ .   see &&&

/   Bethlehem
// growing, rising
/// Roman
&   cities
&& Jerusalem
&&& urban
$ Rome

9. Urbanization accompanies industrialization and other factors in

_____ development.   see &&&

10. Cities are of great importance to the Church because _____

_____ .   see $

   There are reasons for moving to the cities. In the rural sector of developing nations the machine is replacing farm workers. The man who cultivates a few acres can't compete with machines which prepare the soil and harvest the products. The pressure to leave the country is even greater than the attraction of the cities. Nevertheless, living in urban centers does have its advantages. In the cities men can organize themselves for greater productivity. Urban services and facilities are superior. It is possible to earn more money and buy more things. Greater recreational facilities are available. Medical services and schools are better.

11. Agricultural machines help

_____a) All farmers.

_____b) Those who have large acreages.

_____c) Those who have small acreages.   see ///

12. When a man can no longer sustain his family as a farmer he considers the possibility of leaving the
                    see &   _____ .

13. He seeks employment in the _____ .   see /

14. When children grow up their parents want to move to the city where their are greater opportunities of furthering their

_____ .   see &&

15. In factories work is continuous and a man can earn _____ .
                    see //

/ cities
// more
/// b
& country
&& education
&&& economic
$ most people live in them OR SIMILAR WORDS

16. This regular salary permits a man to establish a budget and give his

_____ to the Church.   see /

17. List some advantages and disadvantages of urban life. From your own experience you will be able to add to these mentioned above.

Industrial decentralization will not change the massive migration to the cities. It will rather distribute cities throughout the whole country. Planned cities such as Brasilia can rise up to contribute to the tendency toward urbanization. This phenomenon is seen in the triangle of Rio de Janeiro, Sao Paulo and Belo Horizonte in Brazil. The industrial network of this sector includes eighty-eight cities. Some of the cities, really suburbs, have received half their population in the last twenty years (Read, 1970:249 ff). The Church must face enormous urban populations that are still growing.

18. Industrial decentralization produces _____ smaller cities.   see &&

19. The inhabitants of these new cities have come from the

_____ during recent years.   see &

20. Decentralization means that there will be _____ throughout the nation.   see ///

21. How to win these urban multitudes is the problem of the

_____ .   see &&&

22. These churches should experience the three types of growth which are
see //   _____ , _____ and _____ .

tithe
// biological, transfer, conversion
/// cities
& country
&& many
&&& Church

23. Nevertheless, continuous and rapid growth will be by means of

_____ .   see //

The task of the Church is to make disciples, baptize and teach these urban multitudes. However the Church is not growing well in many Latin American cities. During the 150 years of the modern missionary movement vigorous congregations in the country and static churches in the cities have characterized much of Protestant Christianity in Latin America.

24. In many cities the churches have not grown much.   They have been

_____ .   see &

25. More rapid growth has occurred in the _____ . see $

26. In the midst of the urban masses the Church must _____ .
                                                      see ///

Success and Failure in the Cities

In spite of the possibility of increases by membership transfer from rural churches, the churches in some cities have not grown well. The failure of the Church in its desire to grow in the cities has not been for lack of resources. The administrative centers of Churches and missions are in the cities. Many of the missionary resources have been invested in the cities. But these resources were used in institutions instead of in the formation of new churches.

27. Because of urbanization city churches should have gained many members by

_____ from the rural churches. see &&

28. However, in view of the available resources urban churches have grown

_____ .   see /

29. Most foreign funds have not been spent in evangelization but in maintaining

_____ .   see &&&

/   little
// conversion
/// grow, make disciples
&   static
&& transfer
&&& institutions
$ country

30. Generally lack of growth has not been for lack of available

_____ .   see ///

31. How many missionaries or national workers of your denomination live in cities?

_____

32. Of those who live in cities, how many spend full time in
urban evangelism?

_____

33. How many give part time to urban evangelism? _____

Many conditions favorable to church growth are found in urban
centers. Migrants, after having severed their rural ties to start
a new life in strange surroundings, have come to the church to
satisfy their need for companionship and social support. These
recent arrivals have left the strict controls of their families.
The priest who had so much influence over them in the town where
they lived doesn't even know where they are. These persons are
open to mass media. Every day they are accepting new ideas, new
ways of living, new values.

34. In order to arrive in the city individuals have made a change
in

_____ .   see //

35. In the anonymity of the city they have loosened social

_____ .   see &&

36. One of those who had exercised influence over their religious
life was the

_____ .   see &

37. The old ways of living were associated with the disagreeable
life in the country. Men are ready for many

                    see /   _____ things.

38. Men become lonely. They seek the _____ of other
persons.   see &&&

/ new
/// residence
/// resources
& priest
&& controls
&&& company OR
     SIMILAR WORDS

39. One of the institutions that should offer companionship is the
_____ . see /

40. Christians should take advantage of the need of recent arrivals to make contacts of a
_____ nature. see $

41. Man needs the security of belonging to a _____ .
see //

However there exist conditions in the city which are not so favorable to church growth. The population in new neighborhoods is unstable. The man to whom we speak today tomorrow may have gone to another neighborhood or perhaps returned to the country. Working hours are long and in the larger cities many people waste hours daily going to and from work. A high percentage of city dwellers are indifferent to religion. Movies, radio, television and other diversions attract them more readily. Preaching can not compete as a means of entertainment. After they have lived in the city for a while they form other circles of friendships and other relationships.

42. The man who has moved once can do it _____ . see &

43. When someone leaves early for work and arrives late, he doesn't have much
_____ to devote to the church. see ///

44. A man who doesn't attend any church for some time becomes
_____ to religion.   see $$

45. In the city there are _____ distractions than in the country.   see &&&

46. In order to win the interest, time and financial support of people, the church must compete with
see &&   _____ .

/   church
//   group
///   time
&   again
&&   other groups or
      activities OR
      SIMILAR WORDS
&&&   more
$ social
$$ indifferent

47. List all the ways in which the urban church can communicate the gospel.

48. Mention activities for men, women, young people and children that can attract the attention particularly of those who have recently arrived in a city or neighborhood.

The urban puzzle that confronts the Church consists of this open and shut nature of the cities. In urban sectors where some conditions are favorable and others unfavorable, some churches grow and many do not. Why? It is very important to discover why a church in the city grows and another is static.

49. Although there are unfavorable factors also, generally the city is more

_____ than the country.   see /

50. Not all churches have been successful. It is necessary to discover why

_____ . see //

/ receptive
   some grow OR
   SIMILAR WORDS

Almost half the evangelicals in Ecuador live in Guayaquil or the surrounding area. The importance of this city for the Church consists not only in the members that live there but also in the many who were converted or first heard the gospel in the city and later returned to other regions of the country. We have already mentioned the tremendous success of the Foursquare Church in establishing new congregations in the city as a result of a campaign. The central Christian and Missionary Alliance church has also grown continually. This strong church located in the center of town has loaned its members and resources to form some eight congregations in other neighborhoods or nearby towns.

51. Due to urbanization city churches gain more members by

_____ .   see ///

52. Nevertheless, many are converted in the _____ and later return to the country.   see /

53. When a church in the center of the city grows greatly it is advisable to establish

_____ . see &&

In the cities of Mexico, one denomination, the Apostolic Church of Faith in Christ Jesus, has prospered. In 1967 it had reached a total of 30,000 members without help from outside. That year it entered the city of Los Angeles, California and established fifty congregations among the Latins in that city and its suburbs. Why has this Church been so successful when other denominations have failed? The answer is found in the book The Serpent and the Dove (La Serpiente y la Paloma) by Manuel Gaxiola.

54. The case of the Apostolic Church of Faith in Christ Jesus demonstrates that it is possible for a Church to grow in the cities without help from

_____ . see //

55. Many of the converts in Los Angeles were undoubtedly of

_____ nationality.   see &

/   city
// outside or other churches
SIMILAR WORDS
/// transfer
&   Mexican
&& other churches

56.   These Mexicans should be (more/less)_____ open to the gospel in the United States than in Mexico.   see &&&

57.   Among the Mexicans in Los Angeles the gospel could be communicated best by a missionary who was a

_____ . see /

In Brazil the traditional denominations have hundreds of congregations in the cities. In 1967 the Baptists had 250,000 members; the Methodists, 60,000; the Presbyterians, 150,000 and the Lutherans (Missouri), 80,000. What is the secret of their success? In the city of Sao Paulo the Baptists have established 130 congregations. Many of these are small, but they function as churches, win their neighbors, and grow.

The largest church in Brazil is that of the Assemblies of God. In 1967 its membership was 1,400,000. The structure of the church is built around 200 mother churches that are located in the nation's principal cities. These central churches, that have as many as 40,000 members, administer the work in certain geographical sectors. Under their supervision many smaller congregations and churches in homes are organized. All the Christians in these smaller groups consider themselves to be members of the central church.

58.   Although there is a central administration the Church grows by means of

_____ congregations.   see &&

59.   One country in which the Church has been successful in the cities is

_____ .   see ///

60.   Because of this success it is the _____ Church in Latin America.   see &

61.   The central churches of the Assemblies of God are located in

_____ .   see //

62.   Small congregations depend on these central churches for the

_____ of the zone   see $

Mexican
the cities
Brazil
largest OR
SIMILAR WORDS
many, small
more
administration
evangelization

/   Mexican
///   the cities
//   Brazil
&   largest OR SIMILAR WORDS
&&   many, small
&&&   more
$ administration
       evangelization

63. All the believers who meet in these small congregations
are members of the

_____ . see ///

In view of the fact that some Churches have grown rapidly in
cities and others have been static there is a real need for an
intensive investigation of the problem. We must determine the
activities, ways of living and means of communication that produce
evangelistic fruits in the cities. It would be useful to know
what are the concrete results of literature distribution, radio,
and other efforts to reach large numbers of the urban dwellers.

Some Churches have loaned one or more of their leaders to
collaborate in the promotion and administration of Evangelism in
Depth in their country. The Churches need to do the same thing
for a study of the problems and possibilities of urban evangelism.
Men are needed who have studied social sciences and had experience
in the pastorate and evangelism and who can dedicate themselves
to this study. The designation of a man to make this study over
a period of a few weeks or months would be a good investment.
The conclusions and recommendations of such a man could increase
the effectiveness of what the rest are doing.

64. The first thing which must be determined in urban evangelism
is:

_____a) The best place to live.

_____b) The sectors most open to the gospel.

_____c) The best methods of preaching.   see //

65. In order to determine the effectiveness of literature one must

_____a) Read the literature.

_____b) Ask evangelicals if they like it.

_____c) Ask evangelicals what effect it has had in their lives.
                                                  see /

/ c
// b
/// central church

66. It is suggested that to study the urban problem in depth

_____a) All pastors should set aside their other responsibilities to devote themselves to this investigation.

_____b) One pastor from each denomination should do it.

_____c) The study should be left for others to do.   see /

67. The designation of one of the best pastors of your Church to make such a study for several months

_____a) Is wasting his time.

_____b) Is a good investment.

_____c) Is to take a step backwards.   see //

68. In Evangelism in Depth many committees, etc. were headed by missionaries since capable pastors could not leave their churches. For a study of the cities do you think it is better for the missionaries to do it or for some pastors to leave their congregations in the hands of laymen or even ask the cooperation of the missionary in the local church if necessary? Explain your answer.

Six Keys to the Cities

Since such a study has not yet been made everywhere there exists some doubt as to the best methods for communicating the Christian faith in the cities of Latin America. Nevertheless, on the basis of investigations carried out in some sectors of the world six keys to the cities are suggested. They are general principles that can be adapted to specific circumstances. These ideas are offered so that God's servants who struggle daily with the problems of urban churches will develop them. They are as follows:

Give emphasis to house churches.
Develop voluntary lay leaders.
Recognize difficult sectors of the population.
Concentrate on receptive peoples.
Resolve the barrier of property.
Communicate a positive and convinced faith.

When the Church begins to grow in the cities groups of evangelicals are formed. Each individual, family or larger group must find a place to worship God and learn more of Him. Many new Christians are not interested in going to a central church or one in another neighborhood. Therefore it is necessary to seek a nearby place for Christians to meet. The easiest way is to buy a plot of land and erect a church. That is, it is the easiest way if the money is available. If the believers think that every congregation must have its own building specially designated for services, the progress of the Church will be limited according to the funds available. But even beyond the economic problem there is another disadvantage, in some areas, in buying or renting a building and putting up a sign which identifies it as the evangelical church or mission. Sometimes a place of worship just dares the opposition.

69. Christians can not live apart from others of like faith. They need a place where together they can
see /   _____ God.

70. Christians learn about the Christian life not only from reading the Bible, but also from
see &   _____ .

71. For this reason Christians need to organize themselves into

_____ .   see ///

72. Many new converts don't want to attend a church which is far from home. They prefer a church which may be humble, but is located in their own

_____ .   see //

73. Generally those who live in a certain neighborhood are of

_____a) The same social class.

_____b) Different social classes.   see &

/   worship
// neighborhood
/// churches
&   a Christians OR SIMILAR WORDS

74. For this reason a neighborhood church avoids _____ barriers to the gospel.   see $

75. A meeting place can be rented if there are sufficient _____. see /

76. Non-Christians within a neighborhood will contribute _____ to the evangelistic work.   see &&

77. If the Christians are few in number and poor, funds must come from

_____ .   see //

78. In addition to this economic dependence on others there is another problem. The name "Evangelical Church" painted on the meeting place stirs up

_____ .   see $$

79. It is difficult for many to leave their traditional religion. Focussing attention on the differences between Protestants and Catholics implies that becoming a Christian means ceasing to be a

_____ .   see &&&

80. This implies that the religion which the Catholics follow is

_____ .   see ///

81. Saying that a man has been deceived in religious matters can mean that he is not very

_____ .   see &

82. Inviting a person to become an evangelical is an offense to his

_____ .   see $$$

     The Disciples of Christ in Puerto Rico enjoyed vigorous growth through many house churches. These groups began as Bible studies to which an evangelical family invited its neighbors, or as prayer cells in which some evangelical families met weekly. Other congregations began as Sunday Schools that laymen directed one night a week or as satelite congregations, with regular services, of a central church. Many of these con-

/   funds
//   outside,
     others
/// false, bad
&   intelligent
     OR SIMILAR
     WORDS
&&   nothing,
     little
&&& Catholic
$ social
$$ opposition
$$$ pride,
     religion OR
     SIMILAR WORDS

gregations were organized at no expense to others, but within the resources of the local group. Those that prospered under lay leaders built simple buildings and began to hold services, at first Sunday evenings and later in the morning also. Some of these congregations grew and became strong churches.

83. The student will remember from his study of Chapter V that the notable growth of the Church of the Disciples of Christ began in the years of the economic depression in the United States and that the Church in Puerto Rico did not receive

_____ . see /

84. The groups began through various activities. Some were organized as

_____ studies. see &&

85. Others emphasized a ministry to the children and were formed as

_____ . see $

86. The groups that prospered became _____ . see ///

87. When the congregations grew in number and the homes were inadequate for meetings, they
              see &&&   _____ .

88. These churches were built or rented with _____
funds.   see //

89. The size and style of the buildings was dictated by the

_____ . see &

90. In Puerto Rico many congregations were born as _____

_____ . see $$

    The house church has some disadvantages. If the group does not grow, the people get tired of holding meetings for years under unsatisfactory conditions. Only those who are friendly

/   foreign funds
      OR SIMILAR WORDS
//   local OR
      SIMILAR WORDS
///   churches,
      congregations
&   local resources
      OR SIMILAR WORDS
&&   Bible
&&&   constructed simple
      buildings OR
      SIMILAR WORDS
$ Sunday Schools
$$ house churches

to the owner of the house will attend services there. The
deterioration of a house used for public meetings can be
considerable. Nevertheless, so much growth has occurred in
places of this nature that we should consider this method not
only to begin a church in a town or neighborhood, but also for
the extension of established churches. We must remember that
the Early Church met in homes for the first seventy years of its
existence.

91. By means of house churches the Church in some areas has
experienced

        _____ growth.   see /

92. We must also consider the example of the _____
Church.   see //

93. Indicate the advantages of house churches. You should include in your list some factors not mentioned above.

94. Indicate the disadvantages of house churches. Add some
aspects to those mentioned above.

95. Some Church leaders say that it is better to begin Bible studies in the homes of non-believers. Otherwise everyone will look to the evangelicals to give the right answers to any question and to assume leadership. What is your opinion?

96. What other advantages or disadvantages are there in beginning in a non-Christian home?

97. Do you believe that a church which meets in a home is more appropriate for work among middle class people than among the lower class? Why or why not?

98. Who in your country or city have tried this method?

Have they had much success?

How would you change the methods used by others?

99. The first key to the city is to give emphasis to the formation of

_____ .   see $$

     Another key is to develop voluntary lay leaders. Laymen have always played a major role in the expansion of the Church. One secret of the growth of the churches in some cities of Chile and Brazil is that they are lay movements. When clerks, laborers, craftsmen or truck drivers teach the Bible, lead in prayer, tell what God has done in their lives and exhort the believers, the evangelical faith looks and sounds like something natural for that kind of person. That which these men lack in terms of education and culture is less important than their daily personal contact with the people. They live and work with those whom they seek to win. No paid worker from outside can know an area as well or have as great an influence on its members.

100. The Church does not grow much if it depends on its capacity to pay

_____ .   see /

101. The great expansion which is possible in Latin America will happen only through the efforts of the

_____ .   see &&

102. Many laymen in charge of congregations have had limited

_____ .   see //

103. They preach to those who are of the _____ social class.

                  see $

104. In comparison with a full time pastor these laymen have

_____ contact with the people.   see &&&

105. The one who can influence a group most is one who is a

_____ .   see ///

106. The gospel must be expressed in the _____ of the people.   see &

/   salaries, pastors
//   education, preparation
///   member or leader of the group or SIMILAR WORDS
&   culture, language
&&   laymen
&&&   greater
$ same
$$ house churches

107. The second key to the success of the Church in the cities is to develop

_____ . see ///

Some new converts are capable of becoming leaders. We must discover and develop their capabilities by means of directed experience. One of the most important aspects in the direction of lay leaders is to encourage and support them so that they gain confidence. God has given many gifts to the Church. Good Christian stewardship requires that all these gifts distributed throughout the membership be developed. Our goal is that all men become disciples of Christ and responsible members of His Church.

108. The capacity or gift of leadership is something given by

_____ . see &

109. The Church's responsibility regarding these gifts is to

_____ . see //

110. Some Christians do not use the gifts that they have for lack of

_____ . see &&&

111. God has given spiritual gifts to

_____ a) Pastors only.

_____ b) Christians whether they are pastors or laymen.

_____ c) All men whether they are Christians or not.   see &&

112. The mission of the Church is to produce _____ of Christ and

_____ members of His Church.   see /

Leaders require preparation which goes beyond Sunday School lessons and the teaching ministry of the pastor in the regular services of the Church. This course and others similar to it represent an effort to provide theological education for those who need and can take advantage of it. In Chapter XIV which deals with indigenous principles we will return to this topic of lay leaders and in that context we will discuss more widely theological education by extension.

/ disciples, responsible

// develop

them,
use them
OR SIMILAR
WORDS

/// voluntary
lay
leaders

& God

&& b

&&& confidence
orienta-
tion OR
SIMILAR
WORDS

113. The Church should help its members to develop their capabilities through

_____ .   see &&&

114. All Christians should receive instruction in the _____

_____ .   see &

115. One of the purposes of preaching is to impart _____ .
                                                  see //

116. Nevertheless, something more is needed for those who want to be

_____ in the Church.   see &&

117. By way of review, write the first two keys to urban churches.

●——●

●——●

                    See the list on page 12-13

118. In the expansion of the Church laymen

_____a) Have had an important place in Brazil and Chile.

_____b) Have always hindered the work of the Church.

_____c) Are the paid leaders.   see /

119. The greatest advantage of the laymen is

_____a) Their theological preparation.

_____b) Their cultural refinements.

_____c) Their contact with the people.   see ///

/   a   teaching, instruction
///   c   Sunday School
&   leaders
&&   teaching or
&&&   SIMILAR WORDS

120. If you were the pastor of a church with some fifty members, what would you do to discover and develop lay leaders?

The third key is to recognize difficult sectors of the population. Not all areas of the city are the same. The city is a mosaic composed of hundreds of segments, some open, some indifferent and some hostile to the gospel. The obedient and intelligent servant of God recognizes this fact and makes his plans in the light of the realities of his situation.

121. Not all peoples receive the gospel gladly. In every city there are sectors which are
                    see /   _____ to the gospel.

122. In order to employ well its resources the Church must

_____ these sectors.   see //

It is certain that we do not know that a sector of the population is hostile to the evangelical faith until we try to penetrate it with the gospel. But if after a year it has not been possible to gather at least five converted families it would be better to concentrate the church's efforts some place else. This rule should be applied particularly when we work among cultured and pleasant people. We like to convince ourselves that God has sent us to work among them. However, especially among the middle class, it is very possible to win many friends but few converts. Let us be aware of this danger of wasting a lot of time on pleasant activities with few concrete results.

/   hostile OR SIMILAR WORDS
// recognize

123. A sector of the population that is hostile to the gospel is one that

_____ it.   see ///

124. The only sure way of knowing if a neighborhood will accept or reject the gospel is to
        see //   _____ .

125. The measure of our work is not how many friends we have made but how many
                _____ .   see &&

126. When we enter a town where there is no other evangelical work we should

_____a) Try all areas with the gospel.

_____b) Evangelize just one neighborhood.

_____c) Use the same methods in every neighborhood.   see &

127. If we see scanty results of our work in a neighborhood after considerable time we should

_____a) Abandon the area completely.

_____b) Give it less emphasis.

_____c) Give it more emphasis.   see /

128. If neighbors reject the gospel we should

_____a) Condemn them.

_____b) Find out why.

_____c) Preach with greater fervor.   see &&&

Opposition sometimes arises because of land ownership. A missionary worked for five years in the city of Sao Paulo with little to show for his labors. Finally he discovered that the homes in that area were built on property which belonged to the Roman Catholic Church. Becoming an evangelical meant losing one's home.

/ b
// preach it there OR SIMILAR WORDS
/// rejects
& a
&& converts, disciples
&&& b

129. What errors had the missionary made in this case?

see &&

130. The third key to urban evangelism is to recognize

_____ . see ///

131. If there are difficult areas for evangelism, there are
also other sectors which are more
see /
                 _____ .

    The fourth key is to concentrate on responsive peoples.
The city's mosaic has some responsive elements. The problem is
to find them. They vary from one city to another. And even in
the same city receptivity and the Church's capability to harvest
whitened fields fluctuate.

132. In a city there are always

_____a) Neighborhoods more responsive than others.

_____b) Neighborhoods very open to the gospel.

_____c) The same possibilities as in other cities.   see &

133. Neighborhoods that are open today to the gospel

_____a) Must be open also five years from now.

_____b) May be open five years from now.

_____c) Must be closed five years from now.   see //

    One group that normally has shown itself to be receptive
is that of recent arrivals from the country. For a generation
they are farmers at heart. Generally they live in neighborhoods with others of like backgrounds. They are hungry for
fellowship and are daily forming new relationships of various

/ receptive
// open
/// b difficult sectors
& a persisting for a long time in a difficult area, not finding out the reason for the opposition OR SIMILAR WORDS
&&

kinds. But it would be a mistake to introduce programs financed
with foreign funds. Paternalistic programs do not create stable
and indigenous churches. This is the surest way of founding
small congregations that will always be dependent on others.

134. In the preceeding chapter we learned that two classes of
persons that are generally open to the gospel are:

_____

_____

see /

135. Those who have recently arrived in the city seek other persons who are
_____. see //

136. What dangers are there in introducing paternalistic programs
in new neighborhoods?

137. As a review write below the third and fourth keys to the city.

_____

_____

See the list on page 12-13.

The fifth key is to resolve the property barrier. Congregations need a place for their meetings and house churches provide
a model with which to begin. But in the poorer neighborhoods it
is difficult to find a home with a large enough room. Unless
some way is found to obtain a more adequate location, the multiplication of Christian cells becomes difficult. The commonest
way to resolve this problem is to buy a lot and erect a simple
building. This can serve as the first church. While it grows
the congregation can construct better facilities until it can
erect a large and permanent building.

/ recent arrivals to the city, the masses or SIMILAR WORDS

// of the same class OR SIMILAR WORDS

138. The first urban key is _____ . see /

139. It is unsatisfactory to remain in homes for very long. Finding a home that is big enough for meetings is particularly difficult in

_____ class areas.   see ///

140. For humble people the church building may be _____.
see &

141. In order to have the resources necessary for a large and permanent church building, the congregation must
see //   _____.

Renting a house or room is another possibility. Even a 3000 member church of the Brazil for Christ Church meets in a building that once was a warehouse. A combination of many house churches, rented quarters and a mother church with a large building seems to work out well for the Assemblies of God in Brazil. On the other hand in El Salvador where the average congregation is of twelve members with twelve more believers and their children, the Assemblies depend mainly on house churches.

142. A church can always seek a temporary location. It can _____ space.   see &&

143. In order to satisfy the need for joint worship, believers who meet in house churches during the week can go once a week to the central or

_____ church.   see $

144. These two possibilities fall within the scope of _____ resources.   see &&&

Many people are seeking the manner in which the Church that is relatively rich in some parts of the world can help the Latin American churches to overcome this problem of high prices for property acquisition and construction. When foreign funds are available it is relatively easy to buy property and build a church. But, although some apparently do not realize it, funds from Churches in the United States have their limits also. If a program of building churches with foreign funds only is established, some denominations will have to limit their extension

/   organize house churches
//   grow
///   lower
&   humble OR SIMILAR WORDS
&&   rent
&&&   local OR SIMILAR WORDS
$ mother

to one or two new buildings a year or even less. Besides, this gives people the impression that becoming an evangelical means receiving financial help and direction from foreigners.

145. Comparing the economy of the churches in Latin America with those in the United States we see that those in the north are

_____ . see /

146. Nevertheless, waiting for funds from the United States is placing a

_____ on growth.   see &&

147. In addition this way of acquiring funds leaves the Latin American church in a position of

_____ on those who

donated the funds.   see ///

148. Therefore there are certain problems in expecting that construction funds will come from

_____ .   see &

Missions and Churches have tried to resolve this problem in various ways. The only fixed rule that can be offered is flexibility. What works in one situation will not necessarily be best for other conditions even within the same country. One of the most important considerations is the rate of growth of the congregation. A church that grows constantly soon will have the resources it needs as well as the will to solve the problem of a church building. Therefore the major problem is not that of the building, but how to promote rapid and solid growth. When this question is answered the problem of the building will be largely resolved also.

149. It is better to have services in

_____a) Homes.

_____b) Rented facilities.

_____c) Facilities according to the conditions. see //

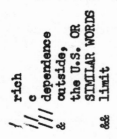

/   rich
c
/// dependence
&   outside,
the U.S. OR
SIMILAR WORDS
&&   limit

150. The congregation should

_____a) Always wait until it can construct something permanent.

_____b) Wait until it receives foreign funds.

_____c) Construct according to its capabilities.   see /

151. If the church does not have adequate income to build

_____a) The pastor should berate his congregation.

_____b) The church should win more members.

_____c) The church should dissolve.   see //

152. Some Christians argue for more humble churches in various neighborhoods and others prefer a large church in the center of town. What are the advantages of each plan?

153. What policy does your denomination have with regard to aid with foreign funds for church construction? What are the advantages and disadvantages of the plan?

The sixth key is to communicate a positive and convinced faith. The primary impulse for the conquest of the cities of the ancient world was an intense faith. This faith shines from the pages of the New Testament. The first expansion of the faith occurred under the persecution which expelled the disciples from the city of Jerusalem. The Early Church was characterized by men and women ready to die for their faith.

154. The first Christians went about preaching in obedience to the words of

_____.   see //

155. They were also impelled by the inner power of the _____

_____.   see /

156. However, the immediate reason for the rapid departure from Jerusalem was the

_____.   see &

157. These men were ready to sacrifice themselves for the _____.
                                                    see ///

The extension of Christianity throughout urban populations was not through human wisdom. The believers committed themselves to God, believed in His revelation, accepted Christ as their Savior and Lord, received the Holy Spirit and as new creatures in Christ with the hope of new heavens and a new earth, they kept and communicated their faith, whatever the cost.

158. The Church spread from city to city according to the plan of

_____.   see &&

159. What was required of these men was _____.
                                                    see &&&

160. The early disciples did not hesitate. They preached a faith which was

_____.   see $

/   Holy Spirit
//   Jesus
/// faith
&   persecution
&&   God
&&& obedience, dedication
$ positive and convinced

161. List some characteristics of the early Christians according to the book of Acts.

Now let us review the six keys to evangelistic success in the cities.

162. The first key refers to the place of meetings. Emphasis should be given to

_____ . see &&&

163. With the multiplication of house churches people were needed who can direct the groups. It is necessary to develop

_____ . see //

164. Two keys have to do with the receptivity of peoples and in particular with the various sectors of the city. The third key is to recognize

_____ . see &&

165. The fourth key is to concentrate on _____ .
                                              see ///

166. The fifth key deals with the economic problem. We must re-solve the barrier of

_____ . see /

167. The sixth key refers to the message and the way of life of the Christian. Evangelicals should communicate a faith which is

_____ . see &

/   property
// voluntary lay
    leaders
/// responsive areas
&   positive and
    convinced
&& difficult sectors
&&& house churches

168. Write the six keys to urban evangelism.

_____

_____

_____

_____

_____

_____

See the list on page 12-13.

13

PEOPLE MOVEMENTS

The concept of "People Movements" may be new for many students. For those who have always considered religion, particularly the evangelical faith, to be a very individual matter, the idea of group decisions seems to be superficial and anti-biblical. But it is essential to know exactly what the term means and how the method can be applied, at least in some cultures. Chapter XIII has to do more with rural sectors where the ties that bind groups are very strong. Nevertheless, there are certain principles that can be applied to all men everywhere. Therefore we must describe various types of movements, indicate the biblical basis of this concept and explain the way of taking advantage of the webs of relationships that exist within Latin American society.

The Importance of People Movements

In order to understand adequately the growth of the Church, some comprehension of people movements is necessary. Such movements have had an important part in the extension of Christianity. This importance is both quantitative and qualitative. At least two thirds of all the converts in Asia, Africa and the islands of the Pacific have accepted the Christian faith through people movements. In Asia and Africa today most Christians are descendents of those converted in people movements. These movements have had their effect in Latin America also.

1.   People movements have been important in winning large numbers of people for the Church. They are important with respect to the

_____ of Christians.   see /

2.   Many times these movements have produced stable and indigenous churches. They contribute also to the

_____ of

Christians.   see &&

3.   These movements have occurred more frequently in the three continents now in economic development which are _____,

_____ and _____ . see ///

     We must remember that sweeping movements toward Christ were the normal way in which the peoples of Europe, Asia Minor and northern Africa became Christian. In the same way, after the Reformation, the Protestant faith was diffused through Germany, Switzerland, Scotland, England, Scandinavia and other nations in a series of people movements of various types.

4.   After Constantine people movements were the means of extending the Christian faith throughout the whole _____

_____ .   see &

5.   In the same way the Protestant faith was spread throughout northern

_____ .   see //

     We can even say that great growth in the future will probably occur through this type of evangelization. It would seem impossible to reach large populations by other means. The relative failure of centuries of traditional work among Mohammedans is in sharp contrast with the conversion of literally thousands of Mohammedans in Indonesia from 1966 to the present. These multitudes did not enter the Church individually. They entered by communities, by whole extended families, by whole peoples. As we have already seen it could be that the resistance of adherents to Islam and other religions toward Christianity is more social than theological. If we can eliminate these social factors they will be able to listen openly to the gospel. People movements are a way of overcoming social resistance to the gospel.

/ quantity
// Europe
/// Africa, Asia, South America
& Roman Empire
&& quality

6.   The great expansion of the Church in Indonesia in recent
years has been among those who were, at least nominally,

_____ .   see //

7.   When large numbers enter the Church together the _____
barriers are removed.   see &

8.   It is possible to reduce social opposition to the gospel by
means of

_____ .   see ///

9.   Has there been a people movement among one of the Indian
tribes in your country? Investigate and describe it.

People Movements Described

    People movements demonstrate a quality which is lacking in
individual evangelism. In people movements whole communities
enter the Church without social conflict, without the bitterness
among members of the same family, without severing normal social
relationships, as has frequently occurred in Latin America. The
congregations that are formed have a complete social structure
with leadership and family loyalty. Instead of mixing converts
of diverse backgrounds, the congregations that are formed in
people movements are composed of a single class of persons who
are already accustomed to working and living together. Therefore
churches born in people movements are more stable, less dependent
on others and better able to resist persecution. Religious convictions are reinforced by social cohesion.

10. In people movements there is (more/less) _____
social conflict.   see /

/   less
// Mohammedans
/// people
    movements
&   social

11. In people movements there is (more/less) _____ social
interaction.   see &

12. One of the Church's problems is developing leadership. But
when a whole community is converted there are already leaders
within the social
                    _____ of the group.   see /

13. In these movements the family of a convert will be (in favor
of/opposed to)
                    _____ his new faith.   see &&&

14. There is greater probability that the congregations formed
in these movements are made up of persons of the same
                                      see $ _____.

15. When a community is converted, the discipline of the church
is maintained by the
                    _____.   see ///

16. Churches founded in movements are (more/less) _____
indigenous.   see &&

17. Because of the social cohesiveness of the group these congregations are better able to resist
                    see //   _____.

       Discipline can be more effective and indigenous. The Christi
community knows how to maintain its standards. It observes what
it really believes. When men become Christians in groups they
can eliminate certain community sins. If Christians decide
that there will be no more liquor at wedding feasts there is no
difficulty in keeping rules set by common consent.

18. Look up I Corinthians 5:11 in your Bible. Would this disciplinary measure be stronger if the whole community is Christian?
Explain your answer.

/   structure OR SIMILAR WORDS
//   persecution, opposition
/// community
&   more
&&   more
&&& in favor of
$ class, cul-ture OR SIMILAR WORDS

19. Congregations formed in people movements are better able to enforce

_____ . see &

    In spite of their importance for the extension of the Church, people movements present a new concept which needs definition. First we must clarify that by "people" we mean a tribe, exclusive society, social class or lineage. For example, the Auca Indians are a people. A people is a grouping of persons that identify themselves as a well defined group.

20. What is it that distinguishes the Aymaras as a people?

_____ . see /

21. What is it that distinguishes the Jews as a people?

_____ see &&

22. The members of a given people know who they are in relation to other peoples. A member of a people can

other members. see /// _____

23. Write in your own words a definition of "people."

    Now, in order to begin to say what is a people movement, we must first say what it is not. It is not just a large number of persons who become Christians. It is not an evangelistic campaign in which many persons go forward. Generally people movements are characterized by a series of small groups that make decisions, one group after another, over a period of weeks, months or even years.

24. By means of campaigns and through people movements many persons enter the Church. One difference is that in campaigns the decisions are made

_____ . see //

/ culture,
language OR
SIMILAR WORDS
/// individually
recognize,
identity
& discipline
&& the conviction
of being God's
people OR
SIMILAR WORDS

25. In people movements decisions are made _____.
see &

    A people movement results from the collective decision of a number of individuals - perhaps five, perhaps five hundred - all of the same people, that become Christians without social conflict, while they remain in complete contact with their non-Christian relatives. In this way they permit other groups of the same people, over the years, after adequate instruction, to make similar decisions and form Christian churches which are composed exclusively of members of that people. It is not necessary to memorize this definition. Nevertheless, it must be studied carefully because every phrase of the definition contains one facet of the total meaning. The whole definition helps to understand church growth which is of the people movement type.

    In order to consider the significance of the phrases in other words, place the letter of the phrase that appears in the column at the right next to the number of the corresponding phrase on the left.

26. ___ Collective decision
see /

a. With the creation of minimal opposition.

27. ___ Without social conflict
see &&

b. Congregations of like persons.

28. ___ Complete contact
see ///

c. Preaching and teaching of the faith.

29. ___ Other groups ... make
see &&&

d. Concern for the well being and unity of the group.

30. ___ Adequate instruction
see $

e. Preservation of all social relationships.

31. ___ Church composed ...
members of that people
see //

f. A continual process of evangelism.

    For a wider understanding it will be necessary to compare people movements with the more common method of evangelizing individuals one by one. This method can be called evangelization by extraction and is the second important way in which the Church

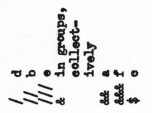

has grown. According to this method the pastor or missionary
seeks only the conversion of isolated individuals. This was
the way in which the pastor himself was converted and therefore
he believes that it is the way in which the few persons he has
seen accept Christ have done so.

32. Most pastors and missionaries who work in Latin America
came to Christ through

_____ decisions.   see //

33. Therefore these pastors believe that becoming a Christian
individually is for

_____ .   see &

When the gospel is preached, the Bible is studied and men
come into contact with Christianity, some individual is attracted
to the Christian faith. He attends the meetings, reads the Bible
and fearing the opposition of his family becomes a secret believer. Finally, mustering his courage, he declares his faith and
in spite of persecution perseveres and is added to the Church.

34. In the evangelization of individuals the convert expects the

_____ of his family.   see /

35. When the individual is won the door is closed to the

_____ .   see &&

36. In effect, the person must decide between his family and

_____ .   see ///

Many pastors, missionaries and workers believe that this is
the biblical pattern. They quote "He who loves father or mother
more than me is not worthy of me..." Other passages come to
mind to support their belief. Therefore evangelists declare that
this way of conversion is not only their own experience but the
only correct and biblical way. Men must expect to suffer for
their Lord. When Christian workers present the gospel, they present this model of conversion as the correct manner of becoming
a Christian.

37. Do you believe that it is better to suffer for your faith
when it may not be necessary? Explain your answer.

/ opposi-
   tion
// indivi-
   dual
/// Christ
& all
&& family

The non-Christian community, noting that men become Christians in the face of family and community opposition, decide that Christians are rebels against society. In the mind of many the idea is planted that becoming a Christian is an antisocial act. Once this conviction is established it is very unlikely that a people movement will occur even where it was possible before.

38. Because of the individual decisions that have been made, becoming a Christian may be seen as an action against the

see / _____.

39. Becoming a Christian is identifying oneself with another

_____ , see ///

40. Those who value highly the identity and integrity of their people

_____ Christianity.   see &

Some Christian leaders reject people movements for theological reasons. They believe that the idea of group conversions is contrary to the individual faith which leads to salvation. They say that men, one by one, followed the Lord Jesus. He called them individually out of the multitude. Following the crowd is not conversion, these Christians say. But this is a misunderstanding of people movements. There is no such thing as a group conversion. A group has neither mind nor body. It can't decide. The phrase "group conversion" is an inexact description.

41. Because of their emphasis on the individual nature of faith many reject

_____ . see //

42. But there can be no conversion of a _____ . see &&

What really happens is the conversion of many individuals that influence one another. What we affirm is that conversion does not have to be a solitary decision against the wishes of one's family. On the contrary, it is better to seek decisions on the part of many individuals related to one another. Many persons participate in the act. Each person decides for himself. He hears of Jesus Christ. He thinks it over and discusses with others whether it is a good thing to become a Christian. He

/ society OR SIMILAR WORDS
// people movements
/// people, group
& group
&& reject OR SIMILAR WORDS group

believes or does not. If he believes he joins those who are becoming Christians. If he does not, he joins those who do not
become Christians.

43. In people movements no one has to become a Christian against
his

_____ .   see &

44. No one decides for someone else, but one's decision _____
that of another.   see //

45. The individual decides, but after discussing it with _____.
see &&

46. The decision is not that of an isolated individual but of
someone who is

_____ to others.   see ///

This interdependence means that all who make the decision
know each other and take this step thinking about what others
will do. It is not only natural for many people to make decisions this way; it is moral. It is immoral, generally, to decide what one will do no matter what happens to the rest. If
Jesus Christ is the Savior, the pearl of great price that a person has found, and if this person is a loyal member of his family,
he will not want to enjoy this salvation in secret. His first
impulse will be to share his treasure that he has found with
his loved ones. The person who loves the Savior will try to
bring his family and friends to Him. Andrew first found his brother Simon, the Bible tells us.

47. He who loves his family will want them to be _____.
see &&&

48. Therefore he will not make his decision in such a way that
his family

_____ .   see /

49. He who finds eternal life should _____ it with his
family.   see $

In a people movement the members of the group try to persuade their loved ones of the benefits of believing in Christ
and becoming Christians. Often they wait to declare openly

/ rejects Christ OR SIMILAR WORDS
// influences OR SIMILAR WORDS
/// related OR SIMILAR WORDS
& conscience, will
&& others, the group
&&& saved OR SIMILAR WORDS
$ share

their faith until they can be baptized together. Perhaps a man
will wait six months or a year so that he can confess Christ together with his wife or brother. It is important to make the
distinction here between the decision and the public confession
of faith. What men do in groups is identify themselves with the
Christian faith or the Church.

50. Many persons do not know the moment of their _____
to become Christians.   see &

51. But later in a meeting they _____that they had
accepted Christ.   see //

52. What is done individually is the _____ . see &&

53. What is done collectively is the _____ . see ///

In any event, the individual is saved, not because he follows
the crowd in a collective action, but because of his participation
in the decision. Almost always he can remain outside the movement. There are groups within groups. If a person does not trust
in Christ he simply joins those who are not becoming disciples of
Jesus. This means of escape ensures that the decision is significant for those who make it.

54. Conversion results from the decision of

_____a) The whole group.

_____b) Individuals within the group.

_____c) The evangelist.   see &&&

55. When a group considers embracing Christianity each member
must first

_____a) Accept the gospel.

_____b) Reject the gospel.

_____c) Wait to see what others will do.   see /

/   c
// proclaim OR SIMILAR WORDS
/// proclamation, confession
&   decision
&& decision
&&& b

56. The action of the group is to

_____a) Accept Christ.

_____b) Identify themselves as Christians.

_____c) Oppose the decisions of its members.   see &&

57. The member of a cohesive group does <u>not</u> have to consider the effect of his decision on

_____a) The life of his family.

_____b) The life of his people.

_____c) The life of another people.   see //

58. The first person to decide to become a Christian should

_____a) Forget it.

_____b) Be quiet about his decision.

_____c) Convince other members of his group.   see /

59. Those who participate in the group action of declaring that they will follow Christ are those who

_____a) Never heard of Christ.

_____b) Want to identify themselves as Christians.

_____c) Reject Christ.   see &

60. Loyalty to the family or larger group and consideration for them is

_____a) What the group demands.

_____b) Contrary to the Bible.

_____c) Of no importance.   see ///

Probably in people movements an individual or a family is converted first. How can an individual stand the social pressure? How can this man maintain his identity with his people? The answer is simple although difficult to put into practice. From the beginning he continues as a member of his people or group. He resists ostracism. He continues to love his people and to identify with them. He spends time with his family and friends to show that although he has become a Christian he still is a good member of the society, perhaps a better member than before.

61. It is easier for a man to be converted if at the same time

_____a) No one else is converted.

_____b) One other person is converted.

_____c) The whole family is converted.   see //

62. With respect to his family the convert should

_____a) Abandon it.

_____b) Be indifferent to it.

_____c) Maintain his relationship with it.   see /

63. There is greater possibility of winning groups instead of individuals in

_____a) New York.

_____b) Buenos Aires.

_____c) An Indian tribe.   see ///

Multi-individual decisions are powerful. They permit individuals to do what they could never do alone. It is very hard for a woman to leave her parents in order to follow Jesus, but when she does so with ten other women it is much more feasible.

64. If a wife is converted but her husband does not want anything to do with evangelicals she should

_____a) Attend church in spite of the opposition of her husband.

_____b) Maintain her faith in secret.

_____c) Postpone baptism until her husband is converted.

_____d) Renounce her faith.   see ///

65. Explain your answer above and write some recommendations for such a woman.

People movements depend on education. Once in a while a movement occurs with apparently little preparation, but we must consider all the forces operating on the people. By means of radio, literature, personal contact and other means the people are educated today with regard to the evangelical faith. For this reason we have great hopes for the future. Never before in the history of Christianity has the gospel been presented so powerfully to those who are not yet Christians. Many people are saying that the Christian religion is good and that some day they are going to become Christians.

We must supplement these vague impressions of Christianity with solid doctrine. We should not prohibit one who understands little from identifying himself with Christ and His Church. However we must provide adequate instruction before and after baptism. The original decision must be confirmed through biblical teaching.

Now let us review the concept of people movements in comparison with individual decisions. Movements have much in common with the evangelization of individuals in spite of the differences. Write movements, individuals or both in the space after each phrase below.

66. The gospel is preached._____ see /

67. There are meetings or services. _____ see &&&

68. A man identifies himself as a Christian no matter what the rest think.

_____ see $

69. A man retains all his social relationships. _____

see &&

70. A man waits to be baptized with his relatives. _____

see ///

71. A man decides to become a Christian. _____ see $$

72. The Church grows through the years. _____ see &

73. The Christian seeks the protection of the mission.

_____ see //

74. A man becomes a Christian in secret. _____ see $$$

75. If it is impossible to begin a movement within a cohesive people after a long time of trying to do so, the evangelist can direct his efforts toward certain individuals. But if he begins with emphasis on individuals it is very difficult afterwards to begin a movement in a large sector of the people. Why is this?

/ both
// individuals
/// movements
& both
&& movements
&&& both
$ individuals
$$ both
$$$ both

76. If you worked for a year among an Indian tribe with the result that many listened to your teaching and attended classes on the faith, but no one had made a profession of faith what would you do?

_____a) Abandon the tribe.

_____b) Concentrate on the individuals who seem most interested so that they would make decisions even if this meant having to leave the tribe.

_____c) Continue with your instruction of the whole tribe. see /

77. Explain your answer above.

78. The efforts of those who hold to search theology have not been entirely in vain. Today we can harvest the fruits of their preparatory work. Indicate the ways in which the people in your part of the country have been prepared to accept the evangelical faith.

79. Suppose that in a small town or neighborhood the majority of the people decided to leave the Roman Catholic Church and join the Evangelical Church. These people know very little of the Bible. Would it be better to organize a congregation immediately or wait until they become genuine Christians? Why do you believe one way or the other?

The Biblical Basis of People Movements

The first ten chapters of the book of Acts mention several times the multitudes that became Christian. The New Testament refers often to the conversion of families. The cases of Cornelius, the Philippian jailer and others may be cited.

80. The New Testament provides us a clear illustration of people movements. The Church expanded among two major classes of people. It began in Jerusalem among the

_____ . see /

81. Later it spread throughout the whole Roman Empire among the

_____ . see &&&

82. On the Day of Pentecost _____ persons were baptized.
(Acts 2:41)   see //

83. These people were not orphans. They had _____ .
see $$$

84. Among the early Christians existed many ties of kinship and friendship. Partly because of this situation they were able to have all things in

_____ . see /// (Acts 2:44)

85. The Church grew among the _____ of the 3000. see $

86. So many persons became Christians so rapidly that the Jewish leaders were not able to

_____ the movement. see &

87. Many Jews had relative who were Christians. Therefore although becoming a Christian meant cutting themselves off from some relatives, it meant also
see $$ _____.

88. Between Judea and Galilee lived another people who were despised by the Jews. Philip went there and preached among the

_____ . see &&   (Acts 8:5)

/ Jews
// 3000
& common stop OR SIMILAR WORDS
&& Samaritans
&&& Greeks, gentiles, Romans
$ parents, friends, families
$$ joining others OR SIMILAR WORDS
$$$ families, relatives

89. Another people movement arose there. All the people were of one accord or

_____ . see $ (Acts 8:6)

90. It seems that _____ were converted. see &&&

91. Because of the animosity between Samaria and Jerusalem probably this Church grew only among the

_____ . see %

92. Among those who attended the synagogues were some proselytes and God fearers that were not Jews, but

_____ . see /

93. At first the disciples of Jesus spoke of Him only to other

_____ . see &&

94. But in Antioch the faith crossed the barrier to another people, to the gentiles who attended the

_____ . see //

95. These Greeks had many _____ in the community.
see $$$

96. When Paul and the other disciples went to other cities they made contact with relatives and friends of the Christians in

_____ . see ///

97. This circle of relationships expanded permitting Paul to have access to the homes of people with Christian relatives in many

_____ . see &

98. Each new group of Christians multiplied the number of _____ with persons open to the gospel. see $$

In Berea the evidence, although scanty (Acts 17:10-14), points to community action because a rather large number of persons or families accepted Christ. They decided to establish a congregation in spite of the opposition of the Jews from Thessa-

/ Greeks, gentiles
// synagogue
/// Antioch, Judea
& cities
&& Jews
&&& all
$ in agreement OR SIMILAR WORDS
$$ contacts OR SIMILAR WORDS
$$$ relatives, friends OR SIMILAR WORDS
% Samaritans

13-18

lonica. All this occurred in the space of a few days. In short, one could say that if the Holy Spirit guided the Church to grow in this way there can't be anything wrong with it. The Holy Spirit can use the same method today.

99. In Berea Paul followed his plan of going first to the synagogue to preach to the

_____ .   see &&

100. But the synagogue community also contained proselytes and other

_____ .   see //

101. It was possible to organize a congregation immediately because

_____ believed.   see &&&   (Acts 17:12)

102. In this panorama of the Early Church three peoples have been mentioned. They are:
     see /
_____ , _____ and _____ .

103. In this way the Church grew by means of a succession of

_____ .   see ///

104. This was the method chosen by the _____ .
                                        see &

105. Study Acts 9:32-43; 16:11-34 and write down your observations of the manner in which the Church grew. Is there evidence here of those principles found in people movements? Explain your answer giving biblical references.

/ Jews, Samaritans, Greeks or gentiles
// Greeks, gentiles
/// people movements
& Holy Spirit
&& Jews
&&& many

Webs of Relationships

If we are to understand people movements, we must become aware of the great variety, each type appropriate for its culture or segment of the population. We have already seen that men like to become Christians without crossing barriers of race, class or language. That is, they prefer to become Christians within their own people. Therefore the norms of each society will determine the way in which they can decide to become Christians.

106. The form that a people movement takes is different in every

_____. see /

107. One key for beginning a movement is to remove _____
barriers.   see &

Among the Spanish or Portuguese speaking peoples of Latin America there are no tribes, but there are many webs of relationships and family ties are extensive. Each individual maintains his relationships not only with brothers, sisters, parents and grandparents, but also with cousins, aunts and uncles, in-laws and God-fathers. All these people are important to him. He is free to visit in any of their homes. His relatives would hide him from the law, help him find a job or celebrate the day of his patron saint. If some member of this extended family becomes a Christian he makes a deep impression on the rest.

108. There are many persons with whom Latins maintain some kind of

_____. see ///

109. A man can expect to receive help and hospitality in the homes of his

_____. see //

110. It makes a difference for him if one of these related persons becomes a

_____. see &&

/ sector,
   people,
   culture
// relatives
/// relationship
   OR SIMILAR
   WORDS
& social
&& Christian

111. It is very important to trace the lines of relationships within the church. Interview at least ten members of your congregation.

How many have no evangelical relatives? _____

How many have at least two evangelical relatives? _____

How many have at least five evangelical relatives? _____

What percentage of those interviewed have five or more relatives who are evangelicals?

_____

The practice of snatching individuals from their families or social ties to become evangelicals causes them to renounce their own people. It assumes that the family will be opposed to the Christian faith. Because of his lack of consideration for the members of his family or other social group, the Christian condemns himself in the eyes of others. Therefore those who reject his testimony are "those of his household." They see him as a traitor and the pastor or missionary as a kidnapper. Once this idea is expressed the Church grows very slowly.

112. Emphasis on individuals reduces the possibility of winning

_____ . see /

113. The one who causes the division is the _____. see //

114. The evangelization of individuals produces more (friends/ enemies)

_____ of the gospel. see //

115. In such a case the Church grows _____ . see &

In contrast with this individual method we must see the webs of relationships which permit a certain kind of people movement. A diagram will illustrate this concept which is very important for the Church in Latin America. We should see not only individuals but individuals who maintain their relationships of kin and friendship with many other persons. We should learn to seek and find the relatives and other intimates who are related to every

/ families, groups
// enemies
/// Christian, believer
& slowly OR SIMILAR WORDS

group of new Christians. Soon we will learn that the faith can
be communicated along these lines of relationships and that if we
do not utilize this means of diffusing the gospel growth can be
cut short.

116. The Church grows only by the conversion of _____. see /

117. Nevertheless, we must see the _____ that each one
of these individuals has.   see ///

118. When a person becomes interested in the gospel we must seek
a way of winning also his

_____.   see &

119. Lines of relationship cross like the designs of a spider web.
For this reason we have adopted the term
                        see //   _____ of relationships.

It will be easier to understand webs of relationships and
their importance by means of a concrete case. The diagram and
its explanation that follow indicate how the gospel spread through
a Mexican village along the lines of kinship. It could be that
in urban areas these relationships are not as strong. However,
certain principles here can be applied in almost any situation.
In the diagram, the numbers indicate the order in which these
individuals became Christians. The circles include those who
acted jointly in becoming Christians.

The first one to become an evangelical was Martin Perez (1).
His action was a shock for the whole village. His wife and sons
reacted in fear and disgust. His father-in-law Fernandez was
angry because of this unfaithfulness of Martin to the Virgin Mary.
Nevertheless, after a few months, Maria his wife, and Leon, his
son with his wife (2), having observed what it meant to be an
evangelical Christian, listening to the Bible and impressed by
Martin's testimony, decided to become evangelicals and therefore
were instructed and baptized. The four met to study the Bible and
pray and they walked to the evangelical church not too far away
for services. These four conducted themselves as good Christians.
Nicolas, his wife, and Maria's younger brother and his wife (3)
attended some of the meetings and at the end of a year they also
were converted.

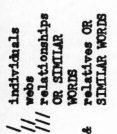

/ individuals
// webs
/// relationships
    OR SIMILAR
    WORDS
& relatives OR
   SIMILAR WORDS

WEBS OF RELATIONSIPS

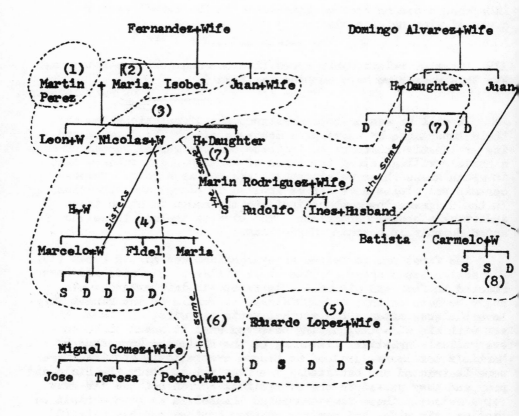

KEY:

Husband+Wife

Son Daughter Son Daughter

Older ————————Younger

120. How did the village react to Martin's decision? _____

_____ see /

121. However those who followed Martin in the evangelical faith were his

_____ and his _____ . see $

122. They were persuaded by the testimony of _____ . see &&

123. They identified themselves as evangelicals by means of

_____ . see ///

124. In addition to their visits to the evangelical chapel the Christians celebrated services in

_____ . see &&&

125. The relatives who were converted in the next stage were those who attended

_____ . see //

126. Nicolas is Martin's _____ . see &

127. Nicolas is Leon's _____ . see $$

128. Nicolas is older or younger than Leon? _____ see %

129. Juan is Martin's _____ . see $$$

130. At the end of a year how many evangelicals were there? _____
see %%

All this did not happen in a corner. Everybody in the village was affected. Some cursed the evangelicals. Others visited them to see them worship and pray. Nicolas' wife had a sister whose husband, Marcelo, was a close friend of Leon and Nicolas. Sometimes they worked together. Marcelo said to his wife "Why don't we become evangelicals? My parents are ready and so is Fidel (4). The evangelicals are good people. They do what the Bible says. I like their services." His decision, however, infuriated Isabel who was estranged from her brothers and spent more and more time with her elderly parents.

131. The conversion of a few had an effect on the whole _____ .
see %%%

/   with fear, disgust
//   services
///   baptism
&   son
&&   Martin
&&&   their home
$ wife, son
$$ brother
$$$ brother-in-law
%   younger
%%   eight
%%%   village

132. Others attended the _____ .   see &&

133. The influence of the evangelicals is felt not only among relatives but also among

_____ .   see //

134. When some accept the gospel and others reject it the family remains

_____ .   see &

    Eduardo Lopez and his wife (5), recent arrivals to the village, were not closely related to the others although they were related in some way to almost everyone there. After attending the meetings off and on for two years they decided to accept Christ. A little later Maria, the sister of Fidel and Marcelo, persuaded her husband to become a believer (6). Maria liked to sing and always attended the meetings.

135. Maria attended the services because she liked the _____ .

                                     see &&&

136. But she waited to become a Christian until she could do it with her

_____ .   see /

    Martin and Maria's only daughter and her husband (7) followed, persuaded by the pastor who visited them and by Maria and Martin. At the same time Ines, daughter of Marin Rodriquez, accompanied her older brother in baptism (7). Marin did not oppose this. He frequently attended the meetings in the church although he was not a believer. Ines and her husband took care of his mother who was a widow. She accompanied them in their faith. Carmelo, second cousin of Ines, had been an enemy of the evangelicals and at first made fun of them when he heard that his cousin and Ines prayed for him. But when he became ill they prayed at his side and he was healed. Therefore he bought a New Testament and read it carefully. When he found nothing about prayers to the Virgin Mary in the New Testament nor mention of purgatory, he concluded that the evangelical religion was the true faith and confessed Christ along with his wife and three children (8).

137. Some relatives were sympathetic to the gospel. Therefore there was hope of their

_____ .   see ///

/   husband
//   friends
///   conversion OR SIMILAR WORDS
&   divided
&&   services, meetings
&&&   music

138. In addition to the influence of relatives, the village was visited by a

_____ .   see &

139. People were also convinced by reading the _____ . see //

140. Many persons, like Carmelo, are more receptive to the gospel when they are

_____ .   see /

141. Make a list of all the elements of the evangelical faith and its expressions in the village that attracted others.

142. How many times was the faith passed from husband to wife?____

wife to husband?____

older to younger?____

see ///   younger to older?____

143. Considering the above data, what conclusions could be made with regard to the lines of communication of the gospel in this type of culture?

This is the simplified story that indicates some of the webs of relationships and the part they play in the growth of the Church. It is worthwhile to consider each of the stages and name the relatives that had already entered the Church. For example, Leon could have said at his baptism, "My mother, my wife and I are joining my father in the true faith." Juan

/ sick, ill
// Bible, New Testament
/// 5,2,7,2
& pastor OR SIMILAR WORDS

could have said, "I am uniting with my sister Maria, my brother-in-law and my nephew Leon." When Ines was baptized, the list of her relationships with other evangelicals would be long.

144. We study webs of relationships because we want to take advantage of them for

_____ .　see //

145. In each stage it was (easier/harder) _____ to become an evangelical.　　　see &

146. It should be the goal of the Church to unite _____ within the congregation.　　　see &&&

The diagram shows us also the members of the family who would be prayed for by other loved ones. After the baptism of the eighth group, Marin Rodriguez and Isabel would be affected by the prayers of all their relatives, as would Fernandez and his wife, particularly if all their children and grandchildren treated them with love and respect.

147. Spiritual conversion is the work of _____ .
　　　　　　　　　　　　　　　　　　　　see /

148. God answers our _____ .　see &&

149. A person is more likely to be converted if many people _____

_____ .　see $

150. The effect is even greater if the person knows that he is the subject of the prayers of

_____ .　see ///

Certainly we can not expect that evangelism along kinship lines will always win whole communities. But we should remember that whole families produce better Christians and more stable churches than do congregations of individuals snatched from their families. These individuals don't even have the opportunity to share the gospel with their families. Therefore we should try to reconstruct these webs of relationships within the church. By all means we will accept solitary individuals when they can not persuade their families to join them. But we must learn what relationships exist among the members of the community and then

/　God
///　evangelism
&　easier
&&　prayers
&&&　families
$　have done
　　his family
　　so, pray
　　for him OR
　　SIMILAR
　　WORDS

carry the good news of salvation to the limits of the extended family and constantly teach that in Christ family relationships are stronger and families are happier than in the world.

151. Christians are more stable if they have the support of their

_____ .   see /

152. When a new work is opened it is always better to try to win first (families/individuals)

_____ .   see ///

153. When a man is won we must find out who are his _____ .

see &

154. One of the motives for conversion is to better _____

_____ .   see //

     Now we need to realize that this series of baptisms occurred in a denomination and area dominated by the individualistic norms of North America. The eight groups delayed four years in deciding to become evangelicals. Each small group made its decision in spite of the opposition of the total community, although as the number of evangelicals increased, each decision meant joining more and more persons who were already evangelicals. Let us suppose that in order to stimulate multi-individual decisions Martin's baptism had been postponed. In this way, while he was still identified with his family he could share his convictions and give testimony of his faith. Suppose that he had said to his whole family - those that later believed and those that opposed - that they should all become biblical Christians together, that they could erect a building for meetings, and that they could continue in their new faith without breaking up the family. Instead of a series of decisions against the group, wouldn't it have been possible to maintain and strengthen their unity? Unified in this way the community could have renounced common sins. They could have received adequate biblical instruction before making their decision. The result would have been the decision of many mutually dependent individuals.

/ family
// family relations
/// families
& relatives OR SIMILAR WORDS

155. Martin's baptism came as a _____ for the group.
see /

156. His individualistic act stirred up _____. see &

157. It would have been better to try for a decision of the

_____. see ///

158. In this way it would not have been necessary to _____
family relationships.   see //

159. In order for a group to decide for Christ it is necessary
that the decision be made by

_____a) An individual.

_____b) The majority of the group.

_____c) Every member of the group.   see &&

     If this had happened the result would have been a larger and
better congregation. It would have been formed with a sense of
unity. On the other hand, it is possible that the group would
have persuaded Martin to renounce his evangelical faith and return to his old religion. Therefore we must weigh all the facts
and decide if it is better to try to win larger groups that will
be strong and stable or if we should win each individual as the
opportunity is presented, knowing that possibly the church will
not grow after a few are baptized.

160. If emphasis is given to the family instead of to the individual the first baptism in a town will be (sooner/later)
                                        see $ _____.

161. If emphasis is given to the family instead of to the individual probably the majority of the town will be baptized (sooner/
later)
              _____.   see &&&   .

/ blow, shock
   break OR
   SIMILAR WORDS
// group
& opposition
&& b
&&& sooner
$ later

162. Explain your answers to questions 160 and 161.

The way in which one begins is what evangelicals and non-evangelicals see. They will believe that the pattern is to become Christians as individuals against the group or as members of the group. When a new work is begun we must consider well the lasting results of the forms of evangelism that are employed.

163. The most critical period in the evangelization of a town is the

_____ . see ///

164. It is then that the evangelist must decide if he will try for

_____ or _____ decisions. see &

165. The concept that unbelievers have of Christianity is based on what they see in

_____ . see /

Care of People Movements

The quality of the churches formed in people movements depends on the pastoral care that the new members receive. In such movements churches are formed relatively rapidly but if these congregations don't receive adequate instruction and guidance Christians will remain nominal. Failure of some people movements has been for the lack of pastoral care, not for the way in which these persons entered the Church.

166. The Church must always be concerned not only for the quantity of Christians but also for their

_____ . see //

/ the Christians,
the Church
// quality
/// beginning
& individual,
group

167. Often in people movements congregations are formed of Christians who know

_____ . see $

168. Generally the quality of Christians is (higher/lower) _____ in people movements.   see ///

169. But this quality is possible only if the Christians receive the

_____ that they need.   see &&

For the first few months after conversion Christians are very open to teaching and they are tremendously hungry for the things of God. But if no one teaches them nor tells them that it is essential for them to grow in their spiritual life, they become accustomed to a nominal form of Christianity. Later it is harder to inculcate important habits and convictions about attending services, studying the Bible and tithing.

170. Habits in the Christian life are formed during a period of several

_____ . see &

171. After this time it is _____ to teach the believers.
                                   see //

172. Without instruction Christians do not become disciples but

_____ Christians.   see &&&

173. Our goal is that they become not only disciples but also responsible

_____ . see /

Regular services must be established and an adequate place for meetings found. Among illiterate people in the country perhaps it is better to have daily services. In the cities this would be impossible. In dealing with illiterates we should overcome our fear of ritualism and use in services memorized passages such as the Lord's Prayer, the Ten Commandments, Psalm 23, Romans 12:6-9, the Apostles' Creed and some hymns. These elements contain the fundamentals of Christian doctrine and will help men who can not read the Bible to establish their faith.

/ members of the church
// harder
/// higher
& months
&& instruction, teaching
&&& nominal
$ little

174. For illiterate persons in the country services should be

_____ frequent.   see /

175. Those who can't read are guided only by what they have

_____ .   see &&

176. Therefore we must teach them creeds or passages that contain the basics of the

_____ .   see ///

177. In the cities also it is necessary to hold _____ .

see &

Training of lay leaders is essential. Voluntary leaders are needed for every congregation. As soon as they learn something they can teach it to others newer in the faith. Theological education by extension should help in the preparation of leaders and also in providing materials and teaching methods that can be applied in the congregations. At the same time there should be a literacy program. The Church is obligated to teach Christians to read the Bible. Only in this way will it be possible to reach a desired level of spiritual maturity. Alfalit now also offers specially prepared materials for persons who learn to read and want to continue their elementary studies without having to attend classes daily.

178. People movements, like other evangelistic methods, can fail. The most common defect is that the people

_____a) Cease to consider themselves Christians.

_____b) Remain nominal Christians.

_____c) Dissolve their social structure.   see //

179. The reason for failure is

_____a) The rapidity of conversion.

_____b) The entrance of many nominal Christians in the Church.

_____c) The lack of pastoral care.   see &&&

/ more
// b
/// faith, doctrine
& regular services
&& heard,
&& memorized
&&& c

180. Movements can be preserved by

_____a) Building large churches.

_____b) Sending well trained pastors.

_____c) Instructing all the believers.   see /

181. Generally Paul stayed in a city to teach the believers until he had to leave because of opposition. If you were in charge of the teaching program for new believers in your church, what instruction would you include as of primary importance?

182. If you were sent to an area where many persons coming into the church lack the preparation necessary to understand the fundamentals of Christianity, what would you do to prevent the movement from failing? What system of instruction could be set up?

e

14

INDIGENOUS PRINCIPLES

In Chapter II the declaration was made that one of the criteria for judging the Church is indigeneity. The concept has been mentioned several times in other chapters with relation to social factors and people movements. Now we are going to examine certain principles which will aid the Church to be indigenous. These principles are very important, but they are not the solution to every problem. Much that has been called indigenous is not. Theological education by extension will contribute to the establishment of an indigenous Church. For this reason, the second part of this chapter will deal with this topic.

Indigenous Principles Defined

Sometimes indigenous principles in church planting are confused with handing over the work begun by the mission to the Church. This step, although good and necessary, does not in itself guarantee that the Church will be governed by indigenous principles. This transfer of the authority and responsibility for the work is only nationalization. Although there may be no missionaries present with voice and vote, their presence is still felt because the policies and practices of the Church are the same as before. Some Churches which have been under the leadership of national pastors and leaders for years are static and can not grow. In order to adopt indigenous principles a change in philosophy and methods is more important than a change in personnel.

1.   An indigenous principle is

_____a) A new idea.

_____b) An idea proposed by the national Church.

_____c) An idea in harmony with New Testament practice.   see //

2.   The most indigenous Church among the following is that which

_____a) Has a national board of directors.

_____b) Depends on foreign funds.

_____c) Grows rapidly.

_____d) Employs methods which fit its culture.   see /

3.   The best way to have an indigenous Church is to

_____a) Change methods which have been imported.

_____b) Cut off all foreign funds.

_____c) Expel all missionaries.   see &

Indigenous principles have been developed for many years.
They were tested and taught by John Nevius in Korea seventy-five
years ago. During the early part of the twentieth century they
were applied by John Ritchie in Peru. Roland Allen, a missionary
to China, wrote books fifty years ago about the need to return
to New Testament methods. These books have more recently been
given the attention and acceptance that they deserve. Perhaps
the best exposition of these principles in Spanish is found in
Edificaré mi Iglesia (I Will Build My Church) by Melvin Hodges.

The simplest definition of indigenous churches is that
they are self-supporting, self-governing and self-propagating.

4.   A church that supports itself is one that receives no funds
from
_____.   see ///

/ d
// c outside,
/// others
& a

5. A church which is self-governing is one directed by

_____.   see &&&

6. A self-propagating church is one that is concerned for

_____.   see &

7. With regard to financial matters, an indigenous church
is one that
_____.   see //

8. With regard to church government, an indigenous church is
one that
_____.   see /

9. With regard to evangelistic outreach, an indigenous church
is one that
_____.   see $

For a wider and more concrete exposition of indigenous
principles let us consider their expression by John Nevius. He
reacted against the policy of his mission which was to pay
evangelists. These evangelists were considered by the Chinese to
be foreign agents to recruit converts in the same way that others
recruited men to work on their farms. Therefore the first principle was to leave a convert in the occupation that he had when
he was called to faith (I Cor. 7:20). Each person should continue the work he had before becoming a Christian. Christianity
would therefore be seen as a way of life for ordinary men.

10. In China where Nevius worked, when a young man was found
who had ability and needed work, he was paid to become an

_____.   see ///

11. The evangelist was considered an agent of _____.
see &&

12. Therefore Nevius thought it would be better not to _____
evangelists.   see $$$

13. Through his usual occupation the evangelist should _____.
see $$

/   governs itself
//   sustains itself
///   evangelist, pastor
&   growth, expansion
&&   foreigners, missionaries
&&&   nationals, local leaders
$ propagates itself
$$ sustain himself
$$$ pay, hire

14. Every evangelist should be a voluntary worker who still continued in the same occupation he had
see /// _____.

15. The evangelist earned his living in the same way as the men whom he sought to
_____. see $$

16. The first principle was that every believer should remain in
_____. see &

17. The evangelist's motive should not be _____. see %

Secondly, pastoral care should be entrusted to lay leaders. These voluntary leaders could pastor the flock. The churches did not depend on paid pastors, but on the leaders who appeared within the congregation itself. These elders and teachers were elected slowly and carefully.

18. The evangelists were _____. see &&&

19. These same laymen could _____ those whom they won to the Christian faith. see //

20. The congregations were led by _____. see $

21. In any congregation it was probable that _____ would have the capacity to be a leader. see %%

22. Capable leaders could be placed over _____.
see $$$

23. These leaders were chosen by _____.
see /

24. The second principle was that _____
_____. see &&

The third principle was a church according to the resources of its members. The congregation could begin in homes of members. It could rent, buy or construct a building when it had the funds to do so.

/ the congregation OR SIMILAR WORDS

// pastor OR SIMILAR WORDS

/// before conversion

& the occupation in which he was converted OR SIMILAR WORDS

&& laymen were responsible for pastoral care OR SIMILAR WORDS

&&& laymen

$$ laymen

% win, evangelize

$$$ the churches

$ money OR SIMILAR WORDS

%% someone

25. The first key to urban evangelism was to give emphasis to

_____. see ///

26. Another key was to resolve the barrier of _____.

see &

27. The important thing was that the place of worship did not depend on

_____ funds.   see %

28. Therefore the congregation had to find a place for its services according to

_____. see $$$

29. The economic level of the congregation determined _____

_____. see %%

Nevius' fourth point was that churches could be supervised by paid workers. These workers baptized the converts and directed the work in general.

30. In the case of the work founded by Ritchie in Peru the work was supervised by five

_____. see /

31. These workers received part of their salary from outside and part from the

_____. see $

32. Supervision of ten to forty congregations required a _____ time worker.   see &&&

33. Therefore it was necessary for the supervisers to be _____.

see //

34. The responsibility of the paid workers was to _____.

see $$

35. Nevius' fourth point was _____

_____. see &&

/   workers, superintendents

// paid

/// house

&   churches

&& property churches

&&& supervised by paid workers

$ full

$$ churches, congregations supervise

$$$ its resources OR SIMILAR WORDS

%   outside, foreign

%% where it met OR SIMILAR WORDS

The fifth principle was to give extensive instruction. The preaching ministry should concentrate on teaching. The congregation should memorize Bible stories, etc. The worship services used these memorized elements. The catequetical instruction was given by lay leaders. Books were used which contained questions based on the Scriptures. These leaders were trained in a month long Bible Institute.

36. The principle cause of failure of people movements is the lack of

_____. see ///

37. Every pastor should instruct the people in his _____.
see &

38. The Korean converts had to memorize teachings based on the

_____. see $$

39. This indicates to us that Nevius' converts had _____ education. see &&&

40. As a part of pastoral care the catequetical instruction was given by

_____. see //

41. Therefore it was necessary to provide some _____ for these leaders. see $

42. They were sustained by _____. see %

43. Therefore their formal preparation would have to be of

_____ duration. see $$$

44. This whole program had the purpose of _____ the converts
see /

The sixth and last principle was that new churches should be founded by other churches.

45. Within a cohesive people exist many _____ of relation-ships. see &&

/   teaching, instruction
//   lay leaders
///   pastoral care, instruction
&   preaching OR SIMILAR WORDS
&&   webs
&&&   little
$ preparation, education
$$ Bible, Scriptures
$$$ little, short
%   themselves OR SIMILAR WORDS

46. Evangelism should be aimed at winning _____. see &

47. A new church should be formed where there are relatives of

_____. see ///

48. The responsibility of the paid workers was _____

_____. see &&

49. Therefore the responsibility for establishing new congregations was that of the

_____. see /

50. The sixth principle was that churches should _____

_____. see &&&

---

51. Now that we have seen an exposition of Nevius' six principles
it will be easier to remember the three briefer principles that
were presented earlier. Write them. An indigenous church should

_____.

see //

---

52. Which of Nevius' principles can be applied in your situation?
Which would not work for you. Explain your answer.

/ laymen OR
SIMILAR WORDS

// sustain itself,
govern itself,
propagate itself
OR SIMILAR WORDS

/// Christians
& families

&& supervise the
congregations
OR SIMILAR WORDS

&&& establish
other churches

The Advantages of Indigenous Principles

At least seven reasons exist for saying that indigenous churches grow better than others. Before examining each one of these reasons a list of key words is presented. The advantages of indigenous principles are:

Extension   Expression
Identification   Multiplication
Leadership   Discipline
Independence

The pastor who follows these principles intelligently considers that the mission of the Church is primarily that of planting churches. The central thrust of these ideas is a passion for propagating the gospel and multiplying churches. The men who have applied these principles have been concerned for the extension of the Church.

53. The will of God is the _____ of man. see /

54. The agency of God in the world to carry out this purpose is the

_____ .   see &&

55. In order to extend the Kingdom of God it is necessary to enlarge also the

_____ .   see //

56. Christianity is spread more rapidly through the application of

_____ .   see &&&

57. Therefore these principles are adopted by those who are concerned for

_____ .   see &

58. The first advantage of indigenous principles is that they can be applied by those who want to
                    see /// _____ .

The second advantage is identification. Non-Christians see voluntary laymen in indigenous churches as people like themselves. In many cases they will be their own relatives and

/ salvation, redemption
// Church
/// extend the Church OR SIMILAR WORDS
& extension OR SIMILAR WORDS
&& Church
&&& indigenous principles

friends. They earn their living in the same way. They live under the same conditions. They are in daily contact with the unconverted. Their changed lives are evident for all to see. The evangelical is like everyone else except that he does not practice certain vices. He has higher standards and shows his love and concern for the needs of others. There is something attractive about being an evangelical.

59. Voluntary lay leaders do not preach to earn _____. see &&

60. Their income depends on their _____. see ///

61. Their standard of living is more or less _____ as that of the rest of the people in their neighborhood.   see //

62. They have more opportunities to testify to the unconverted than the pastor does because they have more
                                    see &   _____ with them.

63. List below the persons with whom the evangelical layman has daily or almost daily contact.

64. With regard to evangelism or the propagation of the gospel the churches depend on

_____a) Voluntary leaders.

_____b) Paid leaders.

_____c) Well prepared leaders.   see &&&

65. The most common method of evangelization according to indigenous principles is

_____a) Evangelistic campaigns.

_____b) Literature distribution.

_____c) Individual testimony.   see /

/   c
//   the same
/// work, job
&   contact
&&   pay, money
&&& a

66. Christians are identified as

_____a) Professionals.

_____b) Another people.

_____c) Their own people.   see &&

  Leaders of local churches learn while they minister to others. When they teach others, they themselves learn much more. In Chapter II the case of the Foursquare Gospel Church in Guayaquil, Ecuador was presented. The Sunday School teachers were named as pastors because they were the best prepared leaders available. These "pastors" grew in maturity and knowledge along with their congregations. The opportunities for theological education by extension that are offered in many areas make it possible today for leaders who need more preparation and orientation to obtain it.

67. A Sunday School teacher learns while he studies the lesson and while he

   _____ it.   see //

68. The one who learns most in the class is the _____.

             see &

69. A Sunday School teacher exercises one of the functions of a

_____ .   see ///

70. Leadership is an important element in the churches. No organization can survive, much less prosper, without leadership of some kind. Local leaders learn most from

_____a) Formal studies.

_____b) The pastor's sermons.

_____c) Their work in the church.   see /

71. The most appropriate theological education for such persons is

_____a) None.

_____b) By extension.

_____c) In residence.   see &&&

/   c
//   teaches
///   pastor
&   teacher
&&   c
&&&   b

72. Leaders are chosen on the basis of

_____a) Formal education.

_____b) Demonstration of leadership.

_____c) Designation by denominational leaders. see ///

73. The third advantage of indigenous principles is that they produce

_____ .   see //

Another advantage is that it does not cost the mission or the "mother" church anything to establish a new congregation. The most capable man available becomes the leader of the group. He serves without salary and seeks the collaboration of the rest. They meet in a home until they obtain the funds necessary to build or rent a building specifically for services. Therefore it is not necessary to await foreign funds to form new congregations. There are no financial limits to church extension. Nevertheless, the church can't go on forever with a minimal budget. When the churches grow indigenous principles suggest that they call full time pastors paid by the congregations. Buildings should be erected also with local funds. As in the case of the Peruvian Evangelical Church, the congregations should contribute to the salary of supervisors. However, for some time these congregations will have to depend on the denomination or mission for assistance in leadership training if they hope to have an extensive ministry.

74. With regard to the property barrier, indigenous principles are not limited in the same way as more conventional methods. It is possible to open a new work when

_____a) The mission decides to do so.

_____b) Funds are available to do so.

_____c) The believers want to do so.   see /

75. Congregations meet in

_____a) Homes for the life of the church.

_____b) Buildings constructed with foreign funds.

_____c) Facilities within the possibilities of the group.

see &&

76. A church that begins in a home

_____a) Attracts neighbors and relatives.

_____b) Attracts all social classes.

_____c) Stirs up greater opposition.   see /

77. These groups should have a full time pastor

_____a) From the beginning.

_____b) When they feel the need and can support one.

_____c) Never.   see ///

78. In addition to local expenses the churches should pay part
of the salaries of

_____ .   see &

79. That which a local church can not do is provide the _____

_____ of supervisors or pastors.   see $

80. In order to establish another congregation there is no need
to

_____ on funds from outside.   see //

81. The fourth advantage of indigenous principles is the

_____ of others for evangelistic work.   see &&&

/ depend
/// b supervisors
&& c independence
&&& preparation,
$ training

82. Do you believe that a church that is not self-supporting can really govern itself? Can it be independent? Explain your answer.

83. Do you believe that a local church which is self-supporting is better motivated to propagate itself? Why or why not?

        The fifth advantage has to do with the expression of the gospel. Natural testimony by all the members of the congregation is more likely when indigenous principles are followed. Local believers know how to express biblical truths in terms that their relatives and neighbors can understand. They may speak of the benefits of being evangelicals. They have a natural interest in the spiritual condition of those who receive their testimony.

        Local expressions and terms used in certain trades or professions may sometimes be used by Christians to give force and relevance to their message. When we are dealing with an Indian culture or other ethnic group the need for testimony by local Christians instead of preaching by outsiders is very important. In Scripture translation certain difficulties have arisen because of cultural differences. For peoples that sacrifice pigs to their gods it is more significant to call Jesus the Pig of God than the Lamb of God. Those who read the Bible in English will find this strange. But an Indian, speaking to members of his tribe can speak naturally and effectively about the Pig of God that takes away our sins.

84. The most effective way of witnessing is to

_____a) Tell your own people the benefits of being an evangelical.

_____b) Explain fine points of theology.

_____c) Invite others to the church where the missionary preaches.
                                                    see //

85. In his testimony a believer should use only terms

_____a) Approved by Webster's Dictionary.

_____b) That are significant for the hearers.

_____c) That come directly from the Bible.   see &

86. Testimony does not have to be eloquent but it must be such that the
_____ can understand it.   see /

87. It is very important for the way of expressing the gospel to be
_____ for the hearers.   see &&

88. The fifth advantage of indigenous principles is that they give meaning to the
_____ of the gospel. see ///

     The sixth advantage is the multiplication of congregations. When all the humble Christians testify of Christ and persuade others to become His disciples and responsible members of the Church, the churches multiply from family to family, town to town, from one valley to the next. A family worship service or a Bible study in a home can become a church without arousing opposition. We must consider the relationship that exists between people movements and indigenous principles.

89. In the first chapter we learned that faithfulness to God that produces church growth is faithfulness not only in multiplying the number of converts but also the number of
                          see &&&   _____.

/ hearers, non-Christians
// a
/// expression
& b
&& significant, meaningful
&&& churches, congregations

90. The use of indigenous principles should result in the conversion of many

_____ .   see &&&

91. These Christians organize themselves into _____ .

see ///

92. If growth takes the form of a people movement the social structure of the churches reflects that of the

see $

_____ .

93. Really each extended family of Christians becomes a _____ .

see &&

94. Therefore an advantage of indigenous principles is that they result in the

_____ of churches.   see //

The seventh and last advantage of indigenous principles refers to discipline. These principles emphasize that discipline be imposed by the local church. What Christian conduct should be in Bogotá should be judged by those who live there. They are the Christian Church in Bogotá. In the same way standards for the Church in Quito must be fixed by the Christians in that city. Rules should not be imposed by people of another culture. We must let the churches be guided by the Scriptures and the Holy Spirit. Lay leaders often avoid the error of pastors in trying to impose discipline alone. If some do not support the pastor in his action, the church is split and the pastor loses part of his authority. Members of a given people can be effectively disciplined only by other members of the same people. We have already seen how the application of indigenous principles in people movements can eliminate community vices such as drinking at weddings and other social occasions.

95. The church can discipline only its _____ .   see &

96. When indigenous principles are followed many of the church members will be

see /   _____ of the Christian disciplined.

/ relatives, friends
// multiplication
/// churches, congregations
& members
&& church, congregation
&&& individuals
$ community, families

97. Because of these relationships discipline is _____ effective.   see &&

98. Standards of Christian conduct can be set only by someone of the same

_____ .   see /

99. Discipline must be determined not by the pastor but by

_____ .   see $$

100. If a whole village is converted it is possible to eliminate some sins of the
_____ .   see %

101. The seventh advantage of indigenous principles is that

_____ is imposed by the _____ .   see &

102. Now let us review the seven advantages. The first is that the application of indigenous principles results in greater

_____ of the Church.   see //

103. In second place voluntary lay leaders have greater _____ with the people.   see $$$

104. The third advantage is that laymen develop into the _____ that the church needs.   see %%

105. The fourth advantage is economic. The church that grows according to indigenous principles can claim
see $ _____ .

106. The testimony of the believers is effective because of their way of
_____ .   see ///

107. The sixth advantage is that expansion from family to family permits the
_____ of congregations.   see &&&

108. In seventh place these principles give force to _____ .
see %%%

/   culture
//   extension
///   expression
&   discipline
&&   church
&&&   more multiplica-tion
$ indepen-dence
$$ the church OR SIMILAR WORDS
$$$ identifi-cation
%   community
%%   leaders
%%%   discipline

109. Write below the key words of the seven advantages of indigenous principles

See the list on page 14-8.

After having said all this we must add that indigenous principles do not always work. It would also be incorrect to say that the church can not grow well using other methods and principles. There is a reciprocal relationship between rapid growth and indigenous principles. The principles contribute to growth, but they can be applied only where the Church is growing. Therefore they should be used in opportunities for good growth and not be adhered to when growth does not result. Where there is much resistance to the gospel, self-propagating, self-supporting and self-governing churches can not be formed. Many factors affect church growth and the use of indigenous principles is only one of them. The mere application of these principles does not guarantee growth.

110. Indigenous principles can contribute to greater _____.
see //

111. But it all depends on _____. see &

112. Indigenous principles function best where the Church is already

_____. see /

113. Therefore they will work better in (responsive/hostile)

_____ areas. see &&

114. Indigenous principles _____ produce greater growth.
see ///

/ growing
// growth
/// sometimes
& the situation,
circumstances
&& responsive

115. Rapid growth is sometimes possible without the application of

_____ .   see &

        A study of people movements will help us to understand indi-
genous principles and the circumstances in which they are effective in reconciling men with God. The Bible furnishes no example
of the use of such principles in resistant populations. Saint
Paul's methods worked because he went to communities of Jews and
gentiles sympathetic to Judaism that were already ready to receive
the gospel. As a result the apostle could organize congregations
after only a few weeks of preaching and teaching.

116. The New Testament gives examples of the use of indigenous
principles only among

_____ peoples. see //

117. Paul could establish congregations because within a few
weeks

_____ believed.   see &&&

118. Indigenous principles work best in the type of evangelism
called

_____ .   see $

        Therefore when the Church is working among a people open to
the gospel it should use indigenous principles. The tremendous
growth of the pentecostals in Brazil and Chile results from
following these principles in the midst of great receptivity.

119. Write true or false before each of the following phrases.

_____We should always use indigenous principles. see /

_____Where the Church is growing slowly it should always
            change to indigenous principles.   see &&

_____In many sectors of Latin America indigenous principles
            would be more productive.   see $$

_____Sometimes it is necessary to use methods different from
            those indicated in the New Testament.   see ///

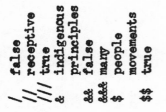

/ false
// receptive
/// true
& indigenous principles
&& false
&&& many
$ people movements
$$ true

_____People movements depend on indigenous principles.   see $$$

_____Indigenous principles should be used in every country.
                                                      see &

_____Saint Paul never used indigenous principles.   see $

_____Among a responsive people indigenous principles should
             always be followed.   see ///

        A common problem is that missions and Churches have al-
ready begun with other systems.   They have an established policy
of paying pastors' salaries and helping congregations to construct
churches.   It is impossible to begin again nor can drastic changes
be made without causing resentments and misunderstandings which
can have serious consequences for church growth.   It would be
better, therefore, to promote the more able pastors and workers
to the position of supervisors and invest in the training of lay
leaders instead of hiring more workers.   It may be necessary to
help retrain unproductive pastors for another trade or profession.
A secondary motive for extending the Church is that of increasing
membership in the congregations to the point at which they can
support, without outside help, a full time pastor if they desire
one.

120. It is very difficult to follow indigenous principles where
others have already employed

                     _____ .   see &&

121. Since supervisors work full time in guiding and instructing
the churches they must receive

                     _____ .   see //

122. The most capable pastors should become _____. see $$

123. The decisions as to whether a pastor should be paid and how
much must be made by the

                     _____ .   see &&&

124. In order to be able to pay a pastor a church must _____.
                                              see /

/   grow
//   pay salaries
///   true
&   false
&&   other methods
        or principles
&&&   church,
        congregation
$ false
$$ supervisors,
        superintendents
$$$ true

125. How many Churches or missions in your country pay pastors' salaries?

_____

126. What plans are there to reduce this subsidy of pastors?

127. If a pastor depends entirely on his local church for his support, will he be very interested in promoting growth in that church? Why?

128. In such a case would the members give more, knowing that the support of the church and its pastor depends on them? Why?

Theological Education

The application of indigenous principles to theological education is an urgent need. For this reason this chapter includes a discussion of the problems in pastoral training and some of the ways suggested for resolving them.

129. No human organization can function without _____ .

see /

130. The second key to the urban church is to develop _____.
                                           see /

131. An essential quality of a leader is to be _____ by the group.   see &

132. Therefore in the discussion of indigenous principles we mentioned the need of
_____ with the group to which one plans to minister.   see //

In Latin America there are some 90,000 congregations, some large and many small. Only a fourth of the pastors or leaders of these congregations have had the opportunity to study in a seminary or Bible institute. Every year some 5000 new congregations are formed. Even if all those who graduated from seminaries and institutes continued in the pastorate they would be insufficient to serve all the new congregations. The number of churches without pastors increases yearly.

133. Most of the men in charge of churches have had _____ formal preparation for their pastoral responsibilities.   see &&

134. It has been said before that the most important aspect of leadership training is what they
     see $ _____ in the church.

135. However, without some orientation from others, the leaders and their congregations are in danger of falling into
     see ///   _____.

136. The principal reason for the failure of some people movements has been the lack of
_____.   see &&&

137. Therefore it should concern us that each year the number of congregations without prepared leaders
_____. see $$

/   lay leaders
//   identification
///   error OR SIMILAR WORDS
&   recognized OR SIMILAR WORDS
&&   no instruction,
&&&   pastoral care
$ learn, do
$$ increases

138. Lack of biblical and theological orientation on the part of leaders can

_____ the extension of the Church. see //

139. The Church must concern itself not only with the number of members but also with their

_____ .   see &

140. To a large degree the number and quality of the believers depend on their

_____ .   see &&&

141. We have already seen that the number of prepared pastors is

_____ .   see $

142. In existing theological education systems there are some defects as to the
see ///   _____ of the pastors which they produce.

The greatest defect of many seminaries and Bible institutes is that they are not indigenous. It is not to be expected that the national Churches would have the funds necessary to invest in founding and operating seminaries. These are very costly institutions. Nor could most seminaries function at present without the collaboration of some North American and European professors. The problem is that these theological schools have imitated the curricula, teaching methods and the student selection procedures of their neighbors to the North.

143. Seminaries are dominated by concepts which have come from

_____ .   see /

144. A Latin America seminary should not have

_____ a) North American curricula.

_____ b) North American funds.

_____ c) North American professors.   see &&

/   outside OR SIMILAR WORDS
//   hinder OR SIMILAR WORDS
/// quality
&   quality
&&   a leaders,
&&& pastors
$ insufficient OR SIMILAR WORDS

145. The problem of the seminaries is that they do not

_____a) Produce Latin American pastors.

_____b) Reflect the conditions of the Church.

_____c) Have the cooperation of the missionaries.   see //

146. With regard to age, most seminary students are _____.

see &&

147. In order to attend many depend on help from _____.

see &

148. Therefore from their student days the pastors have learned to

_____ on funds from the exterior.   see /

149. On the other hand one of the key words of indigenous principles is

_____ .   see &&&

150. Generally the basis for choosing young students is

_____a) Their grades in school.

_____b) Their capacity to teach others.

_____c) Their success as pastors.   see ///

151. In contrast with those whom the seminaries have chosen to become leaders and pastors, the student should analyze his own church or denomination to see who the real leaders are. Of the leaders in your church

How many are married? _____

How many were married before conversion? _____

What is the average number of children that they have? _____

What would be the average age of the leaders? _____

/ depend
/// b
// a
& others,
&& the mission
&& young
&&& independence

How many of them have steady jobs? _____

How many are high school graduates? _____

How many have finished primary school? _____

How many have three years or less of schooling? _____

152. Before deciding if conventional seminaries are reaching the right people in the churches we should consider another aspect of pastoral qualifications. Study I Timothy 2 and Titus 1 and make a list of the requisites for church leaders.

153. Which of these characteristics would not be found in a young single seminarian?

154. Certain other specific problems exist for theological education. The major concern of a pastor should be to

_____

unconverted persons.   see ///

155. But most seminary studies are directed toward the _____
of the saints.   see &

156. The task of the pastor is to teach the people and guide them toward spiritual maturity. But too much emphasis on perfecting produces a

_____ church.   see /

157. Generally evangelical Christians of the first generation have

_____ formal education.   see //

/ static
// little
/// evangelize,
   win
& perfecting

158. In a rapidly growing church many Christians have been under Christian instruction for

_____ time.   see //

159. The Church grows most among those of the _____ class.
                                              see &&

160. A seminary for high school graduates in a large city produces pastors with a

_____ class mentality. see $

161. These pastors find it difficult to _____ with the lower class.   see %

162. Young men from the country who go to the city to study change their way of living. They join another sub-
                              see /
                                                    _____.

163. Often theological education raises a _____ between the pastor and the people among whom he lives.   see &&&

164. It is better for leaders to receive their theological education without a change of

_____ . see $$

    The residence seminaries which follow traditional patterns have several advantages. A student can finish his studies sooner. Some types of studies are offered more easily in residence. The Church needs to produce some theological scholars. Residence studies permit leisure for theological reflection. They also provide a base for other pastoral or leadership training programs.

165. A theological education can be acquired in residence in

_____ time.   see ///

166. It is also possible for such institutions to offer a greater variety of

_____ . see &

167. The Latin American Church should not receive its theological orientation only from North America and Europe. It must produce some

_____ . see $$$

culture
little
less
courses
lower
barrier
middle
culture,
residence
theologians,
scholars
identify

/ &
// ///
/// &&
& $
&& $$
&&& $$$
%

14-26

168. The traditional seminary has its place, but it does not satisfy
_____ . see //

There are several alternatives for the preparation of pastors and leaders. In Korea Nevius directed a month long institute for pastors. The agricultural economy permitted these men to be away from their homes for this period.

169. In some areas it is possible to organize institutes of a
_____ duration.   see &&

170. This would be more difficult for employees in the _____ .
                                                        see ///

171. On the other hand, in the city those who work during the day can study in institutes at
_____ .   see &

172. An advantage of evening schools is that the students can be supported by
_____ .   see &&&

173. Therefore while they study the students are in _____ with the world.   see /

Theological education by extension is a new concept that has captured a great deal of interest. Essentially the seminary goes to the student and can offer him studies at various levels. The greater flexibility permits courses for those who can barely read and also for professionals and university students. They study with others at their own level. The time they have available and their ability determine the time it takes to complete their studies. One key to the program is the text specially prepared for this kind of study. This book is part of a series of some thirty-six texts in preparation for extension studies. Nevertheless, the text must be supplemented by dialogue with others. The stimulus and orientation of the weekly classes is important. This is the advantage of extension studies over correspondence courses.

/ contact
// the needs of the Latin American Church OR SIMILAR WORDS
/// cities
& night
&& short
&&& themselves OR SIMILAR WORDS

174. The student who enjoys most contact with the professor is the one who studies

_____a) In residence.

_____b) By extension.

_____c) By correspondence.   see &&

175. The extension student does not get his information from lectures, but from _____. see $

176. But the application of this information is made in _____

_____.   see ///

177. Extension studies can be adapted for use by

_____a) Those with three years of schooling.

_____b) Those who have a doctorate.

_____c) Any academic level.   see &

178. The student learns where he _____.   see $$

179. It is not so important for the extension student to finish his studies in a short time because he is already
                        see /
                                    _____.

180. How soon can the extension student apply that which he learns in his studies?
        see &&&   _____

181. Besides the traditional residence studies, every day for eight or nine months of the year, there are four alternate forms of theological education. Write them below.

_____ , _____ , _____ and _____.
                                                        see //

/ in the work
   OR SIMILAR WORDS
// extension,
    short term,
    night school,
    correspondence
    weekly classes
& c
&& a
&&& immediately
     OR SIMILAR WORDS
$ books, texts
$$ works, lives,
    serves

182. What system of theological education is most convenient for you? Why?

183. What courses do you most need to study to be a leader of the Church in your area or city? Why are these courses impor-tant?

15

PLANS FOR GROWTH

Chapter XV seeks to apply all that has been studied so far. As has been said, mere knowledge of principles is not of great practical value. This course should not be considered only an academic exercise. It aims to stimulate thinking and investigation. It hopes to change policies and methods. Its object is to produce Christian leaders who will guide their churches in fruitful labor in these years of great opportunity in which we live. Comprehension of this subject should manifest itself not only in the ability to answer certain questions, but even more so in growth in the student's church. This growth probably will be the result of a specific plan formulated on the basis of church growth principles.

The Need for Plans

Many pastors and other leaders act as though church growth occurred automatically without having to make plans. They say, at least to themselves, that if they just continue what they are doing churches will spring up sooner or later. This could be, but we should be concerned that it be sooner and not later. It is possible to spend thirty years in preparation when the Church could have harvested during the whole period. If we believe that expansion is the principal mission of the Church and that all secondary activities should contribute toward this goal, we must make definite plans to reach the desired objective. We must have well defined objectives and measure our progress toward them. Without plans it is possible to float aimlessly swept along by the currents of popular ideas or by many other pressures or influences.

1.   Church growth is more rapid and certain if everyone works according to

_____ .   see /

2.   Even though the Church can not produce political and social conditions it should be ready to take advantage of

see $ _____ .

3.   An important aspect of plans is that of fixing _____ for the work.   see ///

4.   If there are goals it is possible to _____ the success of the Church in reaching them.   see &

It is not sufficient to be faithful in maintaining an institution or program. It is not enough to do "solid missionary work." God demands results consonant with the possibilities. He requires that our efforts be not only dedicated but also intelligent. Our responsibility is to make disciples and multiply churches.

5.   Plans are necessary to

_____a) Give direction to our efforts.

_____b) Measure our success in the past.

_____c) Continue activities already established.   see &&&

6.   Greater growth occurs when

_____a) Plans are made to obtain it.

_____b) We make preparations for a harvest some day.

_____c) We let circumstances guide us.   see //

7.   We should continue present methods

_____a) No matter what happens.

_____b) If they produce good results.

_____c) If there is some way of improving them.   see &&

plans
/
goals
///
measure
&
b
&&
a
&&&
the satu-
ation OR
SIMILAR
WORDS
$

8.   Our primary mission is to

_____a) Extend the Church.

_____b) Maintain the Church.

_____c) Perfect the Church.   see //

9.   Institutions, whether educational, medical or social,

_____a) Should be independent of the Church.

_____b) Should contribute to the Church.

_____c) Should be maintained at all cost.   see ///

10. With regard to the results of our labor

_____a) God requires that we win a certain number of souls.

_____b) Faithfulness implies responsibility.

_____c) We need not be concerned with results.   see /

Church growth rarely occurs unless bold plans are made to promote it. The apostle Paul had a plan which he used in city after city to form congregations. He began with Jews, winning his fellow countrymen for Christ without demanding that they leave their Jewish practices to become Christians. Later he went to the God-fearers and other gentiles to teach them that they could have all the spiritual blessings of Judaism without becoming proselytes and assuming the burden of the law. Paul concentrated his efforts in the cities, not only because they were centers of communication, transportation and commerce, but also because of the Jewish communities found in them. These Jews had relatives in Jerusalem and elsewhere who had already been converted to Christianity. He worked along the webs of relationships of the Jewish people. Paul gained entrance to the Jews by means of the synagogue and later continued with the gentiles who attended the synagogue. In this way the gospel spread and the Church achieved the rapid expansion it needed in the first years of its existence.

11. At least five aspects of Paul's plan can be observed. In the first place his efforts were concentrated in the

see && _____.

12. Secondly he preached first to the _____ . see ///

13. Later he took the universal message of Christ to _____.

see &&&

14. In the case of both peoples he made his initial contacts through the

_____ . see //

15. Paul sought out _____ of Christians in other cities.

see &

16. In this way he took advantage of the _____ that existed among these peoples. see $$$

17. Sum up the five aspects of Paul's plan with a word or phrase for each. _____

see /

18. Paul began in the cities in order to reach the regions of which they were the centers of

_____ . see ⚡

19. His work commenced there also because the cities contained communities of

_____ . see $$

Today also the only way in which the good news of Jesus Christ can reach the earth's multitudes is by fantastic growth of the Church. The only way in which Christian values, economic justice, racial brotherhood and social improvement can be augmented is through the multiplication of ever enlarging groups of believers.

20. For the individual the gospel means _____ . see $

/ cities, Jews, gentiles, synagogues, webs of relations OR SIMILAR WORDS

// synagogues

/// Jews

& relatives, friends

&& cities

&&& gentiles, Greeks

$ salvation

$$ Jews

$$$ webs of relationships

⚡ communication

21. But it also means the transformation of the _____.

                        see ///

      Under the direction of the Holy Spirit and the Word of God Christians develop new forms of the Church and new ways of worshiping and serving God within it. But the Church continues to be God's agency for the evangelization of men and their edification in the things of God. These new forms and methods of reaching certain elements of the population more effectively will grow out of plans and these plans depend on sharing knowledge and experiences among the various evangelical groups.

22. Plans must be made under the guidance of the _____.

                        see &

23. So that Christianity will be expressed in ways natural to various peoples it is necessary to adopt new forms and structures in the

      _____. see $$

24. Although the structure of the Church may be changed, there is no change in its

      _____. see &&&

25. It is more likely that the Church will fulfill its mission if it makes

      _____ to do so.   see /

26. In order to reach other sectors of the population the Church must try new

      _____. see &&

27. Changes of policy and practices should not be arbitrary but should be based on

      _____. see //

28. Knowledge increases if it is shared among _____.

                        see $

      In considering the place of plans in the growth of the Church we might well consider the rapid growth of the Methodist Church two centuries ago. The meetings of Wesley's followers did not just happen. They were formed and governed according to Wesley's plans. Wesley was not just a great preacher; he was a

plans \
knowledge //\
society ///\
Holy Spirit &\
methods &&\
mission, &&&\
purpose $\
all OR SIMILAR WORDS $$\
Church $$

great administrator. He insisted that the new believers form groups to study the Bible. These groups grew and formed churches. Meetings for evangelization and deeper life were organized and a man was not considered completely saved until he had become a member of the Methodist Church.

29. Wesley's groups

_____a) Were spontaneous.

_____b) Did not have any fixed purpose.

_____c) Followed Wesley's plan.   see /

30. Wesley and his followers applied methods which were

_____a) Antibiblical.

_____b) Indigenous.

_____c) Paternalistic.   see ///

The successful extension of the Church in many areas could be attributed to definite plans. Even the success of the pentecostal churches in Brazil, churches apparently without a great deal of structure, was the fruit of certain convictions about the responsibility of the Church and its members. The Assemblies of God in Brazil have baptized hundreds of thousands of persons and not by pure chance. This growth was planned. The Assemblies have grown so tremendously in Brazil because of bold plans well executed by the common believers.

An essential element of their plans was the conviction that wherever a member of the Assemblies of God went he had the responsibility and privilege of winning his fellow men to the same faith in Christ. These converts should meet frequently for prayer, worship and evangelization.

31. It is important for the ordinary believers to

_____a) Develop plans.

_____b) Understand all aspects of the plans.

_____c) Carry out their part of the plans.   see //

32. The members of the Assemblies of God believe that it is their responsibility to

_____a) Attend any church.

_____b) Change the church.

_____c) Plant a church of their denomination.   see /

33. One part of evangelistic plans should be to inculcate in the members certain

_____ .   see ///

34. When making plans we should remember that indoctrination can be as important as organization. In order to promote church growth what convictions should we inculcate in the church members? The student should not be limited to the suggestions in the text.

The Church of Jesus Christ must be concerned about the two billions of persons in the world that are outside the Christian faith. No one knows what proportion of these people will be saved before the Lord returns. But the Church must win all that it can. The mission of the Church is complex. We can not be content to work for the conversion of individuals and groups and the formation of churches. We must teach, guide, exhort. The second half of the Great Commission is "teaching them to observe all that I have commanded you." The Church is responsible for the perfecting of the saints.

35. The Church's mission is to

_____a) Determine how many will be saved.

_____b) Preach the message of salvation.

_____c) Save all that it can.   see //

c convic-
c tions OR
SIMILAR
WORDS
/// /

36. What the Church should do first is to

_____a) Change the society.

_____b) Make more disciples.

_____c) Perfect the saints.   see //

37. With regard to social reform

_____a) It should be the result of the conversion of many.

_____b) It is impossible without Christ.

_____c) It is not the task of the Church.   see &

38. Which of the following is not a legitimate concern of the Church?

_____a) Social action.

_____b) Teaching.

_____c) Speculation.

_____d) Evangelization.

_____e) Planification.

_____f) Theology.   see ///

    Before the Church can dedicate itself to all these activities, congregations must be formed. It is possible to perfect only those who have become disciples of Christ and members of His Church. The influence of the Church in society depends on its size. We can not believe that God prefers to work through those who reject His Son and His revelation rather than working through the Church, the body of Christ.

39. Among all these good things the first obligation of the Church is to _____.   see /

40. The Church's mission, according to Chapter III is to

_____

_____

_____ . See the definition on page 3-7.

41. Therefore the Church is concerned for the _____
and the
_____ of its members.   see &

42. This means that God desires the transformation not only of
the individual, but also of the
_____ . see //

43. Social change which will glorify God can be carried out by

_____ . see /

Carrying Out Plans

The first goal of the student of church growth should be to
develop an intelligent and practical plan for planting churches.
It must be a plan specifically designed for the population in
which he works, although it will occupy many ideas from the work
among similar peoples. It must be a plan that takes into consideration the available resources and even the personal factors in
the situation. If a pastor lives in a town of 30,000 his plan
should indicate how to win those 30,000. It must be a plan which
includes everyone and also that meets certain Christian standards. It is unlikely that the 30,000, or even a large percentage of them will be won in the near future. Nevertheless, his
responsibility is to present the gospel in such a way that becoming a Christian is a live option for each inhabitant of the
city. Therefore a plan or plans are needed which will reach all
the various elements of the population.

44. A plan must be

_____a) Very detailed.

_____b) Very original.

_____c) Very practical.   see ///

/ Christ-
ians,
the
Church

& society

/// c
quantity,
quality
OR SIM-
ILAR
WORDS

45. With regard to the total population the plan

_____a) Gives the same attention to all groups.

_____b) Gives everyone opportunity for conversion.

_____c) Presumes that everyone will be converted.   see //

46. The plan must maintain the Church's

_____a) Exclusivism.

_____b) Identity.

_____c) Prestige.   see &

47. The value of a plan is shown by its _____. see &&

48. We must take into consideration not only the needs but also the

_____.   see ///

49. What part of the population should be included in the plan?
_____   see /

50. Nevertheless the plan should give priority to _____
sectors.   see &&&

     The ultimate goal is to carry out the plans. It is not suf-
ficient to produce a few strategists who sit at their desks making plans. The proof of a plan is seen in the results in lives,
not on paper. The best plan is worthless if it is not acted upon.
It is better to put into effect a plan that has many defects
than to wait until a perfect plan is drawn up. If the administrative committee of the Church does not offer a program, the
worker or layman will have to work out his own plan to the best
of his ability. The only plan of any use is that which is in
effect.

/   all
b
/// resources,
possibilities,
opportunities
b
&   results, fruits
&& receptive, open

51. The mere fact of having a plan does not win the battle. It is only the first step. The best plan is one that

_____a) Considers all the factors.

_____b) Produces results.

_____c) Follows established practices.   see /

52. A plan should be put into effect when

_____a) It has been perfected.

_____b) No better plan exists.

_____c) Someone asks for a plan.   see ///

53. The local believers have the responsibility of

_____a) Developing their own plan if necessary.

_____b) Waiting for a plan made somewhere else.

_____c) Not doing anything beyond plans made by the central committee.   see //

    It is a mistake to think that we can do nothing until the spiritual condition of the Church improves. It is an error to believe that we must go deeper before we can go father. The two processes must take place at the same time. A church that is so concerned with its own perfection that it does not evangelize has another spiritual defect of which it is unaware. It is good to pray for revival, but let us not wait for revival before we visit and preach to those who have no spiritual life to be revived. The evidence of the New Testament indicates that the rapid growth of the first century was by means of a carnal Church. The great missionary movement of the nineteenth century was carried out by Churches that sometimes fought with each other. They certainly were imperfect churches. It is true that many of the leaders of this movement were products of revival. But they were not satisfied to perfect and purify their own churches before planting other congregations in many parts of the world.

54. Effective witnessing does not depend so much on the Christians' perfection as on the power of

_____ .   see /

55. The believer should testify as soon as he

_____a) Receives instruction.

_____b) Is revived.

_____c) Accepts Christ.   see &

56. With regard to the persons whom he tries to win, the first goal of a servant of God is

_____a) Revival.

_____b) Evangelism.

_____c) Instruction.   see ///

57. The Church should include in its evangelistic plans

_____a) The officers of the Church.

_____b) The more spiritual members.

_____c) All the believers.   see //

58. Which of these churches, in your opinion, is more pleasing to God and why?

1) A church that prays for revival in all its meetings and waits until this comes in order to have power to evangelize.

2) A church that uses even carnal Christians in evangelism while it tries to instruct them.

One essential characteristic of a good plan is flexibility. A plan that worked well in Asunción five years ago may not serve there now and even less in Montevideo. By trying out a plan we see that certain aspects function well and others not so well. A plan must be adjusted and modified constantly. The Volkswagen, although its appearance has not changed much through the years, has passed through thousands of modifications. It is not enough that it runs. Every aspect of the product must be perfected. In the same way a pastor should not be satisfied with a plan that results in some conversions. He should study the situation and modify the plan constantly for maximum results. God does not demand the impossible, only the best we can do.

59. If a pastor in Lima reads of a plan that works in Cochabamba, he should

_____a) Adopt it in its entirety.

_____b) Modify it for his situation.

_____c) Reject it completely.   see //

60. Modification is necessary because of _____.
                                                      see &&

61. When should a plan be revised? _____ see /

62. A plan must be perfected to produce _____ results.
                                              see &

63. Adjustments must be made to a plan as to an engine until it

_____ .   see ///

Some Successful Plans

In many ways the conditions in certain sectors of the Philippines are similar to those in some sectors of Latin America. For this reason we include a plan that has worked well there.

/ constantly OR SIMILAR WORDS

/// performs or functions well OR SIMILAR WORDS.

& best, maximum

&& conditions and resources OR SIMILAR WORDS

The Association of Baptists for World Evangelism began its work in the Philippines in 1927. By 1962 it had 215 churches with a total of 12,000 members. At first it subsidized heavily pastors' salaries, but later decided that this was a bad practice. Since the Second World War it has not given this economic assistance. The Association's purpose is to plant indigenous churches according to the plan which follows.

A Bible institute is the center of the plan. The missionary or pastor in a certain area consults the practical work department of the institute about a place to begin a church. Students are assigned to that neighborhood to open and develop a Sunday School. The evangelicals and others interested meet to study the Bible, sing, pray and function as the beginnings of a church.

After a time this Sunday School or congregation invites the missionary to organize a campaign. A Filipino evangelist, workers, students and the missionary hold an intensive evangelistic campaign of six to twelve weeks using every legitimate means for attracting people to the meetings. These converts are added to the already functioning Sunday School to form a new church under the leadership of a student pastor. The church pays his bus fare from the institute to the church and contributes to his support there while he studies. As he dedicates more and more time to the work the student is able to raise a strong church.

Not all the efforts are equally successful. Some students are more capable than others. Some of the new converts are better able to win their families and friends. But there is enough success in constantly producing new churches that the students who graduate from the institute can serve on a full time basis. The students have had valuable practice and instruction in planting and nurturing churches.

The missionary aids each new church with an evangelistic campaign for several weeks every year. New Sunday Schools are opened and churches formed faster than the students graduate from the institute. Therefore when he graduates, a student will generally have invitations from several small churches.

During the month of December every year the young people from all the churches hold a convention. In the services some young men and women from new as well as older churches respond to the call to full time service. Therefore, within a year or two of beginning a new church it will be sending some young person to the institute. In addition to inspirational services for everyone these conventions have the special purpose of recruiting those who will become church planters.

This plan presupposes that the primary mission of the Bible institute and of the churches is to plant more churches. The plan is possible only because every teacher in the institute is more concerned with multiplying churches than he is with academic excellence. Those who organize the youth conventions have as a primary goal the recruitment of the finest young people for the Lord's service. The missionary does not spend his time in whatever worthwhile activity he can find, that perhaps some day will produce evangelistic fruit. He is dedicated to the evangelization of responsive sectors of the population. In short, this plan proposes to multiply congregations in as many cities and towns as possible and measures its success by the degree in which every activity of the Church contributes to this goal.

This example is not included so that others will follow it. It is just an illustration of how one group has used its resources intelligently and with imagination to carry out its mission.

64. With regard to indigenous principles the mission

_____a) Observes them up to a certain point.

_____b) Does not aid the churches in any way.

_____c) Has always followed them.   see //

65. The goal of the Bible institute is to

_____a) Direct all the work.

_____b) Plant new churches.

_____c) Recruit students.   see ///

66. Sunday Schools are directed by

_____a) Students.

_____b) Missionaries.

_____c) Seminary professors.   see /

67. The new congregations

_____a) Need a full time pastor.

_____b) Pay their pastor something from the beginning.

_____c) Pay all expenses for evangelism.   see /

68. Evangelization depends on

_____a) Campaigns.

_____b) Sunday Schools.

_____c) A combination of methods.   see ///

69. When the students graduate from the institute

_____a) They depend on the congregations for their support.

_____b) They don't have anywhere to go.

_____c) They always are very successful.   see &

70. The students of the institute

_____a) Are converted in the youth conventions.

_____b) Have been Christians for many years.

_____c) Come from the new churches.   see //

71. Write in your own words: the purpose of the plan, the resources utilized, the methods of evangelism and the way in which the plan is evaluated.

72. Give your personal evaluation of this plan in the Philippines. What are its advantages and disadvantages? Which of
its aspects could be applied in your situation?

Let us consider now another plan for evangelizing an urban
area. It is the program of the John Calvin Seminary in Mexico
City. The students have participated with their professor of
evangelism in the five aspects of the plan which follows.

House to house visitation. The whole neighborhood is visited to distribute literature and sell Bibles and New Testaments.
The contacts made in visitation indicate the responsiveness of
the area. It is almost always possible to find persons who invite the evangelicals to hold meetings in their homes or who are
willing to go to meetings in the homes of others.

Weekly meetings in homes. When there is an invitation a
definite time for the meeting is set and neighbors are invited.
In these meetings the gospel is preached and presented by means
of film strips. Generally there is a separate class for children. When possible the meeting is changed to Sunday. But it
is better to begin during the week because many non-Christians
do not stay home Sundays.

Continuous and intensive visitation in the neighborhood.
This is the key to establishing new meeting places and continual
growth. Women students are as effective as men in visitation.

Offerings from the start. The offering is an act of worship
and teaches responsibility. It is announced that the offerings
will be deposited in a bank until sufficient funds have been
received to erect a building in the neighborhood. Participation
in giving unites the people through their common investment in a
cause.

Responsive sectors of the city. Various sectors of the city
have been probed. Generally those of the lower class are more
receptive.

73. According to this plan the students try to reach a whole

_____. see /

74. Contacts are made through the sale of _____. see ///

75. According to sales and conversations with the people it is
possible to determine the

_____ of the area. see &

76. When interested persons are found an attempt is made to
set up

_____. see //

77. When these persons are converted these meetings in homes
are organized into

_____. see &&

/ neighborhood, sector
// meetings in homes OR meetings
/// SIMILAR WORDS Bibles, literature
& receptivity
&& churches

78. Because of other diversions on that day it is difficult
to persuade non-believers to attend regular services on
                                                    see /   .

79. In order to extend these groups and form others it is necessary to continue the
                                              . see //

80. To teach Christian responsibility, from the first meeting,
_____ are received.   see &&

81. It is important for everyone to _____ in
the meetings and in the program of the church.   see ///

82. These efforts are directed toward _____ sectors
of the city.   see &

83. What is your opinion of this plan conceived in Mexico City?
What are its advantages and disadvantages? Compare it with the
plan in the Philippines. Which of its aspects could be applied
in your situation?

/ Sunday
// visitation
/// participate
    OR SIMILAR
    WORDS
& receptive
&& offerings

Now we arrive at the application of all that the student has learned in this course. This application is of greater practical value than the final examination. The application will not be graded here, but by God and by those within and outside the Church of Jesus Christ.

The student should present a plan by which his church can reach the area which should be the responsibility of that group of Christians. The student should first describe the social, economic and religious conditions that exist and their influence on the receptivity of the sector. Later he should indicate the various stages or aspects of his plan to carry on the Church's mission in his local situation. The plan should include the following factors:

Determining and exploiting areas of greatest receptivity.
Choosing the best methods for evangelization.
Instructing the new believers.
Providing places of worship.
Training leaders and others in the churches.

BIBLIOGRAPHY

HAMILTON, Keith E.
  1962 <u>Church Growth in the High Andes</u>. Lucknow, u.p., India,
        Lucknow Publishing House.

HODGES, Melvin L.
  1959 <u>Edificaré Mi Iglesia</u>. Springfield, Missouri, Editorial
        Vida.

MC GAVRAN, Donald A.
  1966 <u>How Churches Grow</u>. New York, Friendship Press.

  1970 <u>Understanding Church Growth</u>. Grand Rapids, Michigan,
        Wm. B. Eerdman Publishing Co.

MC GAVRAN, Donald, HUEGEL, John and TAYLOR, Jack
  1963 <u>Church Growth in Mexico</u>. Grand Rapids, Michigan, Wm.
        B. Eerdman Publishing Co.

ORR, J. Edwin
  1965 <u>The Light of the Nations: Evangelical Renewal and Ad-
        vance in the Nineteenth Century</u>. Grand Rapids, Eerdmans.

ORTIZ, Juan Carlos and BENTSON, Keith
  1969 <u>Y Será Predicado Este Evangelio</u>. Buenos Aires, Edi-
        torial Logos.

READ, William R.
  1965 <u>New Patterns of Church Growth in Brazil</u>. Grand Rapids,
        Michigan, Wm. B. Eerdman Publishing Co.

READ, William R., MONTERROSO, Victor and JOHNSON, Harmon A.
  1970 <u>Avance Evangélico en la América Latina</u>. Casa Bautista
        de Publicaciones.

TIPPETT, Alan R.
  1970 <u>Church Growth and the Word of God</u>. Grand Rapids,
        Michigan, Wm. B. Eerdman Publishing Co.

WELD, Wayne C.
  1968 <u>An Ecuadorian Impasse</u>. Chicago, World Missions De-
        partment, The Evangelical Covenant Church of America.

NOTES

NOTES

NOTES

NOTES

NOTES

NOTES

NOTES

NOTES